Urban Child and Adolescen
Health Services

Urban Child and Adolescent Mental Health Services weaves together different strands of mental health work undertaken in one inner-city Child and Adolescent Mental Health Service by professionals working in a range of ways. In particular, it provides examples of how an urban CAMH service has been responsive to, and influenced by, local circumstances, resources and knowledge. The book explores the relationship between professionals and the community context, which provides the background to the lives of individual service users and the families they serve, and how this relationship is integral to the development of a responsive service.

The chapters cover a range of settings and approaches, addressing the social, cultural, political and community contexts impacting on children, young people and families. In this way *Urban Child and Adolescent Mental Health Services* explores challenges and issues emerging in a responsive approach to child and family work in all community settings whether they be urban, suburban or rural.

Urban Child and Adolescent Mental Health Services is intended for mental health and social care professionals involved in therapeutic, social and pastoral work with children, young people, families and communities. The book will be of interest to policy-makers, mental health and social care professionals, health visitors, general practitioners, nurses and midwives, as well as to trainees in these professions including trainee clinical psychologists, social workers or psycho-analytic and systemic psychotherapists. It will also appeal to those interested in responsive communities and critical approaches to therapeutic interventions in mental health work, psychology, psychotherapy and counselling.

Taiwo Afuape is a clinical psychologist and systemic psychotherapist, currently working for the Central and North West London NHS Foundation Trust in a Psychology and Psychotherapy Adult Mental Health department and for the Tavistock and Portman NHS Foundation Trust in a CAMHS. Previously, she has worked with transitional populations, torture survivors in a Human Rights charity and adults in a mental health Systemic Consultation Service. She published *Power, Resistance and Liberation in Therapy with Survivors of Trauma* in July 2011.

Inga-Britt Krause is a social anthropologist and a systemic psychotherapist. She has set up cross-cultural services in London and for the past 14 years has been Training & Development Consultant for Race & Equity in the Tavistock and Portman NHS Foundation Trust, working towards the integration of race, culture and ethnicity as important issues in clinical practice and training. Her published books include *Therapy Across Culture* (1998) and *Culture and Madness: A Training Resource, Film and Commentary for Mental Health Professionals* (2015) with Begum Maitra.

Urban Child and Adolescent Mental Health Services

A Responsive Approach to Communities

Edited by
Taiwo Afuape and Inga-Britt Krause

Routledge
Taylor & Francis Group

LONDON AND NEW YORK

First published 2016
by Routledge
2 Park Square, Milton Park, Abingdon, Oxon OX14 4RN

and by Routledge
711 Third Avenue, New York, NY 10017

Routledge is an imprint of the Taylor & Francis Group, an informa business

British Library Cataloguing in Publication Data
A catalogue record for this book is available from the British Library

Library of Congress Cataloging in Publication Data

Names: Afuape, Taiwo, 1975– editor. | Krause, Inga-Britt, editor.
Title: Urban child and adolescent mental health services: a responsive approach to communities / edited by Taiwo Afuape and Inga-Britt Krause.
Description: Abingdon, Oxon; New York, NY: Routledge, 2016. | Includes
bibliographical references.
Identifiers: LCCN 2015039736 | ISBN 9780415706483 | ISBN 9781315646848 | ISBN
9780415706490
Subjects: LCSH: Mental health services—Great Britain | Community mental health services—
Great Britain. | Child mental health services—Great Britain. | Minorities—Mental health
services—Great Britain. | Adolescent psychiatry—Great Britain. | Urban youth—Great Britain.
Classification: LCC RA790.7.G7 U73 2016 | DDC 362.20941—dc23
LC record available at http://lccn.loc.gov/2015039736

ISBN: 978-0-415-70648-3 (hbk)
ISBN: 978-0-415-70649-0 (pbk)
ISBN: 978-1-315-64684-8 (ebk)

Typeset in Times New Roman
by codeMantra
Printed in Great Britain by
Ashford Colour Press Ltd, Gosport, Hants

Contents

Foreword

As CAMHS director, it is a pleasure to write this foreword, just as the 'Future in Mind' report has been published. 'Future in Mind' reports on the work of the government taskforce designed to identify actions to help increase joined up working across the system and improve outcomes for children and young people's mental health. It is timely because 'Urban CAMHS' is a book that celebrates the work of a range of different clinicians who have been working to achieve these objectives in their different ways over a number of years. The authors describe a service that I myself established and it is both rewarding and instructive to see how those now delivering this service have developed it in a way that reflects and respects differences between themselves and the needs of those with whom they work.

All the authors aim to provide ethical and socially just practice that reduces social exclusion in ways that genuinely place user perspectives at the heart of mental health service delivery. Most importantly, this work often happens where young people and other key individuals live their everyday lives. This is challenging at the best of times, but to achieve all this within the context of increasingly precarious funding is not easy. I was reminded forcefully that 'community' services do not equate simply to services which happen outside of a clinic or hospital setting, but are ones that consider and appreciate the complexity of the meaning of community and the diversity of the outlooks of those living within them. In this context, community mental health work requires a readiness to re-examine, change and adapt models of mental health and practice to have a 'good enough' fit with particular local contexts, including the social, emotional and physical aspects of these.

Each of the authors reflects upon and makes explicit the theoretical underpinnings of their work as well as the personal experiences that have influenced them. It is of interest how this in turn mirrors the diversity of the situations to which the work is applied, demonstrated in case examples the authors describe in order to bring this work alive. The availability of multiple perspectives has been central; just as parents, mental health practitioners and educational professionals can join in their endeavour to help children and young people in their care, the authors bring together complementary theoretical models, which enhance our understanding of how to offer our best to the individuals and populations we are here to help. In addition, all of the authors acknowledge the reality of an unequal and discriminatory society and offer ways of working within this context that builds on the sense of agency individuals and organisations possess, even in the most unequal circumstances. I was so impressed by how the authors have demonstrated ways of helping people find their voice and have tailored the services they offer to the needs of communities and to the particularities of the urban environment within which those communities are located.

With the emphasis on working in partnership, the authors offer us ways of working alongside individuals, families and organisations, and understanding what community and identity means to them, as well as opportunities for shared learning with one another, which, the authors view as essential to managing the challenges of this complex work. The authors' openness to developing new ways of resisting the social constraints imposed upon people's lives opens up a space for creatively engaging with those with whom we work. We are invited to pay attention to and challenge the negative and limiting assumptions implicit in the term 'urban community', as well as the strengths and creativity implicit in difference and diversity. As the authors build on the resilience of those they are working with, the reader is invited to open themselves to the uncertainty and challenge of working in innovative ways that allow for new and relevant meanings to emerge.

Rita Harris
CAMHS Director

Notes on contributors

Taiwo Afuape is Lead Clinical Psychologist and Systemic Psychotherapist in a Community CAMHS at the Tavistock & Portman NHS Foundation Trust and at Central and North West London Foundation Trust Psychology and Psychotherapy Adult Mental Health Department. As a Black African working-class woman she is committed to moving ever closer towards ethical and socially just practice. Taiwo has worked in the community with transitional populations (women escaping domestic violence, homeless people, people misusing substances, travelling communities of Roma and Irish heritage and refugee people), a Human Rights charity for survivors of torture and she managed an adult mental health Systemic Consultation Service.

Leila Bargawi is a Child Psychotherapist who trained at the Tavistock & Portman NHS Foundation Trust. She worked for many years on the inpatient psychiatric ward at Great Ormond Street Hospital for Children and later in various community settings including a primary school, nursery and GP practice. She comes from a mixed heritage background and grew up abroad. After studying she spent some time living in Syria and worked with young children in an orphanage and a refugee camp. This, amongst many things, sparked an interest in working with young children under five and their families in varying cultures and contexts.

Jasmine Chin has been practicing how to be a Clinical Psychologist for the last ten years, exploring the tensions between this and other creative ways of helping people. Throughout, working ethically has seemed the most logical way to be for a psychologist and has become the foundation for her practice. Mindfulness and compassion-based approaches have supported her personally and professionally, helping her to remember that the journey for herself and her clients is as important as the destination. Jasmine is a mother of two bouncing twin boys who have provided her with the best possible insight of parental well-being.

Ana Rivadulla Crespo is a Consultant Child and Adolescent Psychiatrist and a Psychodynamic Psychotherapist. She has worked both in outpatient and inpatient CAMHS settings. She is accredited by the British Psychoanalytic Council and she is a member of The Tavistock Society of Psychotherapists. She currently practices in the NHS and at the Brent Centre for Young People.

Zoe Dale combines her work as a child and adolescent mental health professional, with her role as a Consultant Trainer and Professional Adviser with Young Minds. Since 2002 she has provided a range of training and consultancy to schools and children's services across the UK. For four years Zoe led the Child and Adolescent Mental Health Programme at the University of Greenwich. Her areas of expertise include the treatment of depression, anxiety, stress, self-harm and eating disorders in children and young people. Zoe is a qualified Occupational Therapist and has twenty-five years experience in child and adolescent mental health.

Louise Emanuel is a Consultant Child, Adolescent and Adult Psychotherapist in the Child and Family Department in the Tavistock & Portman NHS Foundation Trust where she is the Under Five Lead for Camden Services. She is course organiser for the PG Dip/MA in Infant Mental Health, teaches on the clinical training for child psychotherapists, and has been convenor of the Infant Mental Health Workshop for many years. She has published several papers and is co-editor of two books: '*What Can the Matter Be?' Therapeutic Interventions with Parents, Infants and Young Children* (2008), Karnac Books, and '*Understanding Your Three-Year-Old*' (2005), Jessica Kingsley.

Chris Glenn is a Systemic Psychotherapist in a community CAMHS team and in a Special Needs CAMHS team. His MSc research was on the educational experiences of Somali refugee children in the UK. He has been a CAMHS representative on the local borough Special Educational Needs and the Education, Health and Care Plan Panels. He has many years' experience of working with schools and families when children present with difficulties. He has edited or co-edited themed issues of Context, the Association of Family Therapy's bimonthly publication, on the political and social context of systemic practice, social class, and attachment.

Rachel James is a Consultant Clinical Psychologist and has over twenty years experience working with children, young people and their families across the health, social care and education sectors, and in partnership with the voluntary sector. She has managed the family mental health provision into the Camden multi-agency children's centre services for over a decade, and has an interest in using evidence based practice and practice based evidence to improve quality in all aspects of child and family mental health and well-being. Rachel particularly enjoys engaging service users in meaningful ways to shape service delivery.

Inga-Britt Krause is a social anthropologist and a Consultant Systemic Psychotherapist. She has carried out ethnographic fieldwork in North West Nepal with high caste Hindus and in Bedfordshire with the Sikh community. She has worked in the NHS with children and families for many years and has helped set up specialist cross-cultural therapy services. She has published papers and several books on these topics and teaches on a variety of clinical courses in the Tavistock & Portman NHS Foundation Trust as well as nationally.

Louise O'Dwyer is a Child and Adolescent Psychotherapist. She trained in the Tavistock & Portman NHS Foundation Trust, and has worked in GP clinics, children's centres and primary schools in inner and outer London boroughs. She has worked in a specialist eating disorder inpatient unit, in which she undertook her doctoral research on parental experiences of having a child hospitalised for an eating disorder. She is particularly interested in eating disorders, under fives work, and work with looked after children and adopted children. She teaches on the Tavistock MA programme in child psychotherapy on emotional factors in teaching and learning.

Kanan Pandya-Smith is a Clinical Psychologist working within the Integrated Early Years Service, supporting young parents with zero- to five-year-olds particularly in the perinatal period. She has extensive experience working with families, couples and children with a range of difficulties of varying complexities and risk. This includes parenting work, mental health difficulties and working with the system around the family. She has also worked with adult mental health in a low secure forensic hospital and within a substance misuse service. Kanan is interested in engaging with and working alongside young parents supporting their journey to parenthood.

Doreen Robinson is a qualified Social Worker and Systemic Psychotherapist. She has experience of over thirty years of clinical practice with a variety of cultural groups across London and adjacent counties. She has worked in areas of community work, child protection, fostering and adoption, mental health with adults, children and families both within voluntary and statutory child and health services. Doreen was a member of staff in the Asian Service in the Tavistock & Portman NHS Foundation Trust and a founder member of the South Camden Community CAMHS Team where she is currently Lead Systemic Psychotherapist.

Esther Usiskin-Cohen has over thirty years of wide ranging experience working with adults, families, couples, young people and children both in the criminal and family courts and with the community as a probation officer and a Children's Guardian. She works in the Tavistock & Portman NHS Foundation Trust in South Camden CAMHS as a Specialist Family and Systemic Psychotherapist, supervisor and trainer and in private practice. She is an AFT registered systemic supervisor. Esther is a fully qualified EMDR practitioner and she is currently developing a multi-family mindfulness programme.

Chapter 1

Introduction

Inga-Britt Krause and Taiwo Afuape

Child and Adolescent Mental Health Services (CAMHS) in the United Kingdom have undergone significant changes during the last ten years or so. Since the publication of *Every Child Matters* (a 2003 government white paper often described as one of the most important policy initiatives and development programmes related to children and children's services in recent times, and leading to the adoption of the *Children Act 2004*[1] and *The National Service Framework*[2] *for Children, Young People and Maternity Services* in 2004), emphasis has been placed on CAMHS aiming to decrease social exclusion, take account of user perspectives and encourage all services working with children to work together. These expectations have led to CAMHS professionals increasingly working outside the clinic or the hospital, in schools, general practices, nurseries and children's centres, than was the case in the past. Fitting in with this commitment to attend to the needs of *all* children, young people and their families comprehensively, there has been a growing realisation that the health of children and young people, to a large extent, depends on the ease of access to services and the possibility of delivering interventions early. This has further underscored the need for CAMHS professionals to work in ways which bring them closer to the populations and the communities who may need their services.

Coming closer to communities necessitates not just a closeness in terms of location and physical proximity, but closeness in terms of the ways of understanding well-being and the interventions that may support it. However, these changes and aims, admirable though they are, have had far-reaching implications not only for service delivery but also for the organisation of services, for funding, models of treatment and theoretical developments. For example, going outside clinics and hospitals have enabled professionals to meet sections of the population who may not consider themselves to be 'clients' or 'patients'. Mental health professional work may also be less defined if this involves brief contact and advice during a visit to a children's centre or school. How should this work be categorised and costs calculated? Who should pay? Indeed as a recent report notes, the commissioning of CAMHS and early intervention services is often precarious, and suffers from reduced, insecure and short-term funding (House of Commons Health Committee, 2014). The same report offers the following summary of the state of CAMHS in the UK in 2014: 'There are serious and deeply ingrained problems with the commissioning and provision of children's and adolescents' mental health services. These run through the whole system from prevention and early intervention through to inpatient services for the most vulnerable young people' (House of Commons, 2014, p. 3).

The daily experience of clinicians of this state of affairs, as well as local organisational changes in our service (an inner-city, urban CAMH service) led to the beginning of the writing of this book in 2012. Professionals in the service were working hard to cope with the growing need to deliver services in the community, that is to say working outside the clinic without other mental health colleagues in close proximity, and with the reduction in funding at a time when success in increasing access had resulted in an increase in numbers of referrals. These two somewhat contradictory processes prompted a change in the organisation of our work, the way we approached our clients and the way we thought about and applied our theoretical models. While all staff in the service have been faced with the changes outlined above, not everyone wanted to write about their experiences. However a sizeable and representative group of professionals felt that they had something new to contribute to the development of contemporary CAMHS work, and two of us, Taiwo Afuape and Britt Krause, took on the task of planning and editing a book based on these experiences.

Taiwo and Britt are both systemic psychotherapists in the CAMHS team. However they work in different subdivisions of the team, and they are different in other ways too. As a Black African woman of working-class and Nigerian heritage, Taiwo was interested in racism and mental health, and after reading *Aliens and Alienists: Ethnic Minorities and Psychiatry* by Ronald Littlewood and Maurice Lipsedge (1989) in 1992 contacted Dr Lipsedge to arrange to interview him about his book. During this interview Dr Lipsedge commented on Taiwo's passion for well-being and challenging questions about racism and psychiatry and suggested that she would make a good clinical psychologist. Taiwo worked on the ward Dr Lipsedge was the consultant psychiatrist on, as an auxiliary nurse in the year before earning a bachelor degree in psychology and during university terms throughout her degree course. In changing her course of action and deciding to pursue clinical psychology rather than social and community activism, Taiwo was adamant that she wanted to train to be a critical (rather than mainstream) psychologist and trained at the University of East London because of the emphasis on critical and political approaches to mental health and psychology there. Two years after qualifying as a clinical psychologist in 2002, Taiwo trained as a systemic therapist, again choosing to train in a training school that emphasised critical and social constructionist approaches to systemic intervention.

Britt, on the other hand, trained originally as a social anthropologist and carried out ethnographic fieldwork with a Hindu population living in North Western Nepal (Krause, 2002) as well as with the Punjabi Sikh population in Bedford, UK (Krause, 1989; Krause et al, 1990). She trained as a systemic psychotherapist twenty-five years ago and has worked in the National Health Service (NHS) ever since amongst other things setting up specialist cross-cultural psychotherapy services. She is a White middle-aged woman with grown children. She grew up in Denmark but has lived all her professional life in the UK. Her experiences as a social anthropologist, speaking different languages and participating in different and to her foreign ways of being and doing has sensitised her to how different and to her often unimaginable, experiences, expectations and hopes can be for persons and groups of persons in different locations. Britt is aware that these circumstances can sometimes lead to clients and client populations from marginalised minority backgrounds experiencing mental health services as discriminating, excluding and even useless.

The Child and Adolescent Mental Health Service

The CAMH service in which the contributors to this book work is a community service. This means that as far as possible mental health services are offered in settings outside of the hospital or clinic, in a domiciliary setting, in the homes of clients, in schools, nurseries or in the surgeries of general practitioners. This alternative to in-patient care was part of the UK government's strategy to increase accessibility to Child and Adolescent Mental Health Services generally and was first set out in the 2000 white paper *Reforming the Mental Health Act.* The term 'outreach' was used in this paper to highlight issues about access, and the paper also emphasised the aims of the reforms to be compatible with the Humans Rights Act, to decrease social exclusion and to place user perspectives at the heart of mental health service delivery. As noted above, the subsequent developments in Child and Adolescent Mental Health Services further emphasised these principles and with the subsequent formation of Children's Trusts[3], emphasised local partnerships which brought together organisations responsible for services for children, young people and families—such as general practitioners, schools, nurseries, health visitors, midwives, social workers, the police and so on—in a shared commitment to improving children's lives. While many of these structures were abolished in the 2012 NHS reforms[4] the principles of working in the community and joining in partnership with other professionals and with community organisations continue to inform our CAMHS work.

In keeping with the 2012 NHS reforms our CAMH service is jointly commissioned by a Clinical Commissioning Group chaired by a local general practitioner. This group jointly with the Local Authority and Social Care (formerly Social Services) commissions all the mental health work with children and adolescents in the borough including Mosaic (integrated service for disabled children), MALT (Multi-Agency Liaison Teams—supporting families known to Social Care), Youth Offending Teams, Infants and Early Years Services and Pupil Referral Units, as well as two community CAMH services for children and adolescents, divided into North and South. The budget for all these services is shared, and regular meetings between the service managers take place, in which both macro and micro clinical decisions are taken or approved. These services together operate a single point of entry (Joint Intake), which is a meeting in which referrals from health and social care professionals are considered and distributed according to clinical need, where clients live, where the identified young person goes to school or where the family's general practitioner is located. At the time of writing, the CAMH service (both South and North) overall was managed by a male consultant child and adolescent psychiatrist. The two sub-teams were managed by two team managers, both women, one a senior social worker/psychotherapist and the other a consultant child and adolescent psychotherapist, who attended the Joint Intake meetings. Approximately half of the referrals came through Joint Intake; the other half of referrals arrived directly from what was referred to as 'outreach', namely from CAMHS work in schools and general practices.

The CAMHS staff are members of a larger training institution/clinic, which is also a national resource for the training of adult and child psychotherapists and other mental health clinicians. The North/South structure of the CAMHS team was created in 2008 out of other clinical teams working in the clinic in accordance with the aforementioned mental health reforms. At the time of writing each sub-team had the equivalent of nine full-time clinicians. These clinicians were also clinical trainers, and trainees from different professions made up another twenty members on each team. Few were full-timers as trainees have other aspects of their studies to see to, and trainers tend to be involved directly in academic training activities. Given that few members of staff worked for the service full-time, and the two teams are large, at times up to forty persons took part in a full clinical meeting. The multidisciplinary teams included administrators, assistant psychologists, child and adolescent psychiatrists, child and adolescent psychotherapists, systemic psychotherapists/family therapists, clinical psychologists, mental health nurses, social workers and educational psychologists. Many clinicians on the team were and still are dual trained in their core profession and a particular psychotherapy modality.

The North and South divisions were further divided into weekly clinical discussion groups, in which cases were discussed with colleagues of different modalities. The CAMH service (both North and South) as a whole carried approximately 1,170 cases of which 670 were new referrals during the 2014 to 2015 financial year (that is between April 2014 and April 2015), including those arising from work in the community. A significant number of these cases were judged by staff to be medium or severe risk. The teams had no waiting lists, but this was because of the high commitment and regular overtime working of staff rather than a surplus of resources. Demand was ever increasing.

Diversity and responsiveness

A book about an urban CAMHS is a book about diversity. The populations of cities all over the UK are heterogenous and multicultural. Therefore providing access to services for people and populations who speak different languages, who may think about their relationships, their bodies, hearts and minds in ways which do not fit with dominant mental health professional frameworks, who may expect different treatments from those on offer or who may feel estranged from the professionals who work in the services, requires a responsive approach. In such a service professionals themselves gain new experiences; they may become in touch with a range of their clients' ordinary issues that are perhaps not directly related to health, such as financial pressures, political pressures, housing pressures, religious persecution, discrimination and so on, from which they might have been protected in the past. Responsiveness may not simply be a question of how to apply professional and theoretical models, it may also be a question of how to develop new models and new theories, albeit against the background of those already in use. This is what the contributors to this book aim to do. We may think of *community CAMHS* as being at the forefront of contemporary changes. And yet, because assessments of community CAMHS have been based on quantitative, centralised measures, they have not always been able to reflect more subtle changes and outcomes, and as a result CAMH services have been criticised and found wanting. We believe that CAMHS work is demanding and complex but also positive and hopeful, and this book is an attempt to show this.

But what do we mean by *community* and *community CAMHS*, and is it possible to be based in the community but not truly responsive to it? Responsiveness and flexibility necessarily imply that while a community-based approach can be advocated and prescribed generally, it is difficult to be directive about detail and each professional group and practitioner will need to reflect for themselves about what community means and find their own style of being responsive to it. This is clearly demonstrated in the chapters which follow. The professionals in our service communicate and collaborate with each other, but they do not all do the same job, nor do they approach the work in the same way. This is partly because of their particular professional orientations, but also because of personal values, preferences and experiences. For example, while all professionals in the CAMH service work with relationships and therefore keep families and carers in mind, we differ in terms of how much we involve families in the actual work carried out. We also differ in terms of how much we emphasise external circumstances and contexts or internalised processes, which may echo past relationships. We differ in how comfortable we are in disclosing details about ourselves. We also differ in the terms we use to refer to those who seek our help; some of us prefer the term 'client', whereas others prefer the term 'patient'. While this choice of how to refer to the persons and people to whom we offer our services sometimes is understood to be a hallmark of the difference between 'collaborative' and more 'hierarchical' approaches, the background to these terms is complex. For example, one might argue that 'patient' medicalises the person coming to services for support and focuses our attention on internal pathology, whereas 'client' gives the service user agency and encourages the service provider's humility. On the other hand, 'client' also fits in with the commodification of services and implies a business-like transaction between service user and provider, whereas 'patient' has more reflective overtones. Finally, while all chapters address diversity in the giving of examples of how the authors work, the CAMHS professionals who are the contributors to this book vary in terms of the way in which they consider culture, class and 'race' differences to be issues which radically challenge our practice. What we hope to do is demonstrate the possibilities which may emerge, despite significant differences in perspectives, experience and theoretical orientation, when CAMHS clinicians prioritise 'community' and 'responsiveness' in their work with service users and with each other. We hope that the distinctiveness of each chapter's 'voice' is regarded by the reader as testimony to the ways in which CAMH services can honour and embrace the opportunities and challenges of diversity both within its service and within and between communities.

The chapters

The rationale for this book is to weave together different strands of mental health work undertaken in one inner-city CAMH service. This certainly requires taking a critical look at services, but it also requires spelling out what we mean by communities as well as the interface between 'services' and 'communities'. In addition it requires demonstrating what responsiveness may look like in different contexts. The book addresses these issues and is divided into four parts.

Part One sets the scene in terms of the challenges of CAMHS professionals moving their work from the 'clinic' to the 'community'. In Chapter Two Inga-Britt Krause discusses the meanings and complexity behind the term 'community' and argues that in the health service, the term 'community' is often pitched against 'the clinic' or 'the hospital' and in this way possibly counteracts the aim of increasing accessibility and preventative work. Britt describes the CAMH team in more detail and discusses the special case of the urban context. She concludes with a discussion of her work with a family and warns against using 'community' as a homogeneous label with only positive connotations. In Chapter Three Taiwo Afuape enquires further into the terms 'inner city' and 'community' and notes that these are often associated with 'problem-talk'. Taiwo shows how she uses Co-ordinated Management of Meaning (CMM) in her work with children, young people and their families, in order to honour the place of 'resistance' in bringing resilience and creativity to the fore. She gives examples of how she aims to be collaborative in her work with clients and concludes by suggesting that collaboration is a cornerstone of responsive and creative CAMHS work.

Part Two contains three chapters, all examples of community CAMHS work in children's centres and general practices. In Chapter Four Rachel James and Kanan Padya-Smith, both clinical psychologists, describe their work in a multi-agency team based in a children's centre. Their places of work are constantly shifting, and often they find themselves working in the homes of their clients. This brings them face-to-face with many of the day-to-day problems faced by families in inner cities and which they are called upon to address. Rachel and Kanan describe their work with one woman and her family in detail. Chapters Five and Six move into the general practice setting and address how child psychotherapy can be used there. In Chapter Five Louise Emanuel describes the Brief Under-Fives model of psychoanalytic psychotherapy with children adapted to work outside the CAMHS clinic. This model is offered alongside a baby clinic in a general practice. Louise describes the theoretical underpinnings of this model as well as the ways in which a standard psychoanalytic approach can be adapted in order to fit with and address the social, cultural and political circumstances in which families find themselves. She notes that issues such as the background of the family and the lack of predictable rooms in the general practice surgery need careful reflection in clinical supervision. In Chapter Six Leila Bargawi and Louise O'Dwyer continue the theme of child psychotherapy offered alongside baby clinics in general practices. Leila and Louise note the similarities between themselves as child psychotherapists in a new setting and many of their clients who do not feel fully included in their local community because of experiences of social abuse, discrimination and oppression. In the description and discussion of several cases they show how their work focuses on issues of cultural 'difference' and identity and can facilitate reconnecting the parents of babies and infants to a sense of community, in their memories, in their daily lives and both.

Part Three contains three chapters describing different aspects of CAMH service work with and in schools. In Chapter Seven, Chris Glenn describes how he uses systemic ideas in his work in a secondary school. Chris describes how the triangle between mental health workers, teachers and parents can place the young person in a difficult and hopeless position receiving blame all around. His case examples show how as a CAMH professional he is able to facilitate discussions between all parties, such that home and school work together to support the development of a young person's strengths and abilities, which might otherwise go unnoticed. In Chapter Eight Zoe Dale reports on her and a male colleague's joint work with a group of teenage boys from a minority ethnic background in an inner-city secondary school. Zoe describes the political and economic context to the lives of the young men and discusses how this context has influenced their experience of family relationships and their emotional outlook. The descriptions of the processes and events which took place in the group show how complex this work can be but also how work of this kind may be able to rekindle hope, by joining the concerns of parents and teachers, whilst centralising the voices and experiences of the young men. In Chapter Nine Esther Usiskin-Cohen describes what CAMH services might learn from a manualised programme such as Families and Schools Together (FAST) with respect to the importance of a non-pathologising, resources-based, preventative approach to family and community wellness. She describes her use of FAST in a primary school and the ways in which the eight-week programme strengthened relationships within families, between families, between families and the school and between families and the community. Esther urges CAMHS professionals, when reflecting on the social constraints on children, young people, adults, and families, to focus as much on prevention as on 'treatment'. Esther is not uncritical and notes that, while funding of FAST continues, in times of austerity other avenues for developing community relations are disappearing.

In the final part of the book, **Part Four**, four chapters address how being more closely involved in the lives of their clients, impacts how CAMHS professionals view their work in relation to wider contexts and the complexity of 'power' and 'difference'. In Chapter Ten Doreen Robinson, a systemic psychotherapist, describes her work with three families from different cultural and ethnic backgrounds. She shows how in such work families may use ideas and meanings which derive from their personal or collective cultural experiences and that it is important for the mental health professional to engage with these meanings in order to help families and persons to move on. In Chapter Eleven Ana Rivadulla Crespo, a child and adolescent psychiatrist, describes her work with an adolescent boy, who has grown up in the care system and received many different psychiatric diagnoses. Ana argues that in such a situation, typically faced by many teenagers, mental health professionals need to turn away from a diagnostic outcome-based approach and instead provide stability, nurturing and containment. This means building relationships with young people in order to foster the 'unrealised hope' lying dormant in the crisis situation. Ana uses psychoanalytic ideas, but she also advocates community projects, which may be able to provide 'family' or 'care' for young people. She argues for mental health practitioners working with young people, not least child and adolescent psychiatrists, focusing more on social inclusion than on mental disorder. In Chapter Twelve Taiwo Afuape and Inga-Britt Krause discuss the challenges which female genital mutilation (FGM) present for clinicians. As well as reflecting on and dialoguing about the political, cultural, social, racial and gendered aspects of this issue, the authors demonstrate that where there are no easy answers or final complete conclusions, dialogue is the most responsive approach to holding contradictory, opposing and/or ambivalent perspectives, both between people and within a person. Britt and Taiwo suggest that it is in focusing on *our* emotional and ethical responses to issues such as FGM, and what they open up and close down in our interaction with 'others', that we might be authentically, rather than tokenistically, responsive. In Chapter Thirteen Jasmine Chin and a parent who she has worked with, 'D', address parental mental health in relation to community connections. Jasmine highlights the importance of working collaboratively with her clients and drawing on their community connections as a way of facilitating their resources. D describes how she felt that Jasmine's ability to join with her, to use her words, and to join with the experience of her children, enabled D to make sense of her experiences and challenge her sense of isolation. Even in the confines of (mainly) individual therapy, 'community' is fostered. Jasmine notes that reflection was central to this process, in order to connect with D's preferences and to bear in mind how her own context and history might differ from that of her clients.

In the final chapter, Chapter Fourteen, Taiwo Afuape and Inga-Britt Krause conclude the book by offering some reflections on the themes which have emerged. The issues raised by the topics in the chapters of this book are at once political/ethical, social, cultural, personal and bodily. In fact, we argue that attempts to be responsive to communities encompass all these aspects.

Notes

1 Since 1908 there have been several Children Acts in the UK. For contemporary professionals probably The Children Act 1989 is best known. This allocated duties to local authorities, courts, parents and other agencies in the United Kingdom to ensure children are safeguarded and their welfare is promoted. It centres on the idea that children are best cared for within their own families; however, it also makes provisions for instances when parents and families do not cooperate with statutory bodies.
2 National Service Frameworks (NSFs) are policies set by the National Health Service (NHS) in the United Kingdom to define standards of care for major medical issues. NSFs are developed in partnership with health professionals, patients, carers, health service managers, voluntary agencies and other experts. The two main roles of NSFs are: 1) Set clear quality requirements for care based on the best available evidence of what treatments and services work most effectively for patients; 2) offer strategies and support to help organisations achieve these.
3 Children's Trusts are local partnership arrangements to improve children's wellbeing. They are not defined in legislation but are underpinned by a 'duty to cooperate' in section 10 of the Children Act 2004. Under the duty to cooperate all local areas are required to have a Children's Trust Board.
4 This was an Act of the Parliament of the United Kingdom. It removed responsibility for the health of citizens from the Secretary of State for Health, which the post had carried since the inception of the NHS in 1948. It abolished NHS Primary Care Trusts (PCTs) and Strategic Health Authorities (SHAs) and transferred between £60 billion and £80 billion of 'commissioning', or health care funds, from the abolished PCTs to several hundred 'clinical commissioning groups', partly run by the general practitioners in England but also a major point of access for private service providers.

References

House of Commons Health Committee (2003). *Every Child Matters*. London, England: The Stationery Office Limited (TSO).
House of Commons Health Committee (2014). *Children's and Adolescents' Mental Health and CAMHS*. London, England: The Stationery Office Limited (TSO).
Krause, I-B. (1989). The sinking heart. A Punjabi communication of distress. *Social Science and Medicine*, 29(4), 563–75.
Krause, I-B. (2002). *The Shahas of West Nepal. Political Autonomy and Economic Dependence in a Former Nepalese Community.* Delhi, India: Ardash Publishers.
Krause, I-B., Rosser, R. M., Khiani, M. L. & Lotay, N. S. (1990). Psychiatric morbidity among Punjabi medical patients in England measured by General Health Questionnaire. *Psychological Medicine*, 20(3), 711–19.
Littlewood, R. & Lipsedge, M. (1989). *Aliens and Alienists: Ethnic Minorities and Psychiatry* (2nd ed.). London, England: Routledge.
Secretary of State for Health & The Home Secretary (2000). *Reforming the Mental Health Act.* London, England: The Stationery Office Limited (TSO).
The Department of Health (1999). *National Service Framework for Mental Health.* London, England: The Department of Health.

Part I

Providing services, thinking communities

Chapter 2

An urban community
Where, whom and what does it mean?

Inga-Britt Krause

Introduction

> *As soon as our attention turns from a community as a body of houses and tools and institutions to the states of mind of particular people, we are turning to the exploration of something immensely complex and difficult to know.*
>
> (Redfield, 1960, p. 59)

This idea of 'community' seems to always have been there. We all in one way or another feel we know what we mean and what other people mean when they use this term[1]. Communities are what we all, whether clients or professionals, live in, and communities make up the background against which we see ourselves, and which may influence aspects of our identities. No-one can live outside some kind of community and people often assert their community participation and membership with pride. In fact 'community' is, at least in our contemporary discourses, what Rapport and Overing following Cranston refer to as a 'hurray' term (Rapport & Overing, 2000, p. 65), that is a term to which we give a positive value. It evokes togetherness and sharing. It suggests people who are doing things together, who may be able to rely on each other, and perhaps even suggests democracy. Certainly in our contemporary political system the term suggests a group of people who have something in common and therefore from some points of view are seen to be representatives of each other. Yet at the same time as the quote above from Robert Redfield, one of the first social anthropologists to study communities rather than 'societies', 'cultures' or social organisations, suggests, the idea of 'community' is complex. So what is the idea and understanding behind 'community' in Community Child and Adolescent Mental Health Services (CCAMHS)? What does it mean to policy makers, to us as professionals and to the persons in the communities we meet, serve, treat and communicate with? Is there something unique about communities according to the geographical context in which they are situated? How far are urban communities different from rural ones? English ones from Bangladeshi or Somalian ones? Or does 'community' perhaps refer to an amalgam of all of these? How does the context, environment, the relationships and the milieu in which we practice and in which our clients and patients spend their lives influence, constrain or facilitate our work, our ideas and indeed the efficacy of our work?

This chapter addresses these questions in order to lay the foundations for an exploration of the complexities and challenges of responsive community mental health work in an urban setting, which is the focus of this book. The chapter begins by describing the particular setting in which the Child and Adolescent Mental Health Service (CAMHS), where all the contributors work, is located. The following section describes the history and structure of the service before moving on to examine the concept of 'community' from a social science perspective. I argue that paying attention to the complexity, which a social science approach can illuminate, can assist professional mental health practitioners working with children, young people and families. I shall demonstrate some of this complexity by considering an example of clinical work and before I describe and discuss this case, I briefly outline my own experiences of 'community' and urban living. In conclusion I summarise the implications for the development of a CAMHS responsive to diverse and particular local needs.

The locality and the city

The Child and Adolescent Mental Health Service in which the different contributors to this book, work, is situated in the midst of a metropolis, in a London borough, one of several in the city. It is a borough with a high population density characterised by a number of contrasts; between a transient population, some refugees and international and national immigrants, others on the move for different reasons, and areas where the population is more stable; between extreme poverty and extreme wealth; between state schools and private schools; national health service and private providers; the unemployed and the ultra-rich; social housing, which is in bad repair and inadequate, and expensive properties, some of which top the house prices in the UK. The borough stretches from the centre of the city to about halfway to its periphery. It includes two major train stations, one of them international; two prestigious teaching hospitals; two world-renowned universities; and many buildings and institutions of special interest, such as a zoo, theatres, museums and so on. The borough is thus a destination for tourists as well as students. At the time of writing the total population of the borough was approximately 230,000 comprised of White British people, Bangladeshis, people from various part of Africa such as Nigeria and Somalia, Irish people, Chinese people, Indians as well as migrants from other European countries. The most widely spoken languages were Bangladeshi/Sylheti[2], Somali, Albanian, Arabic, French, Spanish, Polish and Portuguese as well as English (information retrieved from Camden.data.info, 2014). The borough can thus generally be described as 'multicultural', and this immediately poses the question of the scale of 'community' in this locality. From the point of view of a political and administrative constituency the borough is one 'multicultural community', whereas from the point of view of the inhabitants and those working there, it may be understood to be constituted by many different communities. Thus, as ideas, 'multicultural' and 'community' both tend to be associated with, perhaps be vague about, and even to gloss over, difficult tensions inherent in scale and in the reciprocity of the social relations associated with any given locality (Parekh, 2000; Rattansi, 2011).

The urban context

There has been a tendency amongst sociologists and social anthropologists especially of older generations to overemphasise the difference between rural and urban communities. Redfield himself attempted to plot a continuum between rural and urban, small-scale and large scale, social homogeneity and social differentiation, physical isolation and networks of communication, group solidarity and individualism, face-to-face relations and relations at a distance (Redfield, 1960). I have heard such a romanticised view expressed by people who live in the locality, especially by people who may see themselves as middle class and who may have resources, either financial or emotional, enough to dream of spending time elsewhere. In reality the terms used in these contrasts overstate the differences between the two types of locality. Rural life is not necessarily homogeneous and harmonious, nor are close and face-to-face relationships and communication necessarily missing in urban settings. Furthermore, there are many inhabitants in the city, both UK immigrants as well as those from other countries, who have social and kinship ties to rural areas and whose relationships therefore cross these differences.

Nevertheless urban settings are particular localities. Most people in the city, although by no means all, live in households some distance away from where they work. Most people, again perhaps not everyone, participate in different networks away from their families and kin-groups. Such networks may be based on recreation, sport, schools, services, action groups, neighbourhoods, work, special interests or traffic (the way they get about the city). Riding your bike (less if you are driving your car), taking the bus or the train, tube or metro it is impossible not to meet strangers, and as Hannerz has observed these different networks may intersect to become 'networks of networks' referring to the different relations between these domains (Hannerz, 1980, p. 200). This means that someone you meet on the bus has the potential to become a new acquaintance with whom you may play football, sing in a choir, where you may meet other persons, with whom you may pursue other activities, etc. This may happen in rural contexts too, but the extensiveness and combination of such networks may be more unpredictable because of the faster-changing and greater number of possible combinations of roles and relationships in the city. Cities are thus characterised by offering a wider potential than rural locations for the creation of a mingling plurality on the basis of coincidence. The professionals who work on the CAMHS team experience this too and expect to meet clients in their work who they do not know and whose ideas about mental health and family relationships may be very different from their own.

However, co-location is not the same as collaboration and some of the influences on the way persons and groups of people make choices about their relationships are based on culture, class background and tradition. Therefore the plurality of cities also conveys a multiplicity of cultures and social and ethnic backgrounds. This multiplicity may be in terms of migration histories, religious and educational and economic backgrounds, some of which may not be obvious at first sight, but which nevertheless are important influences on the way persons and groups of persons see themselves and others and where they belong or do not belong. There are other less obvious processes, which may pitch one group or one community up against another. Amin refers to an 'urban unconscious' (Amin, 2012, p. 68), which arises from the conditions and processes pertaining to urban planning, infrastructure and state and social policies. He reminds us of the idea, now generally accepted in social science, that non-human agents such as things, objects, and spaces, are implicated in us becoming and being human in particular contexts (Ingold, 2000; Latour, 2005; Miller, 2010; Amin, 2012). Thus urban traffic systems, timetables, communication systems, data classification, surveillance and architecture influence the way we behave and communicate with each other. The proximity and quality of housing, the availability of parks and public spaces as well as access to services and education all influence our dispositions[3], orientations and social choices even though we may be unaware of this influence. These underlying conditions betray ambiguity, because while all citizens and residents can be said to be existing on the common ground of the city, the infrastructure also points to inequality of provision and participation and therefore a limitation of choice for some. Other mediating factors to equal participation by citizens and residents in the common life of the city may be the extent of entitlement to basic rights conferred by social and state policies. For example, outright denial of rights to work, education, housing, health and hygiene, such as for refugees and immigrants, seriously curtail the ability of such groups to participate in the city. Such processes of institutional discrimination further limit a sense of entitlement, which minorities feel, and in turn may convey the message to decision and policy makers that the suppression of the 'foreigner' is legitimate and perhaps even necessary in order to preserve 'community' (Appadurai, 2006).

These complexities in the visible and invisible differences between persons and groups of persons and the way these are perceived by others are clinically relevant to the professionals working in the CAMHS team. They are relevant not only because they implicate professionals themselves as inhabitants, but also because the CAMHS is an institution occupying a particular space in public life. Gilroy has used the positive term 'conviviality' somewhat hopefully, to convey what 'takes hold when exposure to otherness involves more than jeopardy. It inspires us to applaud settler and other immigrant demands for a more mature polity that, even if not entirely free of racism, might be equipped to deal with racial hierarchies as a matter of politics without lapsing into unproductive guilt and narcissistic anguish' (Gilroy, 2008, p. 58). Here Gilroy highlights the potential in the urban context for providing a background for a mutual recognition and a valuing of difference, because it facilitates encounters and ties between strangers in such places as neighbourhoods, schools, housing estates, health care centres, nurseries, in parks and other public spaces. The CAMHS is such a public space, and it too has a potential for providing a context for encounters between strangers, in this case professionals and clients as well as between clients themselves, which can contribute to the generation of mutual recognition and the valuing of difference in the city. Whether it actually can do this will depend on the social and cultural awareness and the responsiveness of its practitioners.

The teams in the CAMHS

Even though only a few of them live in the borough in which they work, the inner-city CAMHS practitioners are of course themselves subject to the processes described above, and these processes also enter into the relationships practitioners have with each other. Staff may work on their own or jointly, and everyone has a connection with a school—some staff are specifically placed in schools for several sessions—or a general practice in which they both consult to other professionals and directly work with children and their families. All staff carry out generic child and adolescent mental health assessments and treatment. In complex and risky cases clinicians from particular disciplines may join up and team members in the multidisciplinary sub-teams therefore know each other well, help each other out and generally look to each other for support. However, as with all groups (Canham, 2003; Foster, 2006; Vetere, 2007), from time to time staff succumb to group dynamics, which may interfere with the clinical work. The structural subdivision into North and South predisposes the teams to a certain amount of competition and to fantasies or projections[4] about each other, about the other having better working conditions, easier or fewer cases, more resources and inferior treatment models and so on. The regular communication between the two team managers and between individual staff who have cross-team relationships such as expressed in the editing and writing of this book, go some way towards ameliorating this competition and emphasising a collective spirit.

CAMHS staff also work on cases with other agencies, and the dynamics in these relationships may impact the internal dynamics of teams, not least because this kind of mental health work generates anxiety and worry. Together multidisciplinary mental health teams can do great things, but working in teams can also feel powerfully overwhelming with the pressures of containing risk; of facing painful social, psychological, cultural and political realities; of finding solutions;

of travelling around a busy city; of finding time to reflect; of keeping records; and also of worry about outcomes. Coping with these pressures and worries can interfere and distract from the tasks at hand (Bion, 1962; Britton, 1981; Stokes, 1994; Hatcher, 1998) and lead to unhelpful team dynamics. For example, staff from different disciplines may compete with each other about who has the 'best' approach rather than being able to find a way of collaborating with each other. Or team members may respond to anxiety about how they are performing by keeping their heads down and suppressing their differences for fear of provoking conflict. This may result in fragmentation with each professional working by themselves and clients not getting the benefit of the multidisciplinary resource. Thus, just as in the urban context generally and as I will discuss below, in 'the community', the processes and dynamics in the clinical teams and the relationships between team members pivot around the similarities and differences, both professional and personal, between staff members themselves and between staff and clients.

The multidisciplinary professionals differ in terms of professional training and allegiance, and also in terms of gender, class, race and cultural background, ethnic identities, sexual orientation, age, physical ability and personal experiences, and all these differences affect the relationships they have with each other. In fact, the two professional teams contain less diversity than the populations they serve. By far the majority of staff members are middle-class, White, heterosexual, mature women most of whom identify themselves as English with a minority from other, mostly European, countries. There are a small number of men, one of them a consultant psychiatrist, and a small number of persons from other cultural and ethnic backgrounds. The diversity of trainees conveys a similar picture, except that they tend to be younger. Neither of the managers are from minority backgrounds and the proportion of minorities is greater amongst the administrators than amongst the clinical professionals. This profile is not exceptional for CAMHS teams in the National Health Service in the UK generally (Kline, 2014).

Considering this demography of the teams together with the professional trainings of mental health professionals in the UK, which have mostly been slow to address race, culture, diversity and equality issues, it seems that providing an appropriate CAMH service to the multi-cultural population in the locality of the borough presents a challenge for the practitioners, a challenge which is also regularly commented upon nationally. This challenge is accentuated by the ideology articulated in government policies relating to the development of mental health provisions in the community, which I described above. 'Community mental health services' are conceptualised more as services, which happen outside the hospital or clinic, than as services, which consider and appreciate the extent of the meaning and the complexity of the idea of community or the diversity of outlook of those living in them. The impression is thus of a gap between mental health institutions and the populations they serve across which mental health professionals including CAMHS professionals must 'reach out' in order to provide access. In this the 'reaching out' seems to mean 'bringing in' with the suggestion that potential client populations need educating and inducting into the relationships, explanatory frameworks and outlooks articulated by mental health professionals and national bodies such as the National Institute for Health and Care Excellence (NICE)[5]. However, an understanding of mental health and in particular of cross-cultural mental health presents many thornier issues affecting how we might 'reach out', than the practical ones of place and geography (Maitra & Krause, 2014). Ideas about mental health and illness are influenced by political, economic and historical contexts and are embedded in social and cultural conventions and outlooks, some of which are outside awareness. In addition, because mental health professionals themselves are influenced by these social, political and cultural contexts and processes, the wider social relationships and positions of professionals and clients in society generally cannot be excluded from the process of engagement between them. In this way there are at least two aspects to the relationships between the professionals in the CAMHS and their clients, which are relevant to 'outreach in the community'. One, by virtue of professionals offering a service to clients and the latter accepting this, perhaps because they have no other place to go or no other choice; the other by virtue of both parties pursuing social encounters with each other in a situated entanglement of ideas, bodies and things, in which both parties make choices on the basis of prior social, cultural and personal expectations.

In any case this is not a symmetrical encounter because in living with difference, tensions often gather around infrastructures and public places which regulate access to structures such as education, finance, health, credit, safety and food (Amin, 2012). The clinic and the CAMHS constitute such a public space. They are public services to which access is regulated by state and borough policies, for example, in relation to residence, finance and eligibility and by structures and institutions such as intake procedures and ideas about what does and does not constitute legitimate mental suffering.

The CAMHS is positioned between what we might refer to as 'the state', (in the form of the National Health Service) and the wider population, which it is here to serve. With this position comes a potential to regulate and influence relationships between clients and professionals as well as between citizens. The service could thus promote a kind of status quo by affirming a gap between 'mental health services' and 'communities' or it has the potential to work toward the generation of a recognition and equality between all who live and/or work in the borough. To this end the ideas of 'outreach' and 'community' as commonly proposed in mental health literature and in government policies and as generally understood by health professionals do not go far enough. Rather 'community mental health work' requires a readiness to re-examine, change and adapt mental health models and practices to have a good enough 'fit' with particular local contexts.

How we understand 'community'

In what sense do these local contexts constitute 'a community' or 'communities'? It will be clear by now that these terms refer to more than what is outside hospitals and clinics. Over the past decade or so national and local government have been interested in including in their consultations and planning representatives of particular cultural communities as well as voluntary organisations, who tend to have their ears closer to the ground than statutory services. However, who is able to speak for whom? And how may CAMHS professionals make use of the idea of 'community' to inform their mental health work?

The understanding implied in the 'outreach' metaphor is well known from social science. Within a modernist[6] framework of structural functionalism[7] 'community' tended to be understood to refer to a group of persons who belong to a common locale, 'have common interests' or subscribe or adhere to a common social system. This derived from the German sociologist Ferdinand Tönnies who discussed the difference between what he called 'community' (*Gemeinshaft*) and 'society' (*Gesellshaft*) (Tönnies, 1957). He thought that 'community' referring to social organisation based on kinship, friendship and neighbourhood (for example, blood, soil, heritage and language) would be superseded by associations in which social relations would be contractual, based on interest, partial and ego-focussed, rather than group-focussed, superficial, fluid, short-term and impersonal ('society'), as capitalism and individualism developed across the globe. However, communities have not disappeared, not even with the acceleration of the rise of cities and metropolitanism, reminding us that the phenomenon is both robust and complex. Co-presence may afford some opportunities, but it is not the same as co-operation, and we cannot assume that all inhabitants within the political and administrative boundaries of our urban borough, or even some in fairly homogeneous neighbourhoods, relate to each other in the same way, nor that the choice which the urban setting offers is experienced and exercised to equal extents.

Community thus does not necessarily only refer to locality, it is also a symbolic term which is interpreted differently according to context. Persons and groups of persons may find their own identities by defining themselves as different from other persons and groups and these boundaries may be based on differences such as 'race', 'ethnicity', 'religion', 'language', 'a ritual' or 'a practice' (Barth, 1969; Jenkins, 1997; Maitra & Krause, 2014). Such groups may not belong to a particular locality, rather they may subscribe to an idea of sharing something with others far away, such as in the notion of 'imagined communities' (Anderson, 1991). Anderson suggested that the development of printing technology in the sixteenth century eventually provided a vehicle for dispersed populations feeling a sense of commonality, and he too connected this with the rise of capitalism. 'Community' may thus refer to an idea, even a symbol, rather than to actual face-to-face interaction, although of course these two aspects may also overlap.

If 'community' as an idea is slow to disappear and yet may refer to relationships of such differing qualities, what then are we to make of this in the urban setting in which the CAMHS is situated, and where social face-to-face relationships are clearly sustained, while at the same time persons are exposed to networks of networks and faced with 'strangers' regularly during their everyday lives? In social science the interest has shifted from the essential/symbolic dimensions of 'community' to a focus on what kind of concepts of social relations or relational outlooks (sociality) may be associated with this type of modern urban living. For example, in rural communities, particularly in the past, persons might expect to interact and communicate with other persons to whom they were also related through kinship and family ties. This kind of social pattern of interaction may be accompanied as well as sustained by a disposition, which more or less foregrounds the group, the family or a collective as opposed to the individual person. 'Sociality' thus refers to an outlook or an orientation towards others in one's social relationships (Strathern, 1988; Krause, 1998; Ingold, 2000); this reflecting not just individual and personal dispositions and choices but also standardised and routinised expectations. Here again opinions are divided, although all have agreed that something has changed for persons living in contemporary industrialised urban conurbations, which are more or less influenced by capitalism. For Sennett (1998) a community-based sociality refers to an outlook in which persons expect to be different and even to have to negotiate conflict, but where this conflict also cements the feelings of community. 'The scene of conflict becomes a community in the sense that people learn how to listen and respond to one another even as they more keenly feel their differences' (Sennett, 1998, p. 143). Following this line Amit suggests that even in urban network societies collective experiences are transformed into personal intimacies and relationships and it is precisely this process, even in the face of social and other types of mobility, which provides continuity. In turn such continuities provide opportunities for the development of the kinds of communality and permanence conveyed by the notion of 'community' (Amit & Rapport, 2002).

The other side of the argument emphasises the notion of choice and temporary connections and meetings and what this means for an understanding of the 'self' and social relationships. Thus Rapport discusses the possibilities of personalisation by which he means that individuals should be free to move around and to construct identities for themselves on the basis of individual decisions. For Rapport the contemporary (urban) contexts open the possibility that persons can escape from 'communities' as straitjackets to joining communities on a much more voluntary basis (Amit & Rapport, 2002). Wittel also argues for this kind of 'network sociality' related to the contemporary economy and the rise of communications technology, but goes further. 'Network sociality is about social bonds that are continuously produced, reproduced and … consumed' (Wittel, 2001, p. 72). This implies the increasing perception of social relationships as a new kind of social capital[8], namely as fluid resources which are constantly shifting and changing, but which nevertheless like an asset can be converted to something else, such as money, status or prestige.

We may take 'community' to refer to a sliding scale of all these ideas and outlooks and expect to find variations on these themes articulated to different degrees amongst different cultural and ethnic communities in the borough. For example the idea of 'network sociality' may fit some of the clients seen in the CAMHS, whereas others who perhaps are out of work and for other reasons have fewer social relationships, and perhaps little access to information technology, may experience exclusion from these increasingly dominant social processes. Persons, groups and populations or even communities, have different histories, different migratory or sedentary statuses, and have different relationships to each other, to the state and to the locality in which they live. The opportunities, which a locality like our borough affords, must be seen in relation to how individuals and groups of individuals are able to make use of such opportunities against the background of past and current political and economic contexts. Thus a study in the borough in which the CAMHS is located concluded that despite London being designated as a place of dialogue, dissent and negotiation, typical of relations between strangers and in keeping with the spirit of cosmopolitanism, ethnic and class hierarchies 'undermine the realisation of an encompassing cosmopolitan ethics of place' (Devadason, 2010, p. 2961). The study found that the local Bangladeshi population on the whole did not feel at home, but neither did they feel that they could or wanted to move. They felt displaced and without much choice about this. Similarly, a study in another inner-city London borough found that the image of mutual recognition and valuing of difference potentially conveyed in multi-culturalism (Gilroy, 2008) appears not to be realisable for all. In this study Wessendorf found that while a high acceptance of cultural difference is expressed in public spaces, in parochial spaces, by which she means associations and local institutions, this acceptance was lower, and when it came to private spaces the expressions of feelings of divisions and animosity were far more pervasive (Wessendorf, 2014). There is no reason to assume that the way clients who use the CAMH service articulate their most private and intimate feelings towards others around them is any more or less straightforward. Wessendorf (2014) connects this to the poverty and disadvantage which a large part of the population feels and the way this interacts with cultural and racial prejudice. Mental health and wellbeing straddles these intimate, parochial and public domains challenging professionals to work across them.

My work in the CAMHS

A word about my own experiences of these domains. I work as a systemic psychotherapist in the local CAMHS. I have been a systemic psychotherapist for more than twenty-five years, and before that I trained as a social anthropologist and I believe that I approach my CAMHS work as both a mental health professional and as an ethnographer (Krause, 1998, 2002, 2012). I am a White, middle-aged woman of Scandinavian heritage. I grew up in Denmark and consider myself Danish, although my ancestry is more mixed. My own notions of 'community' and 'sociality' are, I suspect, a bit old-fashioned. I grew up in the 1950s and 60s. At that time after World War II Denmark had just emerged from being a mainly agricultural society. In the small Copenhagen suburb (formerly a village) in which I grew up many people knew each other, would stop in the street to chat and members of my family were well known there. Although I lost contact with my father's family, my extended family on my mother's side all kept in touch and some of us were close[9]. However, my most intense experience of a close-knit community context comes from ethnographic fieldwork in several small Himalayan villages in which everyone was related either by kinship or by work relationships based on caste[10].

Denmark is known for a commitment to 'The Welfare State', democracy and relative economic equality with an emphasis on cultural values of 'sameness' (*lighed*) (Jenkins, 2012); at the time of my growing up the only 'strangers' which I met in the course of daily life in the city were people from Greenland (at that time still a colony of Denmark) and tourists. The emphasis on *lighed*, however, did not and still does not denote equality. As the fairy tale the Ugly Duckling (Andersen, 1997)[11] conveys you can be equal if you are similar, but if you are dissimilar you may be ostracised. I moved to the UK in order to study social anthropology in London and was subsequently exposed to other communities both in daily life as a student and later when working as an ethnographer in Nepal and with the Punjabi population in a provincial town in the UK. As a foreigner, albeit a European white-skinned one, I have benefitted from living in a multicultural social context with the possibilities of pursuing networks and connections, accessing diversity and different points of view from a position of relative privilege and wealth and from the creative tensions of 'community sociality', which the multicultural context affords. I have been able to make use of the outlook of 'network sociality' and fluid and fast-changing values. However, through my work I have also become acquainted with many persons less fortunate, for whom the possibility of exercising personal choice may be curtailed by economic, political, emotional and family hardships.

A Bangladeshi family[12]

I worked with a Muslim Bangladeshi family, in which a single parent, a father, Mr Islam, was living with his two children, a boy, Ahmed, aged fifteen, and a girl, Khadija, aged twelve. Mr Islam was born in Bangladesh, and his parents had arranged a marriage for him with a British Bangladeshi woman, after which he had come to live in the UK, where he first worked in a restaurant. Such marriages between spouses from Bangladesh and the UK, respectively, have a long history dating back to the 1950s and 1960s when Bangladeshi men began to come to the UK to seek employment. Labourers tended to find work in restaurants and factories, and this benefited both the UK economy and those men and families who were looking to improve their financial situation in Bangladesh, because people sent money back to Bangladesh enabling families to buy land and build bigger houses there (Gardner, 2008). Since the 1980s and '90s the immigration pattern from Bangladesh into the UK has changed. This followed changes in the labour market as well as restrictions in UK immigration laws, which stipulated that only persons married to a British citizen should be granted residency in the UK. Whereas earlier in the immigration history of the Bangladeshi community in the UK it tended to be women and children who immigrated, the pattern now has changed to involve many more men. Because the Bangladeshi community had previously sent remittances back to Bangladesh, those families associated with the UK had become richer, and it was, and still is, many young Bangladeshi men's dream to come to the UK. For many the only way of doing this is to marry a British Bangladeshi woman (Gardner, 2008).

However, such marriages may pose a challenge to the parties concerned if they, as they often do, position each spouse structurally against the normative expectations of a patrilineal kinship system with possibly difficult consequences for adults as well as children (see also Chapters Four and Eight). In the case of this family the marriage did not last, and the children's mother had left their father two years earlier. Mr Islam refused to see his wife, and Ahmed and Khadija refused to see their mother, but the children also missed her terribly. For example, in their individual psychotherapy sessions both children talked about their mother a great deal. Ahmed articulated his anger towards his father and described how he was trying to keep in contact with his mother. Khadija was adamant that she did not want to see her mother because she had betrayed her and her father. Khadija also spent a great deal of time cooking and cleaning and looking after her father and her brother, as well as herself. Ahmed admitted to being suicidal and having problems controlling his anger. Both children regularly had to suffer other Bangladeshi boys and girls teasing them about their absent mother and calling her rude names.

This case presented several challenges to the CAMHS professionals. One of these related to deciding whether or not there were child protection concerns. Was Mr Islam neglectful of his children in not being able to put their needs before his own? He complained to me and my child psychotherapy colleague that because of his 'culture' and being a Muslim he did not feel that he should touch his teenage, now menstruating, daughter, nor wash her clothes. Therefore Khadija looked after herself. Mr Islam also told us about sleeping on the floor next to his daughter, frequently waking her up because he felt anxious and worried. Again Khadija seemed to accept this, saying that she felt that she was doing her duty looking after her father.

Another challenge related to professionals wanting the children to pursue their relationship with their mother. Khadija was clear that she did not want to see or talk with her mother. Ahmed was much more unsure about this. Mr Islam was adamant that the best thing he could do was to marry again, and while he did not want to stop his children seeing their mother, he was also clear what he thought of her (he used rude words and raised his voice), that she was "bad" and that she would have no rights over her children. Some of the school staff and a social worker were concerned that the urgency of Mr Islam's plan to arrange a second marriage with a Bangladeshi woman, in effect, reflected his wish to replace the children's biological mother with a stranger and in this way 'wipe out' their relationship with her.

Above all as CAMHS professionals we struggled to understand the mother's apparent rejection of her children. As a British Bangladeshi woman did she share her ex-husband's patrilineal outlook on the rights and duties in family relationships, and was that why she did not contact the children and did not want to be involved in the CAMHS work? Or was she, being born in the UK, trying to find a way of living in the multicultural setting of the borough with more choice and more emancipation as a woman? The situation seemed to be permeated by a dilemma between what seemed to be expected in a traditional Bangladeshi family and expressed both by Mr Islam and at different times by Ahmed and Khadija and what seemed to be expected by schools and mental health services according to contemporary ideas of 'community sociality', namely emphasising individual choice above collective expectations. We never met the mother and so could not find out more about how she might have understood this dilemma. However, I and my child psychotherapy colleague also felt that the tension between these different points of view was unduly located in the children and that in the current context it was difficult for them to choose. We therefore decided to let Mr Islam know that we supported his plan of remarrying a woman from Bangladesh since this would provide more help and support for him at home, a female companion for his daughter in the house and, we hoped, in this way allow both Ahmed and Khadija to be less preoccupied with their father's problems.

The new wife arrived in the UK and settled in. The children addressed her as *mai*[13] and Khadija explained to me that as far as she knew this term is an old form for the term 'mother'. She called her own mother *amma,* and she was pleased that she could distinguish her stepmother from her biological mother in this way. Khadija also spoke in our sessions about the relief of not having to cook and clean and no longer being the only one who worried about her father. I think that our acknowledgement of the importance of this new marriage for Mr Islam helped him feel more hopeful about his current multicultural context, and this seemed to facilitate some other changes. Thus, in her individual therapy sessions, which took place in her secondary school, Khadija began to talk about other things such as her friendships in school, music and the pressure of school tests. She was particularly keen to find ways of being Bangladeshi and Muslim in a way that suited her contemporary context. She said that she did not want to be a woman who only cooks and cleans, and she talked about friendships she had made with Christian girls. She also began to be interested in contacting her mother. At the same time Ahmed who was still arguing with his father, had re-established occasional contact with his mother and was a bit more settled in school.

In this case the idea of community had different points of reference. For Mr Islam this was an 'imagined community' connecting Bangladeshis in the borough with the Bangladeshi community in his home locality in Sylhet. This was where he was looking for a new partner and the relationship between the two localities was expressed in idioms of kinship and arranged marriages (Callan, 2012). For various reasons, and some of these related to local discrimination, he seemed to feel much less reassured in his orientation to the multicultural community in the borough. Perhaps he exemplified the cases discussed by Devadason (2010) earlier, in which persons did not feel at home and yet did not feel that they had the luxury of choosing to live elsewhere. By not dismissing his idea about how to find solutions for his situation I think I and my colleague signalled our recognition of his needs within the constraints of his own expectations of kinship and family relationships. For the mother perhaps this 'imagined community' also had meaning, and she perhaps felt that she had to stay away or that she had no rights vis-à-vis her ex-husband and her children, but we can also speculate that through her childhood in the UK she had experienced a community sociality presenting persons with individual choice as an important point of collective focus. While the children understood and could relate to these orientations, they were at the same time growing up and being socialised into a much more fluid context in which other types of networks and relationships and new information technology influence the way persons communicate with each other.

Conclusion

This chapter has drawn attention to the complexity of the concept of 'community'. Health service literature and policies convey an idea of 'community' as a place, as a locality outside and perhaps in contrast to the hospital or clinic where mental health professionals carry out their work. Hence 'community services' involve going out of the clinic and hospital. Our work with Mr Islam and his children took place in the community, in the children's school and in their home as well as in the clinic. While it is certainly helpful for professionals to engage in life outside their institutions, these are not the only places we find 'community'. Ideas of 'community' exist in the minds and hearts of clients wherever we meet with them. A consideration of 'community' as a symbol of connectedness therefore informs us about the relational orientation of a person, a family or a group. In this sense we can do 'outreach' in our clinics, hospitals and consulting rooms. However, everywhere the quality of this work depends on mental health professionals recognising that community is a gloss on social relationships including the cultural, social, class, sexual, emotional and psychological content of such relationships. These aspects combine in unique and unpredictable ways, but the potential for 'community sociality' becoming a resource for mental health for all sections of the populations will depend on CAMHS being seen as public spaces where strangers despite their different ideas about relationships and about the world in general can be recognised and respected.

Notes

1 In different cultures and languages the actual term used may be closer to 'families', 'clans' or 'locality'.
2 Sylheti is a dialect of Bengali.
3 Pierre Bourdieu, a French philosopher and social anthropologist, called such dispositions 'doxic experiences' referring to the way we all grow up learning and acquiring a set of practical cultural competences—the sense that we occupy a position in a social space, which provides a kind of immediate understanding which nevertheless may be an illusion (Bourdieu, 1990).
4 In psychoanalysis 'projection' refers to a theory which suggests that persons may want to distance themselves from unpleasant impulses by denying that they have these impulses and instead attributing them to other persons. In psychoanalytic thinking this process is thought to be a human characteristic.
5 The National Institute for Health and Care Excellence is an executive non-departmental public body of the Department of Health in the United Kingdom. It disseminates research for best practice and publishes guidelines for all services and treatments in the National Health Service.
6 Modernism is a philosophical movement in the arts, that along with cultural trends and changes, arose from wide-scale and far-reaching transformations in Western society in the late-nineteenth and early-twentieth centuries. Among the factors that shaped Modernism was the development of modern industrial societies and the rapid growth of cities, followed then by the horror of World War I. Modernism rejected the certainty of Enlightenment thinking, and many modernists rejected religious beliefs.
7 Social functionalism is a framework for building theory that sees society as a complex system whose parts work together to promote solidarity and stability.
8 Pierre Bourdieu described 'social capital' as 'the aggregate of the actual or potential resources which are linked to possession of a durable network of more or less institutionalized relationships of mutual acquaintance or recognition' (Bourdieu 1986, p. 248).
9 Danish kinship, like English kinship, emphasises relationships traced from a person through both parents, and the nuclear family tends to be the main unit of reference.
10 Caste is a form of social stratification characterised by endogamy, hereditary transmission of a lifestyle, which often includes an occupation, ritual status in a hierarchy and customary social interaction and exclusion based on cultural notions of purity and pollution.
11 In this story a swan egg is hatched by a duck in her nest in a domestic farmyard. The little signet is not recognised by the other animals and because of being different is chastised and eventually hunted out of the yard. He is lonely and

excluded and thinks of himself as worthless until the next year when he catches sight of himself in the water. At this point he realises that he has grown into a beautiful swan.

12   Names and some details have been changed.

13   *Mai* means 'mother' and is commonly use among Hindus (in Northern India, from Sanskrit *matri*/Hindi *mata*), though *ma* is also common among modern urban Bengali Hindus, but may also suggest class and rural/urban differences. *Amma* is more common among Muslims in Bangladesh—but also the 'norm' among Hindus all over Southern India. Khadija's usage reflects how markers of religion, class and modernity separate and unite Muslims and Hindus in Bengal, where these differences may be fraught (personal communication, Begum Maitra). These differences may be reflected in Khadija's use of the two terms, while at the same she wanted to differentiate her two mothers.

References

Amin, A. (2012). *Land of Strangers.* Cambridge, England: Polity Press.

Amit, V. & Rapport, N. (2002). *The Trouble with Community. Anthropological Reflections on Movement, Identity and Collectivity.* London, England: Pluto Press.

Appadurai, A. (2006). *Fear of Small Numbers. An Essay in the Geography of Anger.* Durham, NC & London, England: Duke University Press.

Andersen, B. (1991). *Imagined Communities: Reflections on the Origin and Spread of Nationalism* (rev. ed.). London, England: Verso (first published 1983).

Andersen, H. C. (1997). *Complete Andersen Fairy Tales.* (pp. 251–60). Hertfordshire, England: Wordsworth Editions (first published 1843).

Barth, F. (1969). *Ethnic Groups and Boundaries: The Social Organisation of Culture of Difference.* Oslo, Norway: Universitetsforlaget.

Bion, W. R. (1962). *Experiences in Groups and Other Papers.* London, England: Routledge.

Bourdieu, P. (1986). The forms of capital. In: J.G. Richardson (ed.), *Handbook of Theory and Research for the Sociology of Education.* (pp. 241–258). New York, NY: Greenwood Press.

Bourdieu, P. (1990). *The Logic of Practice.* Cambridge, England: Polity Press.

Britton, R. (1981). Reneactment as an unwitting professional response to family dynamics. In: S. Box, B. Copley, J. Magagna & E. Moustaki (eds.). *Psychotherapy with Families: An Analytic Approach.* (pp. 48–58). London, England: Routledge & Kegan Paul.

Callan, A. (2012). *Patients and Agents. Mental Illness, Modernity & Islam in Sylhet, Bangladesh.* Oxford, England: Berghahn Books.

Camden.data.info (accessed 29 November 2014).

Canham, H. (2003). Group and gang states of mind. *Journal of Child Psychotherapy,* 28(2), 113–27.

Devadason, R. (2010). Cosmopolitanism, geographical imaginaries and belonging in North London. *Urban Studies,* 47(14), 2945–63.

Foster, A. (2006). Living and working with difference and diversity. In: A. Foster, A. Dickinson, B. Bishop & J. Klein (eds.). *Difference: An Avoided Topic in Practice.* (pp. 5–24). London, England: Karnac Books.

Gardner, K. (2008). Keeping connected: Security, place, and 'social capital' in a 'Londoni' village in Sylhet. *Journal of the Royal Anthropological Institute,* 14(3), 477–95.

Gilroy, P. (2008). Melancholia or conviviality. The politics of belonging in Britain. In: S. Davidson & J. Rutherford (eds.). *Race, Identity and Belonging.* (pp. 48–60). London, England: Lawrence & Wishart.

Hannerz, U. (1980). *Exploring the City. Inquiries Toward an Urban Anthropology.* New York, NY: Columbia University Press.

Hatcher Cano, D. (1998). Me-ness and One-ness. In: P. B. Talamo, F. Borgogno & S.A. Merciai (eds.). *Bion's Legacy to Groups* (pp. 83–94). London, England: Karnac Books.

Ingold, T. (2000). *The Perception of the Environment. Essays in Livelihood, Dwelling and Skill.* London, England: Routledge.

Jenkins, R. (1997). *Rethinking Ethnicity. Arguments and Explorations.* London, England: Sage Publications.

Jenkins, R. (2012). *Being Danish. Paradoxes of Identity in Everyday Life.* Copenhagen, Denmark: Museum Tusculanum Press.

Kline, R. (2014). *The "Snowy White Peaks" of the NHS: A Survey of Discrimination in Governance and Leadership and the Potential Impact on Patient Care in London and England.* London, England: Middlesex University.

Krause, I-B. (1998). *Therapy Across Culture.* London, England: Sage Publications.

Krause, I-B. (2002). *Culture and Family Therapy.* London, England: Karnac Books.

Krause, I-B. (2012). *Culture and Reflexivity in Systemic Psychotherapy. Mutual Perspectives.* London, England: Karnac Books.

Latour, B. (2005). *Reassembling the Social: An Introduction to Actor-Network Theory.* Oxford, England: Oxford University Press.

Maitra, B. & Krause, I-B. (2014). *Culture and Madness. A Training Resource, Film and Commentary for Mental Health Professionals.* London, England: Jessica Kingsley Publishers.

Miller, D. (2010). *Stuff.* Cambridge, England: Cambridge University Press.

Parekh, B. (2000). *Rethinking Multiculturalism. Cultural Diversity and Political Theory.* Basingstoke, England: Macmillan Press.

Rapport, R. & Overing, J. (2000). *Social and Cultural Anthropology. The Key Concepts.* London, England: Routledge.

Rattansi, A. (2011). *Multiculturalism. A Very Short Introduction.* Oxford, England: Oxford University Press.

Redfield, R. (1960). *The Little Community, and Peasant Society and Culture.* Chicago, IL: Chicago University Press.

Sennett, R. (1998). *The Corrosion of Character: The Personal Consequences of Work in the New Capitalism.* New York, NY: W.W. Norton.

Strathern, M. (1988). *The Gender of the Gift. Problems with Women and Problems with Society in Melanesia.* Berkeley, CA: University of California Press.

Tönnies, F. (1957). *Community and Society.* New York, NY: Harper (first published in 1887).

Stokes, J. (1994). Problems in multidisciplinary teams. The unconscious at work. *Journal of Social Work Practice,* 8(2), 161–7.

Vetere, A. (2007). Bio/psych/social models and the multidisciplinary team working. Can systemic thinking help? *Clinical Child Psychology and Psychiatry,* 12(1), 5–12.

Wessendorf, S. (2014). 'Being open, but sometimes closed'. Conviviality in a super-diverse London neighbourhood. *European Journal of Cultural Studies,* 17(4), 392–405.

Wittel, A. (2001). Toward a network sociality. *Theory, Culture & Society,* 18(6), 51–76.

Chapter 3

Creative resistance and collaborative relationships

Working with inner-city young people and families

Taiwo Afuape

Introduction

I am a clinical psychologist, systemic therapist, Black African, working-class woman, who grew up in an inner-city borough of London. My parents are from a Nigerian town called Abéokuta, and came to live in South London in the early 1960s. Throughout my professional training I was niggled with doubts about whether I wanted to be a clinical psychologist and whether the profession wanted me. I was not convinced that it did enough to challenge social inequality and injustice. I often felt categorised as 'different', with respect to being African, a Black woman and a working-class person from an 'inner-city', in ways that emphasised pathology, deficit and difficulties. The richness of who I was, who my family were and the communities I lived within, seemed obscured by this tendency within the profession to focus on problems.

It is not surprising then that I developed a keen interest in social constructionist systemic therapy, narrative therapy, community psychology and liberation psychology[1]. These frameworks validated my critique of a 'scientific' approach to psychological practice that centres on 'expertise' as though science, research or indeed 'evidence' can ever be value-neutral and devoid of political, social and cultural context; my critique of what seemed to be a 'disembodied', 'head-based' and 'knowing' approach to well-being; and my critique of an obsession with theory linked to practice, at the expense of process. They were also helpful in legitimising the ways I wanted to engage my whole self, including my heart. Engaging my heart meant being open to the social constraints on people's lives *and* the creative ways they resist them.

The inner-city/urban context

When looking for definitions of 'inner-city', the phrase 'associated with problems' came up a number of times. For example, the Cambridge online dictionary gives the following definition: 'the central part of a city where people live and where there are often problems because people are poor and there are few jobs and bad houses' (Cambridge Dictionary & Thesaurus, 2013). Similarly, the Oxford Pocket

Dictionary (2008) explains that, 'inner-city is the area near the centre of a city, especially when associated with social and economic problems'. It is not surprising, then, that young people and their families from the 'inner-city' also become associated with deficit; defined as victims or perpetrators; seen as a threat to the social order (particularly if coming from Black and Minority Ethnic communities) or as 'chavy'[2] and unsophisticated (particularly when coming from White working-class communities).

Similarly, the term 'community' in the context of an 'inner-city' can come with various negative and limiting sets of assumptions which, in themselves, can be oppressive. For instance, I have noticed that when highlighting the demographic area of the Child and Adolescent Mental Health Service (CAMHS) in which I work, the vague phrase "the Bangladeshi community" is often used as a prelude to describing some sort of obstacle, lack or problem. This problem-orientation unhelpfully obscures the complexity of 'community', as well as the resources and abilities that can be harnessed by those interested in promoting well-being in an inner-city (I will go on to describe how we might understand the term 'community' towards the end of the chapter). Particularly when working with young people, it is often important to recognise the creative forms of expression and resistance that emerge in, and are facilitated by, an urban context.

> As I watch the film *Take the Lead* (2006) featuring actor Antonio Banderas, about a ballroom dancer (based on Pierre Dulaine[3]) who teaches classic dance to teenagers serving school detention, I am struck by how young people are portrayed. Although these young people add flavour to the classic form of dance, the premise of the film seems to centre on a good and loving teacher who rescues hopeless and directionless young people with his ability to shape them into something other than what they are; in so doing he engenders hope and direction. This theme, of taming unruly inner-city youth through teaching them new and more sophisticated forms of cultural and artistic expression, seems to have interesting parallels with popular themes in wider social and political discourse. Although I have not done a comprehensive analysis of the (varying) portrayals of young people in modern films, this storyline seemed to echo what young people tell me about their experiences, with respect to the dual positions of being exotically romanticised and yet perceived as out of control, reckless and lacking direction.
>
> Although I accept that new narratives and ways of being can be liberating, what strikes me about this film, is the implicit assumption that the more young people curb their cultural forms of expression in favour of ones instructed to them by adults and the closer they move towards an idealised (often synonymous with middle-class) image of youth, the better (and healthier) they are.
>
> Alternatively, we might be interested to learn more about the creativity of young people *as they are*, as well as the structural and systemic changes that are needed to support young people's own forms of creativity. What might emerge from such curiosity might be even more surprising, inspiring and owned by young people themselves.

I am particularly interested in how we (CAMHS) are viewed by the children, young people and families we serve. Are we just another adult/service/agency, among many, attempting to rescue, treat, change or punish them, because the problems that they *experience* are viewed as problems that they *have*? This chapter is based on both personal experience (having grown up in an 'inner-city' and currently living in one) and professional experience (working collaboratively with children, young people and families living in an 'inner-city', who experience multiple life stresses and traumas, as well as remarkable resilience and creativity). I attempt to describe collaborative ways of working with young people and families in context, that a) starts with *what is*, rather than *what is not*; b) reflects on the link between creativity and resistance; c) moves people in *their* preferred direction, not ours; and d) aims to support and voice a set of experiences that have previously not been recognised[4]. One theory that helps me attend to social context is Co-ordinated Management of Meaning (CMM), which was devised by communication theorists Barnett Pearce and Vernon Cronen.

Working creatively and responsively with young people and families

Co-ordinated Management of Meaning (CMM)—levels of context

The CMM levels of context framework (Pearce, 2007) invites us to reflect on the several levels of experience happening at any given moment, some of which form the context for other experiences. Levels of context have been depicted in many different ways. Figure 3.1, on the top of the next page, is the version presented by Afuape (2011).

Some contextual factors

Young people, families and inequality

It is recognised by treaties like the UN Convention on the Rights of the Child (UNCRC), that well-being thrives in the context of social equality. The emphasis on equality rather than disadvantage per se, is supported by research that suggests that it is the disparity between the richest and the poorest in the UK that impacts on well-being and causes unhappiness (see *The Spirit Level* by Richard Wilkinson and Kate Pickett, 2010). Children from disadvantaged backgrounds do worse in education than those from advantaged backgrounds, by a greater amount, in the UK than similar countries (DfES, 2006).What is most shocking is that the UK has one of the worst rates of child poverty in the industrialised world, with four million (30 percent of) British children living in poverty (UNICEF, 2010) and 1.6 million children living in overcrowded, temporary, or run-down accommodation (Rice, 2006). Despite being one of the wealthiest countries in the world, the impact of 'austerity' and the government's

Contextual force: The effect different levels of context have on experience. Higher levels have a powerful effect on lower levels. The effect of powerful contexts on a person can make them feel obliged to think and behave in certain ways.

Political—Meanings that are influenced by global/political context *

Spiritual—Meanings related to systems of faith or belief **

Cultural—Meanings that are shared within a cultural group or context

Family—Meanings that are shared within a family

Interpersonal relationship—Meanings derived from relationships

Identity/life script—Meanings that come from personal experiences

Episode—The event which adds meaning to what is communicated

Speech act—The act and/or utterance and meanings that are communicated

Bodily sensations—Bodily feelings/experiences

Content of speech—What is said/a statement

Implicative force: The effect of lower levels of context on higher levels of context. It may be regarded as the way we respond to powerful forces in our lives and how our responses shape our experiences.

These levels are not fixed and change depending on what the highest context (i.e. the most powerful contributing context) in a given moment seems to be. Contextual forces tend to be more powerful than implicative forces; but implicative forces can still have a powerful effect. For example, political context often has a determining effect on our cultural stories, which can have a powerful effect on our family lives, which can influence our individual life experience. However, at times we may resist the power of a particular social discourse, and this resistance might have a ripple effect continuing right up to the political context.

* Addition made by Nimisha Patel, November 2005, personal communication.
** Addition made by Karen Partridge, May 2007, personal communication.

Figure 3.1 CMM levels of context

response to it has meant that the disparity between the richest and poorest in the UK is ever widening. For example, University of Cambridge research commissioned by Shelter found that cuts to housing benefits were pushing more children further into poverty (Rice, 2006) and the 2010 UNICEF report on child well-being ranked the UK *bottom* out of 21 OECD (Organisation for Economic Co-operation and Development) countries (UNICEF, 2010). In addition, government discourse has tended to *individualise* rather than *socialise* poverty. For instance, in 2013 Iain Duncan Smith developed so called 'better' measures of child poverty compared to the original *poor measure of poverty* based on income. This new measure does not measure poverty at all but focuses on negative behaviour, such as poor levels of educational attainment, and parental "worklessness" and addiction. The focus away from material deprivation and disadvantage, meant that Duncan Smith could plan to repeal the 2010 Child Poverty Act, which committed the government to eradicating child poverty in the UK by 2020 (Wintour, 2015) and turn our focus on problem(atic) families.

Young people and the media

Despite the limited ability to determine their own lives, children and young people are often blamed for their circumstances and the ways they act in response to them. Media discourses on the whole imply that young people have choices and simply choose badly, despite many young people living a life not of their choosing, and many families trying their best to function in the context of dwindling resources and increasing social disadvantage, discrimination and traumas.

Young people are often vilified for their forms of self-expression and protest. As a result, current media discourses seem to fall into one of three camps: youth as "bad" (for example, David Cameron's speech post – August 2011 riots), "mad" (for example, 2013 *Guardian* article about 'psychiatric illness' among gang members) or "sad" (for example, the emphasis journalists often put on Camila Batmanghelidjh's words, despite the fact she is often talking about social abuse)[5]. The tendency of the media to focus our attention on young people (or their families) as problems misses out the creative ways people *respond* to their circumstances (Wade, 1997; 2005).

Some implicative factors

Coherence, co-ordination and mystery

In contrast to a problem-focused approach, CMM highlights both the impact of contextual factors (how experiences influence us) *and* the existence of implicative factors (how we respond to our experiences) in our lives. As well as experiencing the world and attempting to make meaning, we also actively interact with our world, and each other; in addition, there are intangible and subtle aspects of the social world. Pearce (2007) referred to this in terms of *coherence, co-ordination* and *mystery*. Creativity, too, requires these three elements:

- Coherence—how we understand the world and our experience
- Coordination—how we interact with the world and each other
- Mystery—how we understand life beyond the rational sense of it

Creativity and collaborative processes

Creativity helps us develop new ways of being collaborative, and collaborative processes seem to encourage creativity. Both open up the limits of what can be expressed and how we imagine alternatives, create possibilities and actualise them. As creativity is everywhere, its theory is in life not just in books. My personal experience is that creativity seems to connect me to myself and to others (as we create in the context of relationships with others, and for others, even when we do this activity on our own) and involves active engagement as well as receptivity. The late artist Georgia Totto O'Keeffe (November 1887 to March 1986) wrote: 'You put out your hand to touch the flower—lean forward to smell it ... or give it to someone to please them. Still—in a way—nobody sees a flower—really—it is so small—we haven't time—and to see takes time, like to have a friend takes time' (quoted in Cameron, 1995, p. 22). Creativity seems to allow pauses in our experience so we can take time to see and to reflect. It can also get us to the other side of our experience and help us move on; as such, creativity seems to both help us encounter life and escape from it. To demonstrate the ways in which creativity has helped me to work more collaboratively with children, young people and families, I will reflect on: *Creative ways of being as a CAMHS clinician* and *drawing on the creativity of others*.

Creative ways of being a clinician

The body as a context for experience

Despite associations with our mind, I view creativity as an embodied process. In the Minority World[6] the body seems largely viewed as a) a commodity and consumer; b) a distraction from the superior expressions of the mind; and c) a machine that either works well or breaks down, which makes it difficult to conceive of how new understanding, meaning and ways to move on can come from it.

Table 3.1 The body, coherence, co-ordination and mystery

The body making meaning	The body is a natural living process constantly building upon itself *and* in constant interaction with its environment, which is a form of meaning making (Gendlin, 2003). If the body is a process rather than a machine it must be capable of new understanding.
The body co-ordinating actions	Living organisms only exist as part of interactions with their environment. As we meet people in our bodies, it is the first meeting place we have with each other (Shotter, 2010). Thus the body is an intrinsic part of any relational and social co-ordination process.
The body and mystery	Most of what the body does it knows to do without us exercising conscious control over it. The heart beats and lungs enable us to breathe; the body's system, including the skin and areas of our brain, knows how to monitor and maintain us at a given temperature.

Alternative perspectives view the body as a living process (Gendlin, 2003). In fact, the body makes meaning, co-ordinates and is subject to the whims and quirks of mystery, just by being (see Table 3.1).

When attempting to be responsive to the people we work with, we may need to reflect on our taken-for-granted ways of being, even down to our embodiment. Our natural or learned ways of carrying ourselves and responding bodily to others may not invite connection from children, young people and families, who may have different ways of life, cultural backgrounds or peer groups, to our own. Reflecting on the nature of our orientation when we meet others enables us to creatively adapt, in order to truly meet another body.

Many people I work with, who were not born in the UK or not of British origin hug me at the start of the session, which means together we foreground aspects of our culture that give credence to bodily contact as a form of affection and respect. In those moments, it feels important to respect both what makes sense to them and what I am comfortable embodying.

***

My intention when doing family work is always to try my hardest to fully understand each person with whom I am in contact. Despite useful conversations in supervision and with a reflecting team (discussed in more detail later in the chapter) there are times when this intention is in mind but not body. By tuning into my body I try to notice these occasions and spend time (even just a few minutes) with my body, before the session, to use various techniques (such as meditation or focusing[7]) to create space for my bodily experience to move in the direction of my intention (see Afuape, 2016).

***

I might ask myself questions such as: what are the emotions, and/or felt senses I am embodying as I meet with X? Am I privileging respect for their creativity? Is this expressed by and experienced in my body? How are they experiencing me and how I am within my body?

As well as levels of context, CMM also reflects on aspects of self, such as gender, age, skin colour, class and so on, that involve overt experiences as well as those that are more implicit. As such, CMM recognises the concrete and practical as well as the intangible and subtle aspects of experience. As we live each situation with a body that senses much more than we think or directly know, the information that comes from attending to our bodily felt-sense, although subtle, might lead to new and useful insights.

Shotter and Katz (1999) distinguish between monological and dialogical stances. A monological stance is one in which we are bodily unresponsive to the activities of the other. We observe but ignore any responses that they as other embodied beings invite from us, as though the other person is an object of our embodied perception and not *another* embodied perception. A dialogical stance means that all participants shape and are shaped by the interaction and are mutually involved in making meaning (Seikkula, 2002). A responsive, embodied, dialogical approach means co-creating with others what boundaries (for example, where to sit, when or if ever to make physical contact and how to respond when people cry) make most personal and cultural sense to them.

Trusting uncertainty and trying not to know too soon

When we are responsive we fully enter into and honour the experience of the other which includes a willingness to question what we think we know, as we can never know with certainty what is behind another's words and actions. This involves asking more questions (about the other person's thoughts, ideas and preferences), than making statements (based on ours). As there is no way of knowing in advance the way a collaborative conversation will unfold, trusting uncertainty involves being open to the unforeseen. Suspending certainty turns dialogue into an improvisational, generative and creative activity (Anderson & Gehart, 2007).

In the same vein I try to resist being taken over by other people's descriptions of a young person or family before I have met them. Often the language surrounding a referral is problem-laden. In collaborative processes we update and evolve our understanding with service users and try not to come to a complete understanding too soon. To paraphrase Julia Cameron, I try to think *mystery not mastery*, as a mystery draws us in, leads us on and lures us (Cameron, 1995). Sometimes we are so accustomed to the familiar that we miss the mystery.

Listening and speaking creatively

If it seems helpful I try to share my thoughts with young people and families, so that they understand why I am asking certain questions, as well as share any dilemmas I might have. I try to share my ideas tentatively, as a possibility that is open to discussion, debate, doubt and challenge from them. To make the conversation *creative* and *emergent* I do not overly direct it; I stay open to unexpected newness and try to be a combination of curious and uncertain ("I could be wrong, but I was wondering. ...", "have I got that right or wrong?", "what do you think?"). Possibilities emerging from the process do not come from one person, but the co-construction and co-joint process. As young people and families co-construct new possibilities with me, the emerging ideas are consistent with their values and world view and they seem, and experience themselves as, more resourceful than in need of rescue.

Drawing on others' creativity

Reflecting processes and multiple voices

Multiple perspectives, a willingness to move in and out of different positions and openness to positions not previously envisioned seem to be key to all forms of creativity. Similarly, inviting as many different viewpoints into my encounter with young people and families as possible is central to a creative approach to intervention. One way of bringing in multiple perspectives is through the use of reflecting processes. For example, reflecting teams (Andersen, 1991; 1995) are two or more people other than the therapist who listen to the conversation and when asked, make reflections to each other about what they have heard. Differences in the team with respect to ethnicity, gender, class, culture and so on, mean they have greater potential than the individual therapist to offer a range of perspectives that might be helpful (Selvini & Selvini Palazzoli, 1991).

If I cannot work with a team I try to minimise monologues—'the same thoughts continuing, like a tune in one's head' (Anderson & Gehart, 2007, p. 51)—by dialoguing with as many people as I can (service users, colleagues, supervisors and my manager). In particular I try to hear reflections from colleagues who are not psychologists or systemic therapists, given that another way of being tripped up by monologues is seeking out those who reinforce my worldview and avoiding those who challenge it.

Recognising resistance as creative

Rather than taking an expert position, we can look more closely at the creative ways that people resist power over them that *pre-exist* contact with us. As Watts et al (2003) and others have pointed out people always resist oppression and abuse. When people view their actions as forms of resistance congruent with their values, they are more likely to feel resilient (Wade, 2005). As well as despair, frustration and struggle, there can also be a validating energy that comes with resisting adversity and indignity.

Respecting resistance to expertism in therapy

Despite what my professional training encouraged me to believe, I do not make change happen, or unilaterally determine another person's perceptions, feelings or behaviour. Although we inevitably influence each other, we cannot influence in a predetermined way. Nevertheless, change is a constant energy; our feelings, meanings and bodies are in constant flux. Responsivity means, not just respecting service user expertise, but expecting and respecting their resistance to any unhelpful attempts by us to be their agent of change. Creative and collaborative processes do not necessarily mean the absence of difference, disagreement and tension. In fact respecting the resistance of young people and families in therapy, and being shaped by it, turns interaction into a more dynamic and responsive activity. Despite psychology and therapy literature generally presenting 'service user' resistance as something to avoid, I would argue that creativity in therapy does not require the (impossible) absence of therapist power, but the acceptance of 'service user' power, such that each participant's contribution is valid (Guilfoyle, 2005).

Respecting resistance to social abuse

Given our relative voice and power as professionals it is also incumbent on us to challenge the forms of social abuse that contribute to distress. A recent example of this has been the development of the group *Psychologists Against Austerity* and both their briefing paper and week-long action (in the run-up to the general election in May 2015) challenging austerity by disseminating real-life stories, as well as research, that highlights the impact of gross government spending cuts, on the well-being of individuals, families and communities (Harper, 2015).

Increasingly, young people and families highlight to me how important my awareness of their resistance practices is, to them and our relationship. Young people may resist oppression by creating niches and identities for themselves that are not mainstream. Understanding this better enables me to support and engage with multiple modes of expression, participation and the demonstration of abilities. Young people may express resistance in ways that are harder to encourage, such as through being angry and defiant, rejecting authority, nightmares, showing fear, displaying disinterest and worrying about the future. Rather than viewing these forms of resistance as symptoms of emotional disorder we might view them as responses to adversity that point to young people's desire for well-being. In these 'small' acts are often unarticulated protests that can be creatively harnessed (Wade, 1997; 2005; Afuape, 2011).

Resistance can be creative and expansive, restrictive and destructive or a combination of both, opening up possibilities whilst creating more difficulties for self or others. How we view acts of resistance depends on our position, the viewpoint we take and the issues we reflect on. We could argue that destructive resistance is a response that is misguided and misdirected towards harming individuals and communities, usually in more disadvantaged and vulnerable circumstances. It stops being creative because it disrupts co-ordination between people by replicating or reinforcing other forms of domination. Creative resistance opens up opportunities and possibilities rather than causing further limits and constraints on people's ability to live well with each other (Afuape, 2011). Whether we engage in reactive or reflective resistance is often influenced by the social circumstances, opportunities and restraints we experience. However, even when challenging unhelpful forms of resistance, we can always harness the *creative potential* of resistance; after all, creativity (no matter how quiet) is *never finished,* as there is always more to learn and ways of refining what we do to live creatively (Afuape, 2011).

Simon, a single father of African-Caribbean origin was referred by his GP for depression. He arrived with his two small children, twin boys Tarik and Taseem, aged seven. As I engaged in creative play with the twins Simon explained how upset he was about his housing situation. He had been "fighting a losing battle" with the council for a year prior to our meeting, to have his family moved, due to sex work and drug use taking place in communal areas of the estate where they lived. Directed by what was most pertinent to the family, our sessions focused on the impact of the family's housing on their well-being, as well as the resources they drew on to cope. For instance, we explored the ways in which Simon was vocal, articulate and persistent, despite the gendered-racist responses of people he came into contact with, and being perceived as 'an angry Black man'. The children and I playfully explored the history of their resources, drawing a 'time tree' based on the 'Tree of Life' methodology developed by Ncube (2006)—an idea that emerged from our conversation—to map the development of their personal and collective qualities. The roots were akin to the past including past characters in the fictional life of the children who demonstrated these qualities, as well as significant people in Simon's family and ancestry; the trunk represented their body and the strengths and skills they embodied in their moment-to-moment experience (for instance, Tarik talked about being able to run very fast and how being active helped him feel more relaxed. Simon felt that he had a "strong walk" that prepared him to meet adversity or challenges, as well as soft hands for caring for others and reading important knowledges); the branches represented the people they drew on for support and the twins suggested that the leaves represent their dreams—for instance, Taseem wanted 'to be able to fly' and Simon 'to live somewhere that feels like a home, a community'. Using this tree metaphor, we explored the beliefs the family had about the importance of environment and of 'home'; not just as a physical place and dwelling but as a doing (with others), a feeling (in the body), a memory and a wish. We reflected on their embodied experiences of resistance as much as the negative impact of their surroundings on their sense of who they were in the world. For example, the tension in their bodies as they walked home was regarded as their rejection of the pressure to simply adjust to deprived conditions.

A significant part of our meetings consisted of contacting local MPs, liaising with the local council, as well as writing a letter to the housing department about why it was imperative that the family be moved (at the request of the boys this letter included a photocopy of some of their artwork, in particular a picture of Tariq 'flying' and his verbatim words from a session where he likened flying to freedom and space, whilst describing his family dwelling as 'a cage'. After a few months the family were moved and unsurprisingly Simon's mental health improved, his sons began to sleep better and reports of their 'problem behaviour' in school dwindled.

***

Sixteen-year-old Nancy, a UK-born teenager of Scottish origin, came to family therapy with her mother Dionne, after Nancy was excluded from school for persistently walking out of class and being abusive to teachers. Dionne explained that she would get into horrendous fights with Nancy when she tried to get her to attend school.

Dionne told me that she felt that Nancy's behaviour was the result of witnessing past domestic violence from Nancy's father to Dionne. Nancy told me she feared I would make assumptions about her and what she should talk about and I explained that we could talk about things that were meaningful to her. I asked Nancy how she spent her time. Dionne answered by saying 'sitting around watching movies all day'. To interrupt the conflict that ensued and encourage a new way of listening, we agreed that Dionne would watch the session in the viewing room with the reflecting team while I spoke to Nancy, swapping round in the next session.

Nancy told me that her favourite film was *Million Dollar Baby* (2004), a film starring Clint Eastwood, Hilary Swank and Morgan Freeman about a boxing trainer, called Frankie, estranged from his own daughter, who develops a close relationship with a waitress and amateur boxer called Maggie Fitzgerald and helps her achieve her dream of becoming professional[8]. Whereas I found the tragic ending distressing, the film had sparked Nancy's passion for boxing and she trained regularly in her local gym, even though it was very difficult at first to find a place training females. She told me that her mum thought she liked boxing because she was violent like her father, or because she was trying to learn how to defend herself from bullies. Nancy said that boxing to her was an art form and she was good. It challenged her to be herself, rather than what was expected of her as a female.

When Dionne joined us, Nancy wanted her mum to talk with her directly rather than with the reflecting team. Dionne wondered if Nancy was drawn to the father figure in the film, 'Frankie'. Nancy said she liked 'Maggie' and her persistence and hard work, commenting, 'Maggie is a natural. She knows in her body she is good even when no-one else does'. Dionne commented that she thought it was a sad film as Frankie has no family. Nancy responded saying, 'No, family are people who believe in you; Maggie is his family. He is hers'. Dionne said, 'But she dies', and Nancy responded, 'Not before she got what she most wanted in life'.

Dionne went back behind the screen in the viewing room where the team still were. I asked Nancy, 'What is boxing about for you?' to which she replied, 'Boxing is everything … it is not about the past but about how I am now and about the future … getting what you really want out of life while you can'.

I looked at the screen, which from the therapy room was a mirror and from inside the viewing room was a window. I wondered if boxing for Nancy was like a mirror *and* a window. The mirror helped her see what was important to her, her values; the window helped her envision what else might be out there, and in their future. Whereas the mirror reflects back just her, the window makes an opening to a wider world beyond her. I wondered what curiosities Nancy had about her mum's life and what was meaningful to her mum, which we agreed to explore in the next session. At the end of the session Dionne shared that she had learned something about what her daughter most valued and had started to see the ways Nancy stood for those values.

Recognising creativity as resistance

As well as exploring resistance as a form of creativity we might recognise creativity as a form of resistance. I have had conversations with young people about creative activity such as parkour[9], listening to/making music, writing, reading, photography, theatre/drama, knitting, fashion, cooking, dance, drawing, sculpture, writing rhymes/poetry and sport. Creative forms of expression often give people a sense of joy, purpose and competence. Through creativity they connect to infinite unexplored potential, despite a context of adversity. Creativity is an energy that reminds us that we are always becoming and never fully reach our destination. Because creativity is both individual expression (related to coherence/meaning making) and participation in something greater than individual experience (co-ordination and mystery), it is important to create spaces for dialogue between people (such as in a family) or between different systems (such as between a family and a school), as this allows new possibilities to emerge in multiple relationships, based on previously unnoticed aspects of people's creative and ethical being. The idea of 'community' is therefore essential to collaborative processes.

What is community?

My understanding of community is influenced by my personal experience, being brought up by my siblings, aunts, uncles and cousins in addition to my parents. My parents also helped to look after other children in our wider family and known to our family. Nancy Chodorow (1978) and Patricia Hill Collins (1995) suggest that collective child rearing generates very different understandings of self than does the nuclear family with mother as primary or sole caregiver. Chodorow (1978) contends that 'studies of more collective child rearing situations suggest that children develop more sense of solidarity and commitment to the group, less individualism and competitiveness, [and] are less liable to form intense, exclusive adult relationships, than children reared in western nuclear families' (Chodorow, 1978, p. 217). As a result of my experience of community I believe that we experience ourselves more richly and feel more connected to what is important to us if we are in some way connected to community, because community can help us access and hold onto preferences for living.

But what is community? Peterson (2001) argues that in the Minority World community is normally defined with respect to similarity among members (for example the Black community, the gay community, the deaf community). This type of definition can obscure the heterogeneous nature of such communities. In fact, 'community' can be a term used to describe as many different experiences as people describing it. For some, it is linked to a concrete place or geographical area, for others it is an abstract concept that links together different aspects of identity. For some, community is where you live, for others it is where you grew up. For some, there is no such thing as community only a universe of living beings. Community might result from transition and movement rather than being a static place. For some, community is a locus of relatedness, identity and belonging, based on a network of people who matter but may not live in the same place. For some, community is a place imposed on you, for others community is a choice. Community might be defined in terms of who gets included (for example, when we refer to the 'global community' or 'a world without borders') or in terms of who is left out (for example, right-wing and xenophobic ideas about 'Englishness'). For some, community is a political gathering of resisters against marginalisation, for others community stifles individuality, creativity and freedom. For some community represents an oppressive place to escape from, for others a sanctuary to retreat to.

For some, community comprises of the people who live or work close by, for others community is an active attempt to maintain relatedness across distance. For some, community conjures up images of small minded thinking and narrow concerns, for others community has connotations of solidarity and collective responsibility. Of course community might be none, any or all of these (Afuape, 2011). How we understand community is influenced not only by our personal experience (as a place where we experience lack, or a place where we feel full, or both), but also by the theoretical lenses we use; whether we are defining community from the point of view of geography, sociology, history, political science, economics, social anthropology, capitalism, socialism or cultural studies, for example.

We can draw on 'community' in our CAMHS work by enquiring about the people in the lives of young people and their families who might appreciate and stand behind their efforts to develop in their preferred ways, bringing them in, through letter writing (Madigan, 2007) or invitations to join the collaborative process. This can help develop a therapeutic sense of community by reflecting on relationships that are highly validating of what people give value to; and that notice and encourage people's creativity (White, 1995; Afuape, 2014). Community in this sense is not determined by physical closeness, but by how closely the contribution of others to our identity, fits with our preferred identity (Afuape, 2011).

Concluding reflections

I have argued that collaborative relationships are creative and responsive because they are open to uncertainty, challenge what we think we know, and are about a sincere interest in other people's experiences, values and preferences. We move from a preoccupation with theory to a focus on our *embodied* ethical stance, and process so that we co-ordinate meaning making in ways that have local relevance and usefulness. A focus on creativity honours the inventiveness of people and helps us notice the ways service users and clinicians might be constrained by dominant discourses/social structures and freed, to some extent, by creativity. It is a helpful concept precisely because it is not palpable or concrete like a theory. Although it is not something we can touch, it can touch us.

Mainstream views tend to conceive of resistance as disruptive, unhelpful and oppositional; resulting from some sort of failing on the part of the individual or group who exhibit it. Much in our everyday life requires that people, especially young people, are non-resistant recipients of instruction. As a result, resistance is normally thought about as the activity of the *asocial* person, who is against society and needs to be managed. Recognising resistance as a way of living creatively and creativity as a form of resistance, honours the way people who resist are often *pro-social*, with certain hopes, dreams, and ideas about how their life and society should be. Collaborative processes might then create the kinds of relationships with people that allow all participants to access their creativity, challenge social abuses and develop possibilities where none previously seemed to exist. Collaborative relationships provide opportunities for what we all want, which is to have our unique creativity noticed and valued, no matter where we might live or our life circumstances, or how quiet our creativity might be.

> If we had a keen vision and feeling of all ordinary human life, it would be like hearing the grass grow and the squirrel's heartbeat, and we should die of that roar which lies on the other side of silence (Eliot, 1993, p. 162).

Notes

1 Social constructionist systemic approaches: When I use the term 'systemic' I am referring to a social constructionist approach to therapy that differs in epistemology (philosophical foundation and assumptions about knowledge) from traditional forms of family therapy, such as strategic and structural. This type of therapy works with any system and relationship, including, but not exclusive to the family—such as groups, organisations, schools, work contexts, communities, couple relationships, individuals in relation to social context and so on.

   A social constructionist perspective takes a critical stance towards taken-for-granted knowledge, because the ways we commonly understand the world are historically and culturally specific. From this view reality is co-created in daily interaction with each other and our environment (Burr, 2003).

   Narrative/collaborative approaches: Narrative practice draws heavily from Michel Foucault's work on power and knowledge. Foucault argued that society has 'normalising truths' that have the power to construct how people see the world, and therefore their lives. These normalising truths create dominant stories and ideas and subjugate other truths that do not fit these dominant accounts. Given that we cannot be sure of what a useful story or direction might be for a person, a narrative therapist is interested in a person's preferences for being and living. Because no one story captures the complexity of life, there are always alternative, more enabling and liberating stories open to us, which might help take our lives in preferred directions (Morgan, 2000). Narrative practice is about joining with 'clients' to co-construct new and enabling stories that sustain preferred identities, activities and relationships. Community/liberation psychology approaches: Liberation theory has been espoused by people such as W.E.B DuBois, Frantz Fanon, bell hooks, Paulo Freire and Ignacio Martín-Baró, who argued that:

   • We should challenge the idea of a universal, impartial psychology/social science, and develop a field that is critically committed to social justice
   • By understanding distress in social context the solution to mental health problems becomes social change
   • Psychology should address the social conditions and aspirations of ordinary people and critically examine itself so that it can be a force for transformation rather than conformity
   • It is marginalised people who should shape, influence and transform psychology practice.

2 'Chav' originates from the Romany word for 'friend'. Other terms such as the highly offensive 'pikey' or 'gyppo', referring to Travellers (the latter being a pejorative of 'gypsy') were earlier used to describe the white underclass (Preston, 2009).

3 Pierre Dulaine (23 April 1944) is an acclaimed ballroom dancer and dance instructor who invented the Dulaine method of teaching dance in 'Dancing Classrooms', social development programs for ten- to eleven-year-olds, that uses ballroom dancing as a vehicle to change their lives and that of their families, by developing social skills prior to the onset of puberty (Wikipedia https://en.wikipedia.org/wiki/Pierre_Dulaine;accessed June 2013).

4 To ensure confidentiality all case examples, although based on the author's clinical work, are fictionalized.

5 Youth as bad: David Cameron's speech following the August 2011 riots referred repeatedly to 'thugs' and 'criminals', as well as people 'showing indifference to right and wrong', 'with a twisted moral code', 'with a complete absence of self-restraint'; who he claimed are not like 'us' 'good people'(Cameron, 2011).

   http://www.newstatesman.com/politics/2011/08/society-fight-work-rights

   Youth as mad: Emily Dugan wrote an article in *The Independent* (11 July 2013) entitled 'Most young men in gangs "suffer psychiatric illness"', quoting research suggesting the high prevalence of 'psychosis', 'anti-social personality disorder', 'anxiety disorder', suicide attempts as well as 'substance abuse' among young men in 'gangs' (Dugan, 2013).

   http://www.independent.co.uk/news/uk/home-news/most-young-men-in-gangs-suffer-psychiatric-illness-8703986.html

   Youth as sad: The emphasis the media often make when quoting Camila Batmanghelidjh CBE founder of *Kids Company* and *theplace2b* is often on damage, vulnerability and sadness in the experience of young people, despite the fact that when I have heard her speak, Camila mostly focuses on young people's resilience in the face of social abuse. In a *Guardian* interview by Emine Saner, Camila is quoted as saying: "I see human misery every day, but I also see extraordinary courage and kindness" (Saner, 2013).

   http://www.theguardian.com/society/2013/feb/22/camila-batmanghelidjh-interview#start-of-comments

   Referred to as the "August riots", in August 2011 for four consecutive nights people all over England took to the streets to protest about their circumstances and engage in anti-social behavior, such as looting and arson, leaving five people dead, businesses and homes destroyed and communities in shock. The disturbances began after an unarmed African-Caribbean man Mark Duggan was shot dead by the police on the 4th August.

   In a *Guardian* and LSE facilitated research, it was estimated that 61% of those who took part in the August disturbance were between the ages of 10 and 20. However, contrary to public perception, on the whole the role of 'gangs' in the disturbances was significantly overstated (The Guardian, 2011). Those who took part came disproportionately from areas of high deprivation; and although there was no single or consistent motive or explanation, the research suggested that many of those involved were 'quite politicised', and frustrated, about diminishing opportunities in the UK, substantive experience of marginalisation and resentment about feeling targeted and oppressed by those in power, mainly the police and the government.

6 Like Ani (1994) I refer to European culture as Minority World culture since Europeans and the cultures they have created (Europe, Australia, North America and Canada) represent a minority in global terms, and those of Latin America, the Far East, the Middle East, Africa and Asia as Majority World cultures, since they make up the majority of the world.

7 Focusing was developed by Eugene Gendlin more than twenty-five years ago and involves holding an open, non-judgmental, kind, attention to bodily felt-sense which does not yet have words. It is based on the idea of *implicit knowing*; what someone knows but is not yet able to express. *Felt sense* is what Gendlin calls the unclear, pre-verbal sense of something experienced in the body and *focusing* makes a felt sense more tangible, by exploring in non-verbal ways, what comes from the felt sense. It bypasses the rational mind and approaches experience through the body (Gendlin, 2003).

8 In the 2004 film *Million Dollar Baby* directed, co-produced and scored by Clint Eastwood, an amateur boxer Margaret Fitzgerald, is trained by boxing trainer Frankie Dunn, winning many of her fights with first-round knockouts. Estranged from his own daughter who returns his letters unopened, Frankie establishes a paternal bond with Maggie, who he calls *Mo Chuisle*. During one fight, Maggie is knocked out and breaks her neck, which leaves her a quadriplegic. Maggie develops bedsores and undergoes a leg amputation and she asks Frankie to help her die while she can still remember the cheers she heard, saying she got what she most wanted out of life. Before Frankie helps her die, he tells Maggie *Mo Chuisle* is Irish for "my darling, my blood, my pulse".

9 *Parkour* is the art of using effective and efficient jumps, vaults, climbing and swinging to conquer obstacles. It is a physical and mental discipline, philosophy and way of life. Although it could be said to be like martial arts, martial arts is the art of fight, whereas parkour is the art of flight. Parkour enables a person to go from place to place in the quickest and most efficient way possible; overcoming obstacles encountered through the use of their own body. The idea is to not be controlled by surroundings, but move freely despite obstacles.

References

Afuape, T. (2011). *Power, Resistance and Liberation in Therapy with Survivors of Trauma: To Have our Hearts Broken*. London, England: Routledge.

Afuape, T. (2014). The significance of dialogue to well-being: Learning from social constructionist couple therapy. In: K. Partridge & S. McNab (eds.), *Outside In/ Inside Out: Creative Positions in Adult Mental Health*. (pp. 187–202). London, England: Karnac.

Afuape, T. (2016). Supervision as relational responsivity: The body in co-ordinated meaning making. In: G. Fredman, J. Bownas & E. Strang (eds.). *Working with Embodiment in Supervision: A systemic approach*. London, England: Routledge.

Andersen, T. (1991). *The Reflecting Team: Dialogues and Dialogues about the Dialogues*. New York, NY: Norton.

Andersen, T. (1995). Reflecting processes; acts of informing and forming: You can borrow my eyes, but you must not take them away from me! In: S. Friedman (ed.). *The Reflecting Team in Action: Collaborative Practice in Family Therapy*. (pp. 11–37). New York, NY: Guildford Press.

Anderson, H. & Gehart, D. (2007). *Collaborative Therapy: Relationships and Conversations that Make a Difference*. London, England: Routledge.

Ani, M. (1994). *Yurugu: An African-Centred Critique of European Cultural Thought and Behaviour.* Trenton, NJ: Africa World Press.

Burr, V. (2003) (2nd ed.). *Social Constructionism.* London, England: Routledge.

Cambridge Online Dictionary and Thesaurus. http://dictionary.cambridge.org/ (accessed 4 August 2013).

Cameron, D. (2011). Full transcript; David Cameron, Speech on the fight-back after the riots. *The New Statesman,* 15th August 2011. http://www.newstatesman.com/politics/2011/08/society-fight-work-rights (accessed 22 August 2011).

Cameron, J. (1995). *The Artist's Way: A Spiritual Path to Higher Creativity.* London, England: Pans Books.

Chodorow, N. (1978). *The Reproduction of Mothering: Psychoanalysis and the Sociology of Gender.* Berkeley, CA: University of California Press.

Collins, P. H. (1995). Black women and motherhood. In: V. Held (ed.). *Justice and Care: Essential Readings in Feminist Ethics.* (pp. 117–35). Boulder, CO: Westview Press.

Department for Education and Skills (DfES) (2006). *Social Mobility: Narrowing Social Class Educational Attainment Gaps.* London, England: DfES. Can be accessed: http://www.dfes.gov.uk/rsgateway/DB/STA/t000657/SocialMobility26Apr06.pdf.

Dugan, E. (2013). Most young men in gangs 'suffer psychiatric illness'. *The Independent,* 11th July 2013. http://www.independent.co.uk/news/uk/home-news/most-young-men-in-gangs-suffer-psychiatric-illness-8703986.html (accessed 16 July 2013).

Eliot, G. (1993). *Middlemarch.* (New ed.). Hertfordshire, England: Wordsworth Editions. (First published in 1874).

Gendlin, E. T. (2003). *Focusing: How to Gain Direct Access to Your Body's Knowledge: How to Open up your Deeper Feelings and Intuition* (25th anniversary ed.). London, England: Rider.

Guilfoyle, M. (2005). From therapeutic power to resistance? Therapy and cultural hegemony. *Theory & Psychology,* 15(1), 101–24.

Harper, D. (2015). Psychologists against austerity. *The Psychologist,* 28(3), 172.

Houston, D. (2006). Take the lead. Film: US.

Madigan, S. (2007). Anticipating hope within written and naming domains of despair. In: C. Flaskas, I. McCarthy & J. Sheehan (eds.). *Hope and Despair in Narrative and Family Therapy: Adversity, Forgiveness and Reconciliation.* (pp. 100–12). London, England: Routledge.

Morgan, A. (2000). *What is Narrative Therapy? An Easy to Read Introduction.* Adelaide, South Australia: Dulwich Centre Publications.

Ncube, N. (2006). The Tree of Life Project: Using narrative ideas in work with vulnerable children in Southern Africa. *The International Journal of Narrative Therapy & Community Work,* 2006(1), 3–16.

Oxford University Press (2008). *Oxford Pocket Dictionary.* Oxford, England: Oxford University Press.

Partridge, K. (2007). Personal communication.

Patel, N. (2005). Personal communication.

Pearce, W. B. (2007). *Making Social Worlds: A Communication Perspective.* Oxford, England: Blackwell.

Peterson, A. L. (2001). *Being Human: Ethics, Environment and our Place in the World.* Berkeley, CA: University of California Press.

Preston, J. (2009). *Whiteness and Class in Education.* Dordrecht, The Netherlands: Springer.

Rice, B. (2006). *Against the Odds.* London, England: Shelter.

Saner, E. (2013). Camila Batmanghelidjh CBE interview. *The Guardian*, 22nd February 2013. http://www.theguardian.com/society/2013/feb/22/camila-batmanghelidjh-interview (accessed 2 March 2013).

Seikkula, J. (2002). Open dialogues with good and poor outcomes for psychotic crises: Examples from families with violence. *Journal of Marital & Family Therapy,* 28(3), 263–74.

Selvini, M. & Selvini Palazzoli, M. (1991). Team consultation: An indispensable tool for the progress of knowledge. *Journal of Family Therapy,* 13(1), 31–52.

Shotter, J. (2010). Social construction on the edge: 'Withness'-thinking and embodiment. Cleveland, OH: Taos Institute Publications.

Shotter, J. & Katz, A. M. (1999). Creating relational realities. Responsible responding to poetic 'movements' and 'moments'. In: S. McNamee & K. Gergen (eds.). *Relational Responsibility: Resources for Sustainable Dialogue.* (pp. 151–62). London: Sage.

The Guardian (2011). *Reading the Riots: Investigating England's Summer of Disorder.* London: London School of Economics.

UNICEF (2010). *The Children Left Behind: A League Table of Inequality in Child Wellbeing in the World's Rich Countries. Innocenti Report Card 9.* Florence, Italy: UNICEF Innocenti Research Centre.

Wade, A. (1997). Small acts of living: Everyday resistance to violence and other forms of oppression. *Contemporary Family Therapy,* 19(1), 23–40.

Wade, A. (2005). *Honouring Resistance: A Response-Based Approach to Counselling.* Vancouver, British Columbia: Viewers Guide Stepping Stone Productions.

Watts, R. J., Williams, N. C. & Jagers, R. J. (2003). Sociopolitical development. *American Journal of Community Psychology,* 31(1–2), 185–94.

White, M. (1995). *Re-authoring Lives: Interviews and Essays.* Adelaide, Australia: Dulwich Centre Publications.

Wikipedia (2013). https://en.wikipedia.org/wiki/Pierre_Dulaine (accessed June 2013).

Wilkinson, R. & Pickett, K. (2010). *The Spirit Level: Why Equality is Better for Everyone.* London, England: Penguin.

Wintour, P. (2015). Government to scrap child poverty target before tax credits cut. *The Guardian.* Available at http://www.theguardian.com/society/2015/jul/01/government-scrap-legal-requirements-child-poverty (accessed 1 July 2015).

Part II

Prevention and accessibility in children's centres and general practice

Chapter 4

Delivering family mental health services in urban children's centres

Rachel James and Kanan Pandya-Smith

Introduction

We start this chapter with a case study that spanned a number of years and which illustrates how complex multi-agency work in the community, that addresses vulnerabilities and risks whilst building on resilience, can deliver very positive holistic outcomes for children and families. We think that a case study is the most meaningful way to bring the multi-faceted work we do to life as this provides an opportunity to understand our work first-hand, including what this can tell us about the service user experience. For us as clinical psychologists based in integrated multi-agency teams within children's centres, this case highlights the typical challenges and dilemmas we face and which are experienced by families living in particular communities within an urban context. The case also shows the importance of adopting a holistic approach to mental health presentations in order to enhance resilience and ensure the best outcomes for infants, young children and their families. Following the case vignette we will go on to describe and discuss further ways of working with families with infants and young children under the age of five years with mental health needs in an urban context. In particular we explore the challenges and opportunities we face in developing services and engaging service users in ways that are meaningful to them and promote positive outcomes.

Raheema's story[1]

Raheema, a twenty-three-year-old, second-generation Bangladeshi woman, was referred to the children's centre family mental health service by her midwife following the birth of her first child as she was low in mood and struggling with the transition to parenthood. Initial consultation with the referrer indicated that a joint approach would be helpful, and Raheema was allocated a family support worker and a clinical psychologist. To avoid duplication, a joint appointment was offered. This ensured Raheema's understanding of the range of children's centre services available to her, clarification of the different workers' roles, and collaborative engagement. Raheema was struggling to leave the house with her baby, and she asked for a home visit. As is often the expectation amongst the Bangladeshi community, Raheema was living with her extended family and it was felt important to carefully negotiate the timing of the appointment with Raheema to protect her privacy, and enable her to speak freely when no other family members were present. Raheema described feeling very low following the birth, and was concerned that she did not feel connected to her daughter. She described her own history and reported that her parents moved from Bangladesh to the UK forty years ago. She described having a difficult childhood and adolescence, as she struggled with being a Bangladeshi girl born and brought up in the UK by a family with very traditional values. She described feeling caught between cultures, and that her parents, extended family and community did not understand her values or the challenges she faced growing up in an urban London area. Her arranged marriage compounded these difficult feelings, and she also felt misunderstood by her husband who had grown up in Bangladesh. These were significant sources of internal conflict for her and were accentuated in her new role as a wife and mother.

Taking the lead from Raheema, our work focussed on how she could be a 'good' woman and mother according to the cultural expectations of her family and community while also being true to her own needs and wishes as a British Bangladeshi young woman. These two outlooks were frequently in conflict and unhelpful to her in her identity as a mother as she was unsure how to respond to her baby. She had a belief that she was not good enough to look after her daughter, resulting in her often being paralysed by her daughter's crying, which perpetuated her feelings of inadequacy and guilt. When the baby's needs were not being met quickly, her distress escalated and Raheema described often feeling overwhelmed that her daughter was constantly crying and that she was being seen as a failure by her extended family.

We offered Raheema a course of cognitive behavioural therapy (CBT) based on a bio-psycho-social model of postnatal depression, which consisted of fortnightly meetings at home with the psychologist over a ten-month period. As her confidence grew, she was able to progress to attending appointments at the children's centre. During this work Raheema was able to explore the impact of the integration of Western and traditional cultural beliefs on her own ideas and values, and through these alternative understandings she developed greater self-confidence and attunement to her baby, which resulted in significant improvements in the mother-infant relationship and improvements in her mental state. For example, Raheema engaged with helping her own extended family understand the rationale for her increased sensitivity to her baby's cues. She became able to explain to them that at times, she felt undermined by their responses when the focus of the work was to help her become more attuned and responsive when the baby was unsettled. The increased self-confidence also allowed her to broaden her context over time and make changes at a family level by beginning conversations with her parents and husband about how they could better support her. She was keen for couple work, but did not think her husband would engage with this

Western approach to problem solving. We supported her to work around this by facilitating her engagement with a family support worker, who enabled her, in a practical way, to engage in community activities, including drop-ins for parents and toddlers. This period of work spanned a two-year period, with Raheema making use of the service when she was feeling most vulnerable, and this seemed to promote her resilience. This resulted in her opening up discussions with her husband regarding her internal cultural conflicts, which she felt led to a helpful shift in the power dynamic within the couple relationship, as well as with her brothers who had taken on leadership roles within the family following the death of Raheema's father.

The family support worker sustained the therapeutic work by assisting Raheema to leave the house in a step-wise progression, leading to her independently accessing community drop-ins and other activities, such as baby massage. This helped increase her confidence in her parenting capacity and feel better connected to her baby and her wider community. Joint work with the psychologist and the family support worker provided opportunities for the dissemination of psychological knowledge, and enhanced the family support worker's capacity to integrate the therapeutic techniques into her work. For example, she was able to successfully support Raheema to use her new coping skills, such as self-talk and the importance of self-reward, to effectively manage challenges in accessing community activities. Raheema showed a measurable improvement in her levels of distress as measured by standardised assessment tools, and made significant gains with her treatment goals (Goal Based Measure: CORC, 2011), which were to: enjoy spending time with her daughter; engage in activities outside of the family home and develop her social network. Her self-confidence grew significantly to the extent that she went on to successfully start her own business. Raheema was clear that the continuity offered through the children's centre services over a five-year period, was instrumental to her developing greater psychological flexibility. Through this, she was able to make use of the multi-agency services available to her, including: successfully completing training to be a volunteer, and going on to work in a children's centre initiative that offers peer-led feeding support to new mothers; engaging with the employability worker to engage in further education and successfully start her own business. Raheema was very appreciative of the consistent support she had received over time; it is interesting to note that the plant that she gave as a thank-you gift remains a healthy and vibrant focal point in the open-planned office where all the services that supported her are co-located. In addition, Raheema and her husband were supported through the housing application process by the multi-agency team, and ultimately secured housing independent of the maternal extended family, which enabled them to continue to negotiate their roles within the family in a culturally sensitive and acceptable way. Being separate, yet in close proximity to the extended family home, meant that Raheema was more able to manage conflicts that arose out of feeling caught between cultures. This part of the work was not without its challenges. For example, the extended family had strong beliefs rooted in Bangladeshi cultural ideas and outlooks, which meant that they perceived the service as encouraging her independence, which they felt was a threat to their traditional values and meant that they often undermined Raheema's engagement in therapeutic work.

Who we are and where we work

We are clinical psychologists working within the National Health Service. RJ is a Consultant Clinical Psychologist, of Caucasian origin from the north of England, and has over twenty years of experience working across the health, social care, education sectors, and in partnership with the voluntary sector. She has managed the family mental health provision into the multi-agency children's centre services for almost a decade. She is also a mother of three children and has firsthand experience with negotiating the demands of single parenthood. KP-S is a Specialist Clinical Psychologist, of British-Indian origin, and has over ten years of experience working across similar sectors. She has been a member of the family mental health team for four years and has a lead role for the young parent service. KP-S has recently become a mother for the first time, and like many of her clients she is adjusting to life juggling the demands of being a working mother with a young child. The family mental health team is multi-disciplinary and includes staff and clinical trainees from a range of disciplines including clinical psychology, psychiatry, nursing, family therapy and psychotherapy.

Within the local authority there are fourteen children's centres delivering services to families with young children across our borough. The goal for children centre services is to build and promote positive outcomes right from the very start of life. Children's centres offer nursery and childcare places and provide a range of other services, such as family support, healthcare, employability training and welfare rights advice right in the heart of the community. The service has clear pathways for partnership working with a range of health, education, social care and voluntary organisations. The service targets the needs of oppressed families (such as teenage parents, homeless families, families from Black and Minority Ethnic groups) with children from conception up to the age of five years. In order to meet the varied needs of these different client groups, the service offers proactive outreach, which we describe below. A key feature of the children's centres, which stands out as unique compared to a 'traditional' CAMH service, are the child-focussed environments which actively encourage and facilitate interactive play and communication between adults and young children. Raheema's story provides an example of how we were able to deliver these outcomes for her and her family. Our aim was to improve her and her daughter's emotional well-being, as well as enhancing the quality of life for the family through partnership and collaboration with all services. This ensured a holistic approach taking all aspects of family life into account as well as greater economic and environmental sustainability for the whole family.

Our ethos

We believe that becoming a parent is both exciting and challenging for everyone, and that all parents want their children to have the best start in life. We aim not to take up a position of being 'experts' with regards to the experiences of families, rather we consider that the team has expertise in particular domains, including child development, family relationships, mental health and well-being, and in managing risk and complexity within a multi-disciplinary team. Our partnership working with families includes consideration of where a family would like to be seen and by whom, shared decision making about what approach would be most effective and an open door for further support should it be required in the future. In doing this we promote a culture of 'Team Around the Family'[2].

Inevitably all staff within the service are influenced by their own values and beliefs. Their capacity to maintain an open-minded perspective is supported by team case discussion forums and regular individual supervision. There are high levels of satisfaction in the staff team, meaning that staff turnover is low. This facilitates continuity of care for families, a positive working culture, and a sustainable service. We use systems to elicit on-going feedback from service users and staff (McDonnell & Zutshi, 2006) and methods of integrating this into ongoing service delivery. An example of this is where a parent gave feedback on the Evaluation of Service Questionnaire (Attride-Stirling, 2002) stating that, "The room was too small and not comfortable for me and my child". This feedback was discussed at the next quarterly meeting, and steps were taken to consider altering the room use to ensure that the larger manager's office could be used instead for direct work with families. Integrating quarterly feedback data into the service contributes to service users and staff influencing decision making in an ongoing way.

A fundamental principle that underlies our ethos is to build resilience in an urban context. Factors such as personal resilience to life's challenges, participation in society and the extent to which individuals and communities have control over their lives significantly influence mental health and well-being for individuals and communities. We have seen how certain aspects of inner-city living can promote resilience amongst the communities with which we work. The heterogeneous nature of networks allows for the possibility of experiences of different social groups, for example, cultures, faiths and class affiliations. Many of our families live in high-density social housing and are thus in close proximity to other people. This, of course, can create tension, particularly where there is overcrowding and limited opportunities for positive social engagement. However, we have seen communities where this works well and where families support each other and take advantage of the close proximity such as helping with child care and cooking meals for each other. Communal gardens can bring people together, and shared responsibility for growing vegetables and flowers fosters a sense of community and togetherness across different cultures. Partnership working with voluntary organisations, which can promote a sense of community and pride in the local environment through shared projects, has proved crucial in beginning the process of engaging families with services. These opportunities can result in parents' wishes to provide better experiences for their own children than the ones they experienced themselves.

Despite these opportunities for building resilience, we are acutely aware of the wide-ranging risk factors associated with parenthood in an urban context. For example, poor-quality parental relationships (whether parents are living together or not), especially those characterised by couple conflict are likely to be associated with poor parenting and poor-quality parent-child relationships (Cummings & Davies, 2010). In an urban context, many of the families can be categorised as falling into high-risk groups with complex needs, some having experienced family breakdown and living in homeless hostels and refuges. Many families are transient and lack support from extended family or social networks, often because of high levels of relocation perhaps because of re-housing or fleeing domestic violence. This is particularly apparent in our work with mothers experiencing significant difficulties in the perinatal period. Focusing on early intervention is key to improving outcomes in later life, is cost-effective and reduces the need for a referral later to more specialist services.

Our approaches to work

As we have discussed, the borough is diverse, and through our tailored as well as flexible approach we aim to engage with families and deliver the right intervention to suit every individual family's needs regardless of age, gender, ethnicity, disability or sexual orientation. This involves us valuing good engagement and prioritising certain principles such as flexible outreach, fostering the therapeutic alliance, non-Western approaches to mental health, security and partnership working, and encouraging reflection on the parental role. In what follows we discuss these concepts with regards to the opportunities these afford us in our work, as well as the challenges they generate.

Flexible outreach

Our flexible outreach approach means we have moved away from the traditional idea of clinic-based CAMHS. We deliver our service in non-stigmatising community settings that families already access, such as children's centres and community projects. Those families who may find it hard to come to the children's centre, perhaps because of low mood, high levels of anxiety, or difficulties in managing young children out of the home environment, therefore have options available to them. Assertive community work also means communicating in a helpful way with our clients, such as using SMS reminders and mobile phones that show the caller number to improve communication and attendance rates. We have changed standard practice in this way because normally service telephone systems do not give the caller number, and we have found that service users do not answer withheld or blocked numbers.

On the surface, a home visit may seem like a straightforward task. However, the complexities of working in this way create a different dynamic between the client and the professional. Home visiting may redress the power imbalance that exists in office visits because you are a guest in the client's home and are being allowed a privileged insight into their life. It also allows you to observe a child in their most comfortable environment, and it can be easier to develop a working relationship with the family. For example, clients may be more engaged, making it easier to set goals and discuss issues; the emotional bond between you and the client may be more overt and stronger, and you may feel more empathic and able to grasp their perspective and world view than in a more formal clinical setting. Home visits also give you an opportunity to join with the client by observing what day-to-day life is like for the child and family, and to consider their broader context from a more holistic perspective. Do the children have age-appropriate toys to play with, and what are their living conditions like? We have observed numerous times how housing and financial issues have a direct impact on the mental health and well-being of a parent and their parenting capacity. For example, a parent sharing a damp room with three children in an overcrowded flat can feel hopeless; everyone is tired from the children waking each other up, parents are frustrated that their children do not have sufficient room to play, and that they themselves can never have adult space and privacy. It is a common frustration for us that our work has to be put on hold until the family has accessed appropriate practical help with housing or finances.

Alongside these benefits of being flexible with regards to where we meet our clients, this flexibility inevitably generates a number of challenges. For example, it makes it more difficult to maintain boundaries and gauge the motivation of clients. Being in the client's home is much less formal, and this can alter how the client sees you. In some cases, you are perceived as being more of a friend, and so are more likely to be asked personal questions, and it can be harder to keep the conversation focussed. This may create clinical and ethical dilemmas. At times sharing personal information can be a helpful engagement tool, for example when working with young parents who might want to know about whether you share the same interests, whereas at other times it may seem that clients paying attention to you avoid talking about themselves. In a home there can also be a wide range of distractions—the phone ringing or a parent going off to attend to something while you are there. These can present challenges but can simultaneously provide meaningful information. We need to ensure we are providing home visits for the right reasons, and sometimes a balance has to be struck between engaging families and facilitating their independence on one hand, and the potential to inadvertently enhance their dependence on services on the other. This was the case with Raheema, who was experiencing postnatal depression after initially being seen at home, and subsequently benefitted from attending appointments at the children's centre (O'Mahen et al, 2014).

Fostering a therapeutic alliance

At the core of any therapeutic work is an alliance, which is the main vehicle for facilitating change (Horvath & Greenberg, 1994). The relationships that we have with our families may allow them to focus on themselves as individuals, but also on their communities that constitute the backgrounds to their lives. The therapeutic relationship should allow clients to bring their own knowledge and expertise to explore social contexts, power and privilege in relation to the issues, which face them (Schmitz, 2010). Raheema used her sessions to reflect on feelings of belonging and not belonging, and the expectations that she perceived from her family (to be a submissive woman in a male-dominant system) and British society (to be self-sufficient and an independent mother), which she felt were in conflict with each other. By exploring these ideas, she was able to regain a sense of power and understanding and to find a way to integrate these two identities. Once an alliance is established with a professional in our service, families can find it difficult to move on to other services, even if their needs would be better met by another agency. A common scenario is one in which a parent has their own identified mental health needs that would benefit from the input of adult services. Parents may be reluctant to transfer to a new service, or they may have difficulties engaging with the new service if home visits are not available, or the work is not possible because of a lack of child-care provision. These situations can often lead to feelings of stuckness for clinicians as it is widely accepted that parental mental health strongly influences the well-being of their offspring (Falkov, 2013). To ensure that a parent receives the appropriate intervention and to promote the best outcomes for the family, we can often join our adult mental health colleagues in undertaking this work. This kind of joint working facilitates engagement and promotes clear pathways between services, bridging gaps.

Non-Western approaches to mental health

Being non-judgmental and open-minded helps us to foster safety in the therapeutic relationship, and, in turn, this means that we can be thoughtful about cultural differences and non-Western approaches to mental health. Raheema experienced difficulties in trying to engage her husband in services, perhaps because he grew up in Bangladesh. For her, being supported to introduce new ideas, and open up alternative conversations in a gradual way allowed some thinking to shift. As a British Indian, KP-S is familiar with Raheema's predicament, as the concept of seeking 'psychological' help for mental health difficulties (what might be viewed as spiritual, bodily and/or community difficulties) in her own community is still very much in its infancy. The understanding of 'mental health' often comes from a very different point of view, in which a person's struggle with low mood or feeling 'not quite right', may be expressed as physical symptoms or a spiritual crisis. This understanding means that cultural explanations of symptoms and 'treatment' options are very different (Krause, 1989; Maitra & Krause, 2014) and may include, for example, getting help from a community elder or taking herbal remedies. As in all our work, being reflective of our own background and social context is key. Being curious about our clients' ideas and cultural outlook allows us to respond more flexibly. Nevertheless we have found that facilitating change in families where there are very different understandings of the presenting problems is challenging, and this can be a source of frustration for us. In our experience it helps being aware of where our own ideas originate. Thus we are aware that the approaches we use are based on Western models; this is particularly apparent in parenting. Many families who we have worked with have different views on how to effectively parent children under five. For example, some parents believe that young children should not be spoken to as they are too young to understand what is being said. The importance of play and praise is heavily emphasised in the Incredible Years (Webster-Stratton, 2006) approach and in many other parenting models, however this does not always reflect ideas expressed in other cultures. For example, a common theme in the parenting groups we have run for Bangladeshi parents is that praise is seen to be showing off or spoiling a child, whereas in Western contexts an approach, which positively connotes a child's achievements is considered helpful for the development of a child's autonomy and independence. In response to service users' requests, we have run culture specific parenting groups for some communities such as the Bangladeshi and Congolese communities. This has allowed for open discussion and learning from each other about experimenting with different ways of parenting within the safety of a shared cultural context. The richness of delivering culturally specific parenting groups provides invaluable opportunities for parents to challenge Western parenting approaches and the conflicts with traditional cultural understandings and beliefs (Bornstein, 2013).

Working with South Asian families, we have noticed a recurring theme associated with concerns that their child is underweight and not eating enough. This stress can cause a parent to put pressure on the child at mealtimes, which may have the opposite effect, resulting in children eating less and becoming fussier. In reality, many of these children do have a good appetite and a healthy weight, but the parents struggle to recognise this. We think that this suggests the cultural importance of food, particularly as a medium for the expression of love and generosity and as a subject for close scrutiny by elderly family members. Parents can therefore feel under pressure from their own parents and transfer this worry to the child. In our experience, the most useful approach to this situation has been to open up discussions about the interplay of cultural expectations and food in order to help the parent to see their role in this dynamic and become more relaxed at mealtimes.

Security and partnership working

The isolating nature of outreach work, where the clinician is often the only mental health practitioner in a large multi-agency team, means that having a secure base to work from is paramount. We have a physical base located in children's centres, and emotional security is provided through clear supervisory and management structures. Our experience of security in our work is further strengthened by clear pathways to the local CAMHS team from which colleagues offer multi-disciplinary expertise. Our multi-disciplinary colleagues offer invaluable consultations that enable us to keep psychologically minded and connected to the broader CAMHS network. The benefit for the families that we work with is evident, as we can seamlessly refer families with higher levels of need directly to the multi-disciplinary teams. This is a good example of how our joined up working can facilitate successful engagement with CAMHS teams, which have proved highly valuable when families require longer-term therapeutic support.

The secure base in the community is also strengthened by our high level of partnership working with local hospital and community midwifery services, social care services (including the hospital teams), multi-agency children's centre teams, community CAMHS and adult mental health services, health visiting, primary care and voluntary sector organisations. A common framework for those families who may benefit from support from CAMHS begins with the offer of a joint appointment with the referrer in the first instance. This partnership working model has proved productive in joining client families, enhancing engagement and building trust in the service from the outset. We feel that this has become key as over the last few years we have seen the complexity of our referrals increase in part due to the social and political contexts, such as higher levels of unemployment and changes in the benefit and housing system which have meant that more families are struggling. In such a financially and socially challenging climate safeguarding thresholds for other services are rising, and this has meant that we hold families with higher levels of risk. We are fortunate in that the families typically have developed a trusting relationship with the children's centre family support workers, and through them can access support with regard to practical issues involving their basic needs, such as housing and finances, being met (Maslow, 1943). If families are in this position of security, it is often a good time to consider engaging in CAMHS work, as the family support worker can be the professional to broach this. In addition, the clinician's role often involves indirect work with family support workers to develop their capacity to deliver mental health interventions for those families who are reluctant to engage in CAMHS for a variety of reasons. This approach can also lead to a joint appointment with the family and a family support worker, and this may be the beginning where engaging 'hard to reach' families who otherwise might be unlikely to engage with more 'traditional' CAMHS begins. This kind of referral pathway may also be useful for families who have a non-Western understanding of mental health, and who therefore might not access CAMHS through more standard routes. In addition, as some of the family support workers' ethnicities reflect the local population, this can help to engage parents who may feel their cultural values are better understood by a matched worker, or who may be mistrustful of interpreters being present from their own community. The flexibility reflected in this approach to referrals enables communities themselves to influence the ways in which they connect with mainstream services.

Many of the families we work with have active involvement with local authority social care services and as a result, we regularly need to demonstrate our independence from such scrutiny. Families can find local authority involvement, intrusive and unwelcome and it can have a significant impact on their motivation and capacity to engage. As a consequence we may face the dilemma that families engage with us in a 'superficial' way, perhaps as an outcome of a child protection plan, and therefore their engagement is driven by compliance. In this case it can help to emphasise transparency in our work, and depending on the level of risk we may take up an advocacy position in which we help the families to reflect on how to work alongside social services by understanding better the ways in which their behaviour might be causing concern to others. For example, we will actively promote attendance at peri-natal appointments where there are concerns they are not being prioritised. We have found that it is important to collaborate with partner organisations to enable all agencies to work towards a shared goal of improving holistic outcomes for families whilst avoiding duplication and ensuring engagement with the right service, at the first time.

Encouraging reflection on the parental role

A central aspect of our work is to help parents gain an understanding of the role they play in what they perceive as being their child's difficulties. There is often an expectation from parents that the child under five will be seen individually as they perceive that the child has the 'problem' with for example feeding, sleeping or toileting. Thus, Raheema was able to use the therapy to shift her understanding of her identity as a woman who could cope and be more confident in herself, and have a more sensitive attunement to her baby's needs. This change in turn enabled her to have a different understanding of her daughter, respond more effectively to her cues, and cope better when she was unsettled. The intensity and reciprocal nature of the mother and baby relationship meant that the baby was able to cue in to the shift in her mother's outlook and state of mind and feel more contained in herself. This resulted in Raheema noticing that her daughter was more settled, which in turn positively affected her own mood.

In this way, we consider the parental role as fundamental to the child's emotional wellbeing. Helping parents to see that their own mental health and wellbeing has a strong influence on their capacity to parent to their best ability can sometimes be a challenge. We offer a range of evidence-based interventions, including the Incredible Years parenting approach (Webster-Stratton, 2006) and Video Intervention to promote Positive Parenting and Sensitive Discipline (VIPP-SD: Juffer et al, 2008). The former is a directive approach that helps parents understand that when they give positive attention to their children, their behaviour often improves, whereas the latter increases parental sensitivity to their children's cues through the use of video feedback. Our own personal experiences as parents enables us to be in touch with this dynamic. How able we are to understand and relate to our own children is highly dependent on how we feel, what kind of day we have had and what we expect from them. Young children do not understand this, and may be confused when they act in the same way and then get a different reaction from their parents. Being reflective about what we bring to our relationship with our own children is key but can be particularly difficult at times of high-stress. Working with families affords us a knowledge about different ways of parenting, but it also means that it can be harder for us to empathise with parenting experiences that are different from our own. As clinicians, the family mental health approach can feel overwhelming at times as you are trying to promote mental health, well-being and resilience, and affect change for many people. We use signposting to appropriate partner services, supervision and collaborative working with the family to focus on what work should be prioritised and to get us through this complex task.

Conclusion

The work of the family mental health team within the multi-agency children's centre teams is highly rewarding. Despite the challenges faced, the service is able to demonstrate a wide range of excellent outcomes for infants, children and their families. In this chapter we have described our approaches to our work including, our flexible outreach model; the importance of fostering the therapeutic alliance; how we maintain a cross-cultural perspective on parenting and family mental health and wellbeing; partnership working; and reflecting on parents' roles in facilitating their children's wellbeing. Raheema's story is a good example of this. It tells the story of her journey from being a first time parent, struggling to manage the cultural conflicts between being a traditional Bangladeshi woman living in an inner-city urban context, and a highly competent and confident mother with a career and better understanding of the influences of her cultural context and family dynamics. The team experiences regular frustrations and challenges in this work, and their own resilience and capacity to support each other is crucial in negotiating these. So too are the opportunities for shared learning and case supervision and consultation within the team as well as across the broader CAMH service. Our aims for our future work are to incorporate more service-user feedback to enable us to continue to shape our service around the wants and needs of our clients, for example, enabling them to move more easily between services and make more informed choices about their treatment and support plans (Wolpert et al, 2014). We endeavour to continue to find creative ways to engage populations who for many reasons find it difficult to access services based on more traditional CAMHS models.

Notes

1 Personal details have been changed to protect the clients' confidentiality.
2 The Team Around the Child approach is a well documented model of multi-agency service provision that brings together a range of different practitioners from

across the children's workforce to support children and their families (Children's Workforce Development Council, 2009). Within our service we have broadened this further to encompass the needs of the whole family, hence the term 'Team Around the Family'.

References

Attride-Stirling, J. (2002). *Development of Methods to Capture Users' Views of Child and Adolescent Mental Health Services in Clinical Governance Reviews.* London, England: Commission for Health Improvement.

Bornstein, M. H. (2013). Parenting and child mental health: A cross-cultural perspective. *World Psychiatry,* 12(3), 258–65.

Children's Workforce Development Council (CWDC) (2009). *Coordinating and Delivering Integrated Services for Children and Young People. The Team Around the Child (TAC) and the Lead Professional. A Guide for Managers.* Leeds, England: CWDC.

CORC (CAMHS Outcomes Research Consortium) (2011). *Goal Based Measure, CORC Measures.* Available online at: www.corc.uk.net.

Cummings, E. & Davies, P. T. (2010). *Marital Conflict and Children: An Emotional Security Perspective.* New York, NY: Guilford Press.

Falkov, A. (2013). *The Family Model: Managing the Impact of Parental Mental Health on Children.* Brighton, England: Pavilion.

Horvath, A. O. & Greenberg, L. S. (1994). *The Working Alliance: Theory, Research and Practice.* New York, NY: Wiley.

Juffer, F., Bakermans-Kranenburg, M. J. & van IJzendoorn, M. H. (2008). *Promoting Positive Parenting: An Attachment-Based Intervention.* New York, NY: Lawrence Erlbaum/Taylor & Francis.

Krause, I-B. (1989). The sinking heart: A Punjabi communication of distress. *Social Science and Medicine,* 29(4), 563–75.

Maitra, B. & Krause, I-B. (2014). *Culture and Madness. A Training Resource, Film and Commentary for Mental Health Professionals.* London, England: Jessica Kingsley.

Maslow, A. H. (1943). A theory of human motivation. *Psychological Review,* 50(4), 370–96.

McDonnell, F. & Zutshi, H. (2006). *The "Whole Systems" Model for Leadership and Management.* Leeds, England: Skills for Care.

O'Mahen, H. A., Richards, D. A., Woodford, J., Wilkinson, E., McGinley, J., Taylor, R. S. & Warren, F. C. (2014). Netmums: Phase II randomized controlled trial of a guided internet behavioural activation treatment for postpartum depression. *Psychological Medicine,* 44(8), 1675–89.

Schmitz, D. S. (2010). Developing an awareness of white privilege. *Reflections: Narratives of Professional Helping,* 16(1), 15.

Webster-Stratton, C. (2006). *The Incredible Years: A Trouble Shooting Guide for Parents of Children Aged 2–8 Years.* Seattle, WA: The Incredible Years Press.

Wolpert, M., Harris, R., Jones, M., Hodges, S., Fuggle P., James, R., Wiener, A., McKenna, C., Law, D. & Fonagy, P. (2014). *THRIVE: The AFC-Tavistock Model for CAMHS.* London, England: CAMHS Press.

Chapter 5

'Border crossings'

Reflections on undertaking brief psychoanalytic therapeutic work in community and primary care settings

Louise Emanuel

Introduction

In this chapter I explore some of the issues which arise for practitioners working in a Child and Adolescent Mental Health Service (CAMHS), in this case psycho-analytically trained child and adolescent psychotherapists, when they leave their familiar clinic setting, and 'cross the border' into a community outreach centre to undertake their clinical or consultation tasks. This process, just as crossing from one country to another, raises issues relating to the rules and mores of the country one is entering, as well as the fantasies about the country the 'visitor' has left behind, and is likely to impact on the transference relationship to the visiting clini-cian. I will go on to explain terms like 'transference' and the theory that underpins them later on in the chapter.

As a consultant child and adolescent psychotherapist working in a large CAMHS team, my role is to undertake clinical and consultation work in com-munity settings, as well as supervise and manage the outreach services offered by trainee child psychotherapists. I am a White, British female clinician; the trainees are from diverse backgrounds, including those of White and Black British ethnicity, and from Italy and Taiwan. The demographic of the area we serve is diverse, and includes families from Somalia, Bangladesh, Turkey, Pakistan, France and other parts of Europe. The focus of the outreach work described here is on families with babies and children under five, as this is the area in which my colleagues and I have been most active. We have adapted our approach and technique in order to work with a range of families of diverse backgrounds—many of whom are different to my own—in a range of commu-nity outreach settings.

I will first give a brief overview of the Tavistock Clinic approach to psychoanalytically-based interventions with under-fives, then offer some thoughts about the complex task of working psychoanalytically in outreach settings, describing the impact on a senior clinical trainee, of his first experience of work of this kind. I will then illustrate how the under-five model is adapted to clinical work in community settings, by describing a case involving parents seeking help for their young child's fearful behaviour.

The brief under-fives model

The Tavistock Clinic brief under-fives service, offered as part of a large inner London CAMHS team, offers quick-response, psychoanalytically-based, focused interventions to families with babies and young children primarily by child and adolescent psychotherapists. It is characterised by ease of access and flexibility of approach, which makes it particularly suited to work within community outreach settings. The theoretical framework for this approach is designed to be applied universally to all families, as many of these ideas are considered to be cross-culturally and cross-racially applicable. However, as the clinical vignettes will convey, some aspects of this theoretical approach have needed to be adapted, or re-thought in the light of the community and family contexts.

The basis for this under-five model includes an understanding of psycho-analytic theory, child development research, and well-honed observational skills, gained through undertaking infant and young child observations in a family setting, as part of the psychoanalytic child and adolescent psychotherapy clinical training. The key to the application of these ideas is a deeply embedded under-standing of this framework, combined with a flexibility of approach, allowing for a range of decisions to be made about frequency, duration and type of inter-vention. The focus is on the 'here and now' experience in the room of clinicians and the family, with detailed attention paid to family members' interactions with each other, and with the therapist(s). The way in which the therapist is perceived by parents and child, the expectations that clients bring with them to the clinic and how these are addressed, are key to understanding the flow of conscious and unconscious communications in the consulting room. Alongside these 'transfer-ence' phenomena, the therapist's observations are enriched by her awareness of sometimes powerful feelings evoked in her by the child or parent, and these 'counter-transference' experiences often give essential clues to the meaning of behaviours and interactions taking place.

This model is based on the paradoxical need for the clinician to facilitate the 'slow unfolding' of material within a brief time frame. This 'unfolding' within a session often involves a conversation with parents, and a simultaneous exploration of the infant or young child's communications through their behaviour, play, and drawings – a slow unfolding, at double speed! The dramatic way in which children enact their (and their family's) predicament in the consulting room contributes to what Annette Watillon (1993) describes as the 'speed and spectacular nature of the therapeutic effect' in work with under-fives, which enables this type of 'slow unfolding' (Watillon, 1993 p. 1041) to take place (Emanuel & Bradley, 2008).

Theoretical framework

Clinicians in the British 'object relations' tradition have been inspired by Austrian-British psychoanalyst Melanie Klein's theories, and the many devel-opments built on her contribution. Of central importance is the psychoanalyst

Wilfred Bion's concept of container/contained (1962b) and his notion of 'maternal reverie'. Bion recognised that the baby's psyche is not developed enough to contain powerful feelings of any kind, and described the infant's need for an attentive carer, able to 'take in' and think about his/her intense states of distress or excitement, without becoming overwhelmed by anxiety. Gradually the infant learns, through repeated experience of a thoughtful parent, how to make sense of his/her own experiences, to think for themselves. This shift, from 'evacuation' of overwhelming sensory data to a capacity to investigate his/her own feelings, is vital for a baby's emotional and cognitive development. It is the beginning of his/her development of 'symbol formation'—the ability to internalise a picture of helpful parents to whom he/she can turn in his/her mind in times of distress—emotional development, the evolution of the capacity for thought, and of the development of 'mentalization', (Fonagy et al, 2004), which have in part been described in Bion's theory of thinking.

But what happens when the primary caregiver cannot perform this function of containment or reverie for the baby, or when the baby cannot make use of the receptive attention of the caregiver? How does the baby cope with long periods of inattention or unpredictable responses by a preoccupied or depressed parent? Data from observing babies and from the analysis of children has led to ongoing investigation of the consequences for the child when containment is inadequate. This may arise from internal or external difficulties of the primary care giver or from constitutional impediments in the child's capacity to use what is available, including those situations when a baby is ill or has a disability.

Esther Bick (1968) described what she termed 'second skin' phenomena, in which the child finds substitutes from its own resources, to replace a sense of safety based on dependable relationships. Recognising, through close observation, the infant's terror of falling apart or fragmenting when feeling un-held, Bick suggested that the infant may find ways of 'holding himself together' in the absence of maternal holding in mind—through excessive muscular development; becoming precociously self-sufficient and controlling; excessive sensory stimulation or kinetic activity, thereby creating his own 'second-skin containment' as a defence against falling apart. Toddlers and older children often keep their thick coats on when they arrive at nursery or insist on having their shoe laces tied tight, as if an extra layer of (skin) clothing can help them feel held together. Much of the understanding of young children's behaviour and communications, as well as that of their parents, is based on a recognition that these unconscious infantile defence mechanisms may be resorted to at times of stress or anxiety throughout their development. Difficulties such as sleep problems, tantrums and biting may originate in very early experiences in infancy, relating to the lack of an adequate container for the infant's internal and external experiences that might become intensely persecutory. This may result from the caregiver herself lacking support and containment, as a result of external as well as internal circumstances.

Intervention model

In approaching sessions, the therapist has in mind the theoretical framework, a receptivity to observing all details of the way the family members present themselves, and an awareness of the emotional impact of the family on the therapist. The attitude is one of openness to exploration of all communications until a 'selected fact' (Bion, 1962a) and focus for the work emerges. This is likely to include a gradual exploration of the parental background and social circumstances and its implications for the family, as well as a simultaneous exploration of a child's communications through behaviour, play, drawing and interaction with parent(s) and therapist. A basic tenet of the psychoanalytic training of child psychotherapists is the need to approach each case afresh, 'eschewing memory and desire' (Bion, 1967), without making assumptions or jumping to premature conclusions before having assessed the observational data available in the 'here and now' of the consulting room—wherever that is—as the meeting with the family unfolds.

Applying this approach to community outreach settings: Border crossings

'Crossing the border' into community outreach settings requires the clinician to hold in mind a clear theoretical framework, and well-honed observational skills, part of her portable mental 'toolkit', while remaining flexible and adaptable, not only to the particular outreach setting, but to the cultural and ethnic background of the referred family. He/she needs to take into account the family's experience in their country of origin (if not British) and current community, as these factors are likely to impact on parents' attitudes towards mental health professionals, and the interventions they offer, as well on their views about young children's behaviour difficulties: tantrums, discipline and boundary setting, the meaning and value of play, bedtime rituals, feeding, are all typical areas of difficulty with under-fives.

Similarly, the outreach setting is likely to impact on clinicians in different ways, challenging many of their assumptions about family relationships, and offering new perspectives on clinical practice. The impact on clinicians, who may be used to the clear boundaries operating in a CAMHS clinic, of entering an organisation with a different ethos and culture to which they have to adapt, may initially interfere with their capacity to think, resulting in them feeling as overwhelmed and displaced as their clients. However, being a 'visitor' to an 'outreach' setting, while being expected to abide by its rules, also has advantages. If the dynamics operating within the particular setting can be observed and reflected on, they may become meaningful, and offer an interesting perspective on the work. For example, the clinician's experience of getting to understand the new setting, might enable the clinician to identify with the sense of bewilderment often experienced by clients, who may see a different doctor or health visitor each time they visit the GP surgery, and have to repeat details of their history, just as the clinician might be confronted each week by a different receptionist who does not recognise them, and requests their personal details again. As many of the families and children we are trying to help may be struggling with 'attachment' difficulties in their relationships with each other, it can be helpful to think about how the clinician 'attaches' to the outreach setting, making themselves 'at home' enough to be able to welcome the clients and offer them a 'home' in the clinician's mind, so that they can provide a thoughtful intervention. This is particularly pertinent for asylum-seeking or refugee families, who are often housed in temporary accommodation, and isolated from extended family support.

However, these advantages of flexibility and accessibility, which outreach work offers, also pose challenges to clinicians training to work within the 'standard' psychoanalytic framework. This includes a predictable consistent room and environment (that is, not too many changes of content, pictures, equipment and so on, from one meeting to the next), a consistent timeframe, secure boundaries avoiding unpredictable interruptions, all of which cannot be guaranteed in these settings. What is the effect on the clinicians, and how are they able to harness these challenges to offer an appropriately adapted intervention?

As the clinical vignettes will convey, technical adaptations are required in order to work effectively in outreach settings, where the 'usual' clinical conditions may be far more subject to change, and impingements from the external environment. It may be more difficult for the clinician to gain a clear idea of what may be contributing to a child's state of mind, as there are more variables to consider. To this end, clinicians need to incorporate these changes into their technique, highlighting these factors as they emerge in the setting, to explore the family's areas of difficulty, rather than seeing them as 'a spanner in the works'.

Reflective supervision

These thoughts about the impact of outreach interventions on CAMH practitioners, are based on my experience of supervising the clinical work of trainees in the Tavistock Clinic doctoral training in child and adolescent psychotherapy, who undertake brief psychoanalytically based interventions to parents, infants and young children in a range of early years community-outreach settings, including nurseries, children's centres and baby clinics, as part of our CAMHS team. This brief work is particularly adaptable to community settings because of the flexible and short-term nature of the work, which can also function as an assessment for longer-term work, or referral on to other services, if required. An additional advantage of operating from a community setting, is the opportunity it offers for meeting with early years professionals such as health visitors, and for sometimes seeing families jointly, providing them with an experience of a professional 'couple' (working together with different skills to offer).

Supervision is essential, both to help contain the clinicians' anxieties, and to help them reflect on their own countertransference response to disruptions to the setting. The clinician may be able to consider whether his/her own response (indifference, fury, anxiety), could be reflections of the client's own reactions of shock, anxiety and anger, at unpredictable intrusions or changes which the client may sense are out of their therapist's control. Such states of mind might reflexively give an indication of previous experiences of sudden possibly traumatic events which may have occurred, in which parents have found themselves feeling helpless and out of control, for example at international border crossings, when seeking asylum or in situations of war and conflict in their countries of origin. Such extraneous events, which disrupt the setting, can be useful if the clinician is able to absorb and think about them, without reacting precipitously by conveying anger or shock overtly to the client. Reacting, rather than reflecting, could give a sense to the family of a lack of containment of their own states of mind, and might lead them to feel insecure in the setting, and unheld by the clinician, particularly given any past traumas and experiences of oppression. I will illustrate this in the case examples to follow.

A trainee child psychotherapist's experience in community outreach work

One of the trainee child psychotherapists on our team was based in a nursery school, and another trainee, Mr T, began to attend a local baby clinic one afternoon a week, run by a senior health visitor, Ms H who referred parents for one-off consultations or longer-term work, in the practice. I ran a fortnightly supervision group to support their work. Mr T, already an experienced clinician, brought to the supervision group his shock at the turmoil he felt when he first began to offer services in the baby clinic, because his usual expectations of clinical practice, with booked appointments on the hour, a regular room in which to see families, and set times for case discussion with colleagues, for example in team meetings, were not met; he had to adapt his approach to match the needs of the outreach service. Although the health visitor Ms H was very keen to make use of his input, there was limited time for them to meet and discuss referrals, because of the busyness of the clinic. The appointment booking system was difficult to control, as the child psychotherapy trainee Mr T only attended once a week, so he would arrive to find appointments had been written into a book in the baby clinic waiting room. There were occasional double bookings, or confusion over appointment times, which may have mirrored the parents' struggles to manage routines and structure with very young, demanding infants. Over time we reflected that the health visitor manager, with limited support herself, may have been overwhelmed by the states of anxiety and helplessness of many first time mothers and their infants, possibly transmitted to Mr T, himself feeling slightly out of his depth and uncertain of his role and skills. At this stage, he seemed unable to offer much emotional containment to families or Ms H, and conveyed to the supervision group a feeling that he could never provide enough to satisfy the urgent need he perceived in parents and professionals alike.

In our supervisions in the first few months of his outreach work, Mr T described feeling how easily his internal psychoanalytic framework could become fragmented in this context. His capacity to remain thoughtful, when struggling to locate a room in which to work in, or to deal with interruptions by a nurse or doctor, was threatened despite being in his own analytic treatment, a prerequisite for all trainees. It was shocking to hear of consulting rooms where doctors' equipment and bins of 'sharps' or loose electrical wires, posed threats to babies and young children, so that the trainee had to check the rooms for safety, before inviting parents in. Remaining clinically focused, while adapting to less-than-optimal circumstances was a demanding task, and supportive supervision was essential. In discussion with Mr T, we agreed that he would approach the health visitor and the practice manager in person and by e-mail, indicating his concerns, and these were dealt with efficiently and thoughtfully. We also reflected on the way in which his own anxiety about what he would 'discover' on his next visit, and his nervousness about being taken by surprise, needed to be processed and understood, both in terms of personal issues that might be evoked in him, and as clues to areas of emotional difficulty for the families he was seeing. Many of these families may have been subjected to shocking experiences, which ruptured their sense of predictable safety; a small incident in an apparently 'safe' medical environment might evoke echoes of past dangerous events.

In our work with under-fives, we often felt pressure to offer what appeared to us to be concrete solutions and strategies to families in difficulty, even in the clinic setting; however, this pressure was greater in the GP surgery, where parents came expecting to be provided with medication or a practical solution. This could make the clinician's approach, which is to hear about the problems, and to take the time to observe the underlying dynamics unfolding in a session, difficult for parents to tolerate. The struggle to move from preoccupation with concrete physical concerns to more abstract containment of emotional states of distress, was challenging, particularly as young children often presented with what we viewed as psychosomatic symptoms such as constipation, incontinence, eating problems, which we felt often had an emotional basis, linked to their primary relationships.

Mr T's input over the half day a week he attended the clinic, took different forms, ranging from a brief informal chat to a mother in the waiting room to pre-booked appointments; Mr T was able to adapt and shift from one intervention type to another at short notice. At times a mother would arrive in a state of distress and need to be seen at once. During one busy period, the health visitor asked Mr T to lend a hand and weigh a baby, and at that moment, Mr T's pre-arranged appointment arrived early to see him. It seemed as though seeing the therapist holding another baby had an impact on the little girl whose parents had brought her because of her disruptive behaviours and rivalrous feelings towards her baby brother! It seemed that the little girl's feelings of jealousy and possessiveness were aroused and needed to be addressed in the consulting room.

In our supervision, it became clear that some of the referrals were a function of Ms H's feelings of isolation and wish for another professional's viewpoint, when having to bear overwhelming anxiety about families she was responsible for; in these cases the parent was sometimes unclear why their family had been referred, and it seemed as if further pre-referral discussion might have been needed. This alerted us to the importance of struggling, despite the difficulties, to try and 'grab' five minutes of discussion time with the health visitor manager, either at the start or end of the baby clinic. Mr T found that, when he persevered in seeking out that discussion time, Ms H managed to carve out some time, and they began to work better as a 'united professional couple', jointly discussing cases and their suitability for referral.

Case vignettes

This case illustrates some of the complexity of undertaking community outreach work, and how difficulties experienced in providing a consistent setting for families can have an impact on the clinical process. Three-year-old Pippa and her parents (White, British, English-speaking) were attending the under-five service, which was held alongside the baby clinic, in a GP practice, because of Pippa's huge tantrums at nursery and home. When the family arrived at the GP clinic for their second appointment, Mr T, was helping to weigh a screaming toddler, Mr T invited mother and Pippa in, explaining that they were to be seen in a different room. Pippa ran ahead in the direction of the room where they had met last time and Mr T called her back, commenting on her remembering the previous week's room.

Settling into the 'new' room, Pippa became controlling and demanded that Mr T draw her a picture of a "mummy, big papa and a little girl". Mother and Mr T asked who else was in their family, what about baby sister Jane, was she part of the family too? "NO JANE!" shouted Pippa. Mr T reminded Pippa that last time they had talked about how difficult it is to feel there is room in her family for two "little girls". Mother told Mr T that Jane was an "angel", giving no trouble when starting a new nursery, unlike Pippa, who was "always creating a drama" about separating at the school gates. Mr T said it must be difficult for Pippa to trust that there was enough attention to go around. As if in response, Pippa pointed to two baby dolls, telling Mr T that they were wearing the wrong clothes. She insisted that she was going to change the doll's clothes around, so that the big girl doll should have the nice dress, and the baby doll should have the plain one. Mr T watched as Pippa changed the clothes, and suggested that perhaps Pippa was showing them how much *she* wanted to be the good girl with the nice dress and how hard it was to feel that there could be nice clothes for two girls.

Pippa stood up and, pointing to the wall, asked Mr T who was in the "other room". Mr T asked whether Pippa was referring to the room they had been in last time she had been here. Pippa nodded and repeated her question. Mr T said she wanted to know what was happening in the other room, and felt angry about having been 'pushed out of "her" room'. Perhaps Pippa worried about things that happened that she couldn't see. Also, she hated it when the grown-ups took charge and said "no" which is what happened with the room. She thought she knew where she was going, and she could be 'in charge', then suddenly she didn't know where she was! At this moment there was a knock at the door and the health visitor asked how long Mr T was going to be, telling her that another parent was waiting to see Mr T. In addition, he would have to move rooms again, as the speech therapist was about to see a client in the current room. Pippa was faced with a concrete experience of 'her' therapist being in demand elsewhere, which seemed to leave her feeling deflated and displaced. This was all the more poignant as the interruption occurred just as Pippa was demonstrating how she felt 'trapped' in the role of the 'difficult child', and her longing to change places with the good, obedient 'baby sister Jane', as she changed over the two doll's clothes.

This experience of displacement seemed to tap into Pippa's feeling that a new baby is always waiting to claim her parents' attention, just as another client is waiting to replace Pippa. It seemed understandable that this would arouse feelings of rivalry and jealousy, and needed to be taken up by the clinician, as part of his understanding of the transference to him, as a figure who 'rejects' Pippa in favour of a new baby (new client). This reaction is likely to have happened whether the family was seen in an outreach, or a more predictable CAMHS setting; however, it was unlikely that this kind of interruption would occur in a CAMHS setting, simply by dint of the fact that the clinician takes charge of the start and end of the session. In the outreach setting it was more likely that Pippa would feel pushed out at the end of the session, and displaced by a new client. The difference between the two settings is that these feelings of displacement would have remained at a level of fantasy in the more predictable CAMHS environment, whereas in the outreach setting, in the GP practice, Pippa was confronted with concrete 'evidence' of her therapist's 'betrayal'. The therapist in the GP practice needed to understand this and address the situation through interpreting Pippa's (and the rest of the family's) possible reaction to him and this disruption of their session, or there could have been a danger that the family might have 'acted out' their feelings of rejection and displacement by cancelling or DNA'ing (Did Not Attend – DNA) their next appointment. This might have conveyed to Mr T what it felt like to be displaced in favour of another, more important activity, and projected the feeling of rejection into him.

Underlying this case is the theoretical assumption that sibling rivalry is likely to be present in all cultures and societies, albeit expressed in different ways. In this family, the child's play could be understood to convey her rivalrous feelings towards her sibling, and the additional factor of the child's space in the clinic being intruded on and commandeered for other uses, would serve to highlight an already evident theme to be addressed within the family.

This vignette is a snapshot of the demands on clinicians, especially those still in training, who have to learn to hold onto their capacity to reflect, when faced with interruptions, and to make use of the material that this provides to further their understanding of the patient's communications. In this way, the ways of adapting the 'classic' therapeutic approach to outreach work can be incorporated into the clinician's 'toolbox', and his/her technique can be extended and refined to adapt to the community setting.

Freud, in his paper on *Mourning and Melancholia*, describes how 'the shadow of the object falls on the ego' (Freud, 1953, p. 249), suggesting the trans-generational transmission of unresolved parental loss and trauma, which we recognise as particularly pertinent in parent-infant psychotherapy. The brief intervention model involves a simultaneous exploration of both past and current experiences, considering the impact of unprocessed parental and couple conflicts on young children's emotional development. The countertransference experience of the therapist can usefully alert her to patterns of emotional interaction, which have been transmitted trans-generationally to a young child; or situations where the child's behaviour is an enactment of ongoing trauma in the parents' lives. It is often only in the room with the family that these phenomena are brought to emotional life in the 'here and now', and their emotional impact can be explored.

Enid Balint suggested that 'a mother's general mood is absorbed by the very young infant, who reacts, for example, to her aliveness or deadness and to her unconscious anxieties, which do not necessarily arise from the relation between mother and baby' (Balint, 2003, p. 16) but from a previous trauma in the mother's early life. She suggested that the therapist's countertransference experience may not relate directly to the child's internal or external life but to the parents' lives, and may be being communicated via the child's behaviour. A vignette of a recent case may illustrate this, as follows.

Tariq, an only child aged two and a half years, from a war-torn Middle Eastern country, was referred because of his intense anxiety states, particularly after a serious road traffic accident the previous year. I met with the family five times, together with an Arabic interpreter, alternating parent meetings with family sessions. An increasingly complex picture emerged, of a child whose anxiety seemed linked to past traumatic events in their lives, and anticipatory terror of further impending disasters. Before I describe the intervention, I will say a word about working with the interpreter. Although in some cases I found this to be a challenging experience, at times, as in this occasion, the interpreter contributed in a positive way to the sense I had of working within a professional 'couple'. She was sensitive to the fact that Tariq's mother spoke better English than his father, and seemed aware that this might be potentially humiliating for the father, in a culture where the man is seen as head of the household and where it may not be easy for him to show 'weakness' or a lack of competence in an area, in which, in his home country, he would be fluent. The interpreter also facilitated my conversations with

Tariq, who spoke a mixture of Arabic and English, without being overbearing or intrusive. For my part, I took care to address the interpreter, as well as the family members, maintaining eye contact with her when she was interpreting, and, where I could, I had a brief conversation with her after the session, to endorse our professional link, and pick up on any issues that had been touched on for her. Although there was potential for fragmentation and splitting to occur, I felt that, in this case, the interpreter united with me in offering a 'containing' (Bion, 1962a) setting for the family.

In the first family meeting I heard about Tariq's fear of the doorbell ringing; how he listened out for the sound, running away in terror and hiding behind furniture. He hated loud noises, even a TV set on at high volume would send him hiding under a chair, and I found myself wondering about rows at home, sensing a hint of tension between the couple. Mother described Tariq getting into terrible states of rage and frustration, head banging, tearing at his skin and squeezing his throat and chest so hard that he would vomit. I was shocked by the apparent ferocity of his self-harm. I also heard about his imperious control at home; how he 'forbid' visiting children to enter the flat or remove their coats, screaming and kicking at them. I wondered to myself whether Tariq was struggling with the notion of a sibling invading his exclusive space with his parents, becoming increasingly terrified of retaliation for his own hostile feelings.

As we spoke, I noted that Tariq was taking care to lay the coloured round pegs in neat, orderly rows, concentrating intently. I commented on this to them all, suggesting that Tariq likes to keep everything in order and under his control, otherwise things may feel too frightening. I said that from what they had told me, it sounded as if it was difficult for Tariq to be a little boy, not in charge of things. They sat forward and both nodded, mother telling us: "he does not want me to call him a little boy. He says he is 'a man'". I asked about rows between them and they acknowledged they argue, saying that Tariq gets frightened by their fights. Father described how Tariq takes his mother's side, feeling that she needs 'protecting', whereas dad is strong enough to cope. I was struck by how quietly attentive Tariq was, sitting between his parents and playing with the coloured bricks. He laid all the rectangular green bricks out in a row, then, in a separate part of table, the blue arch bricks. I said that Tariq seemed to want to keep all the same colours together; he did not seem to like the two kinds of bricks to get too close to each other. Tariq nodded and father laughed. I said: "Perhaps he also doesn't like it when his mummy and daddy get too close together ... and he is now sitting right in-between you". Mother and father nodded emphatically, mother telling us how, "He doesn't like us talking to each other, and even if I am on the telephone he tells me to say goodbye". I said he feels he should be in charge and mother should be with him only; no one else should get in the way, not even daddy. As we talked, Tariq moved the blue arch bricks over across to the rows of green, so that they were closer together, and creating some combined structures. I commented on how the bricks were being joined up, suggesting that Tariq may have been responding to the conversation, 'allowing' the parental couple to come together to think about him and his difficulties.

The atmosphere became more sombre when I asked about the accident, and I heard about Tariq's terror, and resulting incontinence after the event. I suggested the accident must have been particularly shocking for a child like Tariq who may have felt completely out of control, feeling even his parents couldn't protect him, and he showed this by becoming like a helpless baby, losing control over his bodily functions. His parents nodded and seemed powerfully affected, father sitting with bowed head, as if reliving the shock. Tariq was filling a truck with bricks, whispering a request to his father, as he tried to pack in more and more bricks until it was full to bursting and starting to overflow. I addressed Tariq and his parents, suggesting how Tariq seems to notice and hear everything, and becomes quickly overwhelmed, filled up with so many sensations and feelings; like the truck, his mind is full of feelings he is trying to sort out. Father agreed, caressing Tariq tenderly, saying, "His brain gets too full up"! As the parents talked about his possessive control, I commented on how Tariq seemed determined there should be no more people in their home, suggesting that he may be preoccupied with the idea of other babies in the family. They agreed, saying that he has ordered them to "fetch a baby brother from the hospital"! I said he seemed determined to stick to the idea that producing a baby would have nothing to do with his parents being together! As we talked, Tariq moved to the toy cradle, covering the dolls and rocking them tenderly. Mother talked about extended family members who also have only one child, saying that Tariq had suggested his cousin and he could be brothers, as neither of them have siblings.

The atmosphere became sad and an unspoken distress threatened to overwhelm me. Taking into account my countertransference experience, which indicated to me that the parents were possibly preoccupied by more upsetting issues than they had been able to express so far, I addressed the parents, wondering whether there had been a pregnancy before, and heard about a lost baby, referring to difficulties around their status in the country. I felt shocked and a feeling of grief entered the session. I suggested that Tariq may have picked up their distress at the traumatic event. This, followed six months later by the accident, may have compounded his anxiety and his subsequent need to take total charge, to evade feelings of vulnerability and dependency. Aware that there may be issues the parents could not discuss with Tariq present, I suggested that I meet them on their own.

In the session with the parents on their own, I quickly understood that my previous thoughts about Tariq struggling with Oedipal anxieties related to possessive control of his mother, and rejection of father, a bid to take over father's role by taking charge of the household, while possibly valid interpretations of his communications, were, in this case not the central issue. As the parents' distressing story emerged, I began to recognise that it was their *own* fear of the doorbell, which represented experiences of real threats from the outside world—UK officialdom, torture and persecution—which was being projected into their son, filling him with terror. A picture emerged of a couple whose marriage was unsupported by extended family, and of father, whose political activities had led to his torture in his home country and a failed asylum bid in the UK. His own aspirations to continue studying had been thwarted by the asylum system, which meant he had no entitlement to grants or benefits. Both parents broke down as they described the father's depression, his waking in terror of being 'taken' in the night and deported, never seeing his family again. Work with the parents over several sessions deepened our understanding of Tariq's difficulties, and their own problems in setting firm boundaries for him. We were able to refer father to an appropriate service for help with his traumatic experiences, and the family were eventually granted leave to remain in the country.

In the fourth family session they reported that Tariq's fears and self-harm had diminished, although he now took 'charge' of the telephone. It appeared that a shift could occur in Tariq's behaviour once we had been able to recognise how burdened he was by projections of parental anxiety and trauma, and how his mind, like the truck he had filled to bursting, was overwhelmed with anxiety and anticipatory fears of imminent traumatic separation. His self-harm may have reflected an unconscious apprehension of states of terror induced through his parents' experience of torture. This was gradually revealed to me, through my countertransference experience in the session, of intense terror of separation and loss, which went way beyond that associated with 'ordinary' Oedipal fear of displacement, as well as my willingness to meet and talk to the parents about areas of their life that I had not been foregrounding, that were pertinent to their experience of acute anxiety and fear; as a result the focus shifted accordingly to a different level of concern relating to wider contextual issues.

Discussion

Several issues arose relating to the family's cultural background, and how this piece of work developed. As I have noted earlier, I think that a basic tenet of psychoanalytic work pertains, which is that one cannot jump to premature conclusions, and that theory needs to take second place to what is occurring in the 'here and now' of the consulting room, whether it be in community outreach or a clinic setting. In this case, my initial assumption, based on my observations of Tariq's play, that he seemed to be in the grip of Oedipal anxieties, and that his parents were having difficulty managing his challenging and frightened behaviour, was only partly correct. This observation was overlaid by a more serious and sombre atmosphere, which overtook the first session, and led me to invite the parents to come and see me on their own, at which point their background story emerged, and the links to their son's difficulties could be explored. An important element of this approach is facilitating the material to unfold in such a way that a key 'selected fact' emerges within an emotional context, as it did in this case; whereas, if I had established the parents' background details through a questionnaire, assuming they would have divulged details of torture experiences, the links between their child's emotional difficulties and the parents' anxieties may not have been so evident. In addition, the parents may have struggled to trust this confidential matter to a form, which they may have feared would be divulged to officials.

One aspect of the work, which I did not anticipate was, that once the father had exposed his distress and vulnerability in the session, he felt unable to face neither me nor the interpreter, and did not attend further meetings. His wife explained that he felt humiliated, and that in his culture he should not expose his weakness to other women. This was exacerbated by having a woman interpreter, whom he may have felt had absorbed his distress and states of helplessness directly, through their shared language. However, we did write to the father, and heard that he had taken up the referral made to the service for asylum seeking survivors of torture.

Conclusion

In this chapter I have described the Tavistock Clinic psychoanalytic approach to brief work with parents, infants and under-fives, undertaken primarily by child and adolescent psychotherapists. I explore how this model of clinical work has been implemented in a range of early-years community outreach settings, illustrating the adaptation of theory and technique to fit the setting, and the cultural context of the diverse families seen within the service. The challenges, which face the clinician, who needs to remain thoughtful and attentive to the conscious and unconscious communications of parents and their young children, while operating out of their 'normal' clinic comfort zone, have been discussed. In my view undertaking clinical work *in* the community is an essential aspect of CAMHS input *to* the community, and it enhances clinicians' clinical skills, challenging them to reflect carefully on those aspects of their theoretical framework, which they might consider to be universally applicable to all families, and those, which may be more culturally determined. Being able to address both of these dimensions offers a 'binocular' perspective, which can deepen the quality of interventions on offer.

References

Balint, E. (2003). 'Before I was I'. In: J. Raphael-Leff (ed.). *Parent-Infant Psychodynamics.* (pp. 121–30). London, England: Whurr Publishers (first published in 1993).

Bick, E. (1968). The experience of the skin in early object relations. *International Journal of Psychoanalysis,* 49(4), 484–86.

Bion, W. (1962a). *Learning from Experience.* London, England: Heinemann (first published 1984).

Bion, W. (1962b). A theory of thinking. *International Journal of Psychoanalysis,* 43(1962), 306–10.

Bion, W. (1967). *Second Thoughts: Selected Papers on Psychoanalysis.* London, England: Karnac Books.

Emanuel, L. (2008). A slow unfolding – at double speed: Therapeutic interventions with parents and their young children. In: L. Emanuel & E. Bradley (2008). *What Can the Matter Be? Therapeutic Interventions with Parents, Infants and Young Children* (pp. 81–99). London, England: Karnac Books.

Fonagy, P., Gergely, G., Jurist, E. & Target, M. (2004). *Affect Regulation, Mentalization, and the Development of the Self.* London, England: Karnac Books.

Freud, S. (1953). Mourning and Melancholia. In: J. Strachey (ed. & trans.) *The Standard Edition of the Complete Psychological Works of Sigmund Freud.* London, England: Hogarth Press.

Watillon, A. (1993). The dynamics of psychoanalytic therapies of the early parent-child relationship. *International Journal of Psychoanalysis,* 74(5), 1037–48.

Chapter 6

A radical synthesis

Child psychotherapy in the community and community in child psychotherapy[1]

Leila Bargawi and Louise O'Dwyer

Introduction: Child psychotherapy in a community general practice

In this chapter we will look at the work of child psychotherapists in an inner-city general practice surgery, in particular the work with babies and their families, which happens in and alongside baby clinics. Infancy and early childhood are times when rapid development occurs, which can evoke 'intense and at times turbulent emotion' (Schmidt Neven, 2005, p. 190). Consequently, many families of young children find themselves needing help. This is perhaps particularly so for families in urban areas with a highly mobile population, who do not have a traditional support structure in place, such as extended families or neighbours. Furthermore, families may also be struggling with poverty, poor housing, discrimination and a lack of community resources, which all increase stress for families. Parents with babies can find themselves in the unfamiliar cultural context of a new country, at a time when they are having to adapt to the culture of parenthood, and are without a model in their mind to guide them. To an extent, child psychotherapists working in the community undergo a similar process as they leave behind the safety of the clinic context and work in a new culture with a different patient group. They have to find a way of reaching out to the community clinic in which they take part, in order to generate appropriate referrals and be of some value to community professionals, such as general practitioners and health visitors, as well as find a responsive and appropriate way of reaching out to members of the community themselves, who may or may not be familiar with what child psychotherapy is, or how it might be helpful to them. Families who are referred may have very different motivations for engaging in therapy compared with families who attend traditional CAMHS clinics. Although child psychotherapists retain their theoretical model of working in their minds, in the community there are significant challenges to this, but there are also ways of usefully adapting our approach and being responsive, which we will explore in this chapter. We will first describe the general practice in which the work takes place and then outline the theoretical framework that underpins our work, as well as ways in which we have been responsive to the community within this framework. We will highlight some of the ways we sought to reach out to the professionals and to the families. We will then discuss three clinical cases that illustrate some of the complexities of carrying out brief psychoanalytic work with a diverse population in the community.

We are child psychotherapists who have been trained psychoanalytically at the Tavistock Clinic. While much of this training has focused on an in-depth psychoanalytic understanding of patients seen at CAMHS clinics, the training also encourages therapists to use psychoanalytic concepts in applied settings in the community. We have both worked in inner London boroughs for some years, in schools, nurseries and hospitals undertaking a range of psychoanalytically informed brief work. We are both from mixed cultural backgrounds (LO'D is from Ireland, but brought up in the UK. LB comes from mixed-heritage parentage and was brought up abroad) and have, probably because of this, developed an interest in working with a wide range of communities, present in many of inner London boroughs. This applied work has also made it possible to work with families that may not be able to access a CAMHS clinic for a variety of reasons as we will discuss below. A key part of our psychoanalytic training is the use of observation as we are interested in trying to understand nonverbal communication as a useful tool for communicating experiences. We observe closely how families relate to one another, and to us, and how we relate to the families. This includes attention to what the family members say, and do not say, as well as their body language, their facial expression and their tone of voice, and the way in which they present their difficulties. This provides important information about patterns of interaction within families, and as part of this, how the families relate to their cultural context. Through observation, we aim to gather a picture of the internal life of individuals within families.

The setting

Recently, general practices have begun to offer a wide range of services on site, so it is not unusual to find marriage guidance alongside acupuncture, physiotherapy and dentistry, as well as employment advice, electrocardiogram recordings and English for speakers of other language (ESOL) classes. For families having a baby, this means that routine midwife and health visitor appointments can be offered under the same roof. A mother may attend the practice to see the midwife for antenatal checks, and once the baby is born, she will attend the baby clinic to have the baby weighed and immunised, and subsequent developmental reviews often take place within the same baby clinics in GP practices.

The baby clinic of the inner-city community practice we are writing about is staffed by a team including one rotating general practitioner, a nurse and two health visitors, as well as a clerk and two child psychotherapists. The clinic is aimed at families with a child under five, although the majority of the families who attend regularly have children under two. The practice serves a wide range of socio-economic and cultural groups as it encompasses both an affluent part of London and large areas with socio-economic deprivation. The baby clinic thus includes groups who are traditionally isolated such as young mothers, refugees and asylum seekers, as well as economic migrants; this clinic is also culturally diverse, with families coming from Eastern Europe, Somalia, Eritrea, Central and West African countries such as the Democratic Republic of Congo, Nigeria and Angola. Within this wide group are many families who would not traditionally access help from mental health services, either because they are concerned about the stigma attached to mental health difficulties, do not view the services offered as culturally relevant and acceptable to them or because they are not yet able to orient themselves to, for them, new psychological ideas. These are families often described as 'hard to reach' by traditional services. However, because of the different functions of the baby clinic, we come across most children recently born in the area. Therefore, the baby clinic provides a good opportunity for child psychotherapists to access families who may benefit from psychotherapeutic help, but who would be unlikely to access it in the traditional clinic model. Frequently, parents attend the clinic for advice around weaning, toilet training, sleep difficulties, home safety, or when there are queries or concerns about the child's development or health. At the end of each clinic, there is a meeting in which the professionals discuss the families who attended that day. This is an opportunity to link with professionals from other disciplines, refer internally to another discipline and to raise concerns or think with others about the families. Referrals to other services are discussed in the clinic, and often this is the point at which a child psychotherapy referral is considered. The main model used is the brief Tavistock 'under-fives' model.

A child psychotherapy approach adapted to an urban setting

Emanuel and Bradley (2008) explain that the Tavistock 'under-fives' model was established to offer quick response, psychoanalytically based interventions to families. Families with babies, toddlers, and children up to five years old, are seen in the service, although as many therapists point out, slightly different techniques are required for the different age groups (Lieberman, 2004; Baradon et al, 2005). Emanuel and Bradley (2008) further explain that the therapist draws on usual psychoanalytic practice in establishing a reliable and containing framework free from interruption and distractions. Through observation, and close attention to detail the therapists can explore with patients their preoccupations and start to get a sense as to how the patient understands themselves, their difficulties and their relationships with others (Miller, 2008). Part of this task, in ordinary psycho-analytic work, is to look at the unhelpful defences that patients rely upon and, if appropriate, link these to experiences that the patient may have had, or perceive themselves to have had.

However, there are important differences in the 'under-fives' model compared with traditional psychoanalytic work. First, the model is based on a brief inter-vention and families are initially offered up to five sessions. Second, as many therapists have argued, it is essential that the parent and child are involved in the treatment together (Lieberman, 2004; Stern, 2004). Therefore, the therapist is potentially relating to a family in the room, or at least a parent/infant dyad; whereas traditional psychoanalytic therapy would involve the therapist working alone with the child, while another 'parent worker' works with the parent. These two factors mean that the therapist's technique must be modified. Traditionally, psychoanalytic therapists have used the relationship that develops between the patient and the therapist, termed the 'transference', to understand the patient, but also as a tool to help the patient reflect upon and modify their interactions. This is usually discussed directly with patients. For example, some patients will feel that the therapist is highly critical of them and respond in a very defensive way so that it is difficult to develop a working relationship. The therapist would be curious about the patient's perception of them, and discuss this with the patient. This may relate to actual experiences that the patient has had with significant others (such as parents), or to the patient's perception of such experiences. Over time and through exploration, in our work in the baby clinic, the patient may develop better understanding of the impact of the previous relationships on their developing relationship with their baby. Therapists using the Tavistock model of brief intervention tend to keep these transference issues in mind and use them to inform their responses, rather than always directly comment on them (Barrows, 1997). We give examples of this in the clinical vignettes that follow.

Given that this work is in the community, there are further challenges to the approach. Creating a therapeutic framework in a GP clinic can be difficult as the context is often medical. Boundaries of space and time are seen differently in the general practice setting and despite an understanding of our work, time pressures sometimes mean that rooms are double-booked or we need to see families in ordinary general practice consulting rooms. Furthermore, one has to think about how child psychotherapists take up their role in the baby clinic. In Daws's (1985) paper, 'Standing next to the weighing scales', she describes this dilemma. She talks about the importance of being visible to baby clinic staff in order to gather appropriate referrals, as well as being able to understand the nature of the clinic and the families who attend. We have to hold on to three hats at the same time, acknowledging that we are working in a general practice context, holding on to our own theoretical models, while trying to adapt to and connect to the culture of the families we see who themselves come from diverse cultural communities. We aim to work with the team of the general practice but remain separate so that we are able to think outside the immediate situation and bring our thinking as child psychotherapists to the clinic. Emanuel in her chapter in this book describes this as child psychotherapists using a 'portable mental toolkit' (Emanuel, this volume). Our double identity, made up of an existing established identity and a newer, less-set one seems to echo something of the changing identity of the new mothers/fathers/families we see, who are often in an unfamiliar culture too.

Cultural context

Many of the families we see in the GP practice have experienced painful loss in leaving their home country behind to come to the UK. While for some families, this loss may partly be mitigated by securing employment and comfortable housing, for many other families this loss will have been quite traumatic in terms of having experienced war, torture or oppression and may be further complicated by the unfamiliar cultural context and a continuing uncertainty about remaining in the UK. In these circumstances, trust in 'the authorities' is understandably diminished and families may feel suspicious about engaging with therapists from a different culture. These are important issues to be curious about and explore with families as they have a bearing on the relationship that the family will develop with the therapist, and will also add another layer of meaning to the family's current presentation of 'symptoms'. Therapists may also need to have greater flexibility in arranging appointments, which we will discuss in the case examples below. Andreou (1999) has written about the challenges that intercultural issues can pose for psychotherapists. She argues that:

> There are no clear formulae and there is a pressing need for the therapists to be able to unpick the interrelationship between emotional distress resulting from individual/family dysfunction in any culture, and cultural issues that are specific to that particular cultural group.
>
> (Andreou, 1999, p. 76)

In our work we have tried to keep this in mind with the families who we have seen, and neither underestimate, nor overestimate the impact of cultural differences. Andreou (1999) also highlights that experiencing racism, and belonging to a culture that is different or unfamiliar to the host culture, has an impact on young people's minds.

Clinical context

It is important to find a way of engaging with staff in the baby clinic, and for families to make a meaningful connection with them. When time is so short and there are other pressures for the team and for the family, it can be difficult to make this connection. In the cases that follow, we will look at the ways we sought to take up our position in the baby clinic, and engage with the referrers and with the families. All names and identifying information have been changed to ensure confidentiality.

Aisha and Hani

This family first came to our attention in our post baby clinic meeting discussion. Over the last few months, the mother, Aisha, had repeatedly attended the baby clinic to have her youngest son, Hani, then aged one, weighed. This was becoming an almost weekly occurrence and despite his weight remaining stable and reassurance from the health visitor, Aisha continued to raise her concerns about Hani's eating at home as he would only eat a handful of different foods. Amongst the professionals, concern about Hani's nutrition also emerged and possible referrals for physical investigations were touched on. The health visitor, Diana, concerned both for Aisha, who she thought was "needy and demanding" and possibly low in mood, and Hani, who seemed withdrawn and was observed in the waiting room only interacting minimally with others including his mother, instead seeming preoccupied with the toys. After a discussion we decided that a child psychotherapist would join Diana in her appointments with Aisha and Hani as this would provide a dual perspective for the family, and it may help the wider group of professionals to better understand the family's difficulties. When families have made good relationships with community professionals, it is important that these are not lost when the family is referred on to a 'specialist' provider. Therefore, working together, we hoped to minimise this risk.

During the baby clinic Diana introduced Aisha to me (LB) in the busy baby clinic waiting area. This was far from ideal, given confidentiality issues, and a busy clinic waiting area is not necessarily a reliable and containing therapeutic space. However, it was clear from Diana's reports that Aisha would not attend an appointment without meeting me beforehand, and in this way I could be introduced as an additional member of the team.

Aisha was a young woman in her twenties, originally from Somalia. Her broken English seemed to me to stand in contrast with her very contemporary, Western clothing and I noticed that she used her non-native language to speak to Hani, which sounded stilted and somewhat cold. Psychoanalytic training teaches us to use our observation skills and reflect on our perceptions of clients, especially when we first meet them. I wondered in this first encounter about her adopted dress and language and her native culture and 'mother tongue'. I also felt that Aisha was rather distant towards me. Hani sat passively pushing a car back and forth away from his mother, and I wondered what he made of her words to him as he reacted so minimally to her. Aisha was concerned about Hani's eating, and this seemed to preoccupy her sense of him. She also talked minimally in what felt to us to be a rather flat and monotone way about their home life. We agreed to meet again the following week, but Aisha missed this session. The health visitor, Diana and I (LB) tried, together, to make contact with her over the telephone and after many attempts arranged another appointment, which Aisha also missed. It was important to think about whether this was a decision Aisha had made about not engaging with us, and whether we should continue to offer appointments. Yet at the same time, given that she had presented as low in mood, and knowing that she was relatively isolated, I wondered about her experiences of rejection, and whether it was important not to replicate this with her, particularly since I was feeling rather rejected. This was my counter-transference: 'the sometimes powerful feelings that can be evoked' (Emanuel, this volume) in the therapist with a particular patient, which is a helpful tool for understanding non-verbal communication. I wondered about my interest in Aisha's dress and words, and this made me wonder if she had been sensitive to these in me too. Maybe she had made assumptions about me and whether I could understand her difficulties. Diana and I were able to discuss our concerns with each other and think carefully about what to do. When she attended the baby clinic the following week, Diana and I wondered if Aisha wanted to meet with us then, which she did. Offering ad hoc appointments is not the way that child psychotherapists usually work, but it seemed important to reach out to this young family, to adapt to the setting we were in and respond to her unique needs. Here are some process notes from that session:

> *Hani played repetitively with the cars. He spun the wheels, one by one, and barely looked around the room. I commented on his play with the toys and wondered what the cars were doing. Aisha repeated the question to him, but he looked at me blankly, and turned quietly to the cars again. I felt useless. He started to move the cars from the sofa to the table and then back again, without speaking, and continued to look rather blank. We asked Aisha what she made of his playing, and she commented that he played a lot like this at home and that he does not seem that interested in things or people. She sounded disappointed. We commented on her sense of disappointment—that she had tried to encourage Hani just now, but he had continued with his game on his own. She nodded and spoke about his lack of interest in her cooking at home. We picked up on what appeared to be her sense of failure and rejection. We linked this to Aisha's uncertainty about engaging in therapeutic work with us, which she acknowledged.*

Following this appointment, Aisha attended all subsequent arranged appointments with us. Our ability to tolerate her ambivalence and possible hostile feelings towards us seemed to engage Aisha and deepen the contact with us. As our work continued, Aisha told us about experiencing multiple miscarriages before Hani was born. As they had always been very early in her pregnancies she had never discussed these. Hani had been conceived quickly following the last of these. Her sense of failure seemed to possibly connect to her wondering about these lost babies and the guilt she felt at not being able to keep them. This was made worse by her confusion about why these miscarriages had occurred because of the piece-meal nature of the medical information Aisha had picked up about nutrition and well-being during pregnancy. The traumas of the miscarriages seemed interconnected with her earlier traumas related to losing her family when she came to the UK. We talked about her worries that she was not able to keep Hani well and feed him. Diana's knowledge of both Hani's progress and her having experienced and seen many pregnancies, as well as babies, helped immensely at this point.

Because Aisha had no alternative possibilities of child care Hani attended all appointments with Aisha and therefore it was important to consider her distress and the impact it had on Hani as he experienced it in the room with us.

Aisha seemed surprised that Hani may be aware or interested in her feelings and moods. This enabled her to find a way of talking to Hani about her feelings, which helped Hani to connect with his mother. As we showed caring curiosity about Aisha and she was able to share the pain of her losses, more space was created for Hani who became more curious about the room, us and the toys and his play and interest in the toys became richer. It was as if he was becoming more accepting of new experiences available as his mother was experiencing feeling more accepted by us. Aisha was visibly proud and touched by our interest in Hani, which seemed to awaken more curiosity in her for Hani and his play. The absence of her own mother was a key loss, but our attention to her and Hani seemed to awaken an internal mother in Aisha who was able to increasingly observe her child.

Aisha still had some concerns about Hani's eating, and so Diana offered to do a home visit to observe a mealtime with the family. We felt that it would be too much for the family to have two visitors, and as home visiting is a service offered by health visitors, we thought that it would be more appropriate for Diana to do this. Aisha seemed enthusiastic about this idea, and I agreed to meet with Diana afterwards to discuss the visit, and I wrote the following notes about this session:

> *Diana seemed rather flat when I met with her and said that she could not stay long as she had another meeting to attend. I was surprised and disappointed as I had been looking forward to hearing about the visit. Diana described feeling uncomfortable in the house, as Aisha had been busily preparing an elaborate meal for Hani, while relatives were watching. Diana was unsure who the relatives were, or what they were eating, and did not understand much of what was being said, as the adults communicated in Somali. Diana felt that she did not have anything to add while she was in the home and felt that Aisha may not have found it helpful. She noticed Aisha did not eat with Hani, but spent her time trying to feed him. Diana described seeing four or five dishes being offered to Hani, but Hani pushing most of them away. I spoke with Diana about the mealtimes seeming to be filled with anger and rejection.*

It became clear that there was a clash in our perceptions of the purpose of the home visit. Diana and I were hoping to gain further insight into the family mealtimes and how to assist with them, but I believe Aisha also wanted to offer us something, feed us, show her appreciation of our work. It was clear that in her culture mealtimes are a time of people gathering together and sharing an experience. We had not anticipated this in advance, and the presence of so many others came as a shock to Diana. When we next met the family, we explored some of these feelings with Aisha and Hani. It emerged that Aisha had very complicated feelings and associations about her cultural background, including feelings of belonging, hostility and exclusion. Aisha spoke about her anger at being in the UK, away from her family and her home, and this feeling like a punishment, while she also felt a sense, from others in the community, that she should be grateful—grateful to be safe.

REFLECTIONS

Aisha's attempts to navigate different cultures were mirrored in my work with Diana, the health visitor. We both had to give up our pure, learned cultures of working and of our profession and trust that we could create something new with our client without losing our skills. Our modelling different ways of thinking and understanding Aisha within her multiple internal and external contexts, as well as being able to communicate this to each other in our joint-professional sessions, offered Aisha a type of responsive, containing parental couple that she was lacking in London. Aisha described being severely traumatised by miscarriages, trauma in her own country, and traumatic separations from her family. This may have been projected[2] into Hani, making it difficult for him to 'take in' new experiences and food (Williams, 2002). When this trauma could be digested in the sessions, it was a relief for Hani and Aisha; it meant that there was more space to think about the anxieties and maybe normalise them. It felt as though Aisha was able to get some nourishment for herself and was no longer preoccupied with Hani's food intake. Aisha may have benefited from long-term psychotherapy to address some of the traumas she had experienced. However, she did not feel able to access professional/mental health services, and she was coping well with a difficult situation. It was important to respect her wishes, and limit the work to our remit, rather than to fulfil our wish to 'rescue' Aisha and feed her more. Aisha and Hani taught us that an unsettled identity may be significant for an understanding of the experiences of families in the community, especially at the juncture in their life of being with a new baby.

Eva and Maya

Eva was a Polish woman in her thirties, an economic migrant, who valued independence and autonomy, but who was also struggling with separation issues. She had worked in a successful career in finance. She had met her husband, also from Poland, through work and had a two-year-old daughter, Maya. Eva had consulted her general practitioner in the baby clinic about Maya's projectile vomiting on several occasions. This GP felt that Maya was "rather clingy to mother" and was keen to refer them to us. He discussed this with Eva and reported that she seemed anxious about being seen by a psychotherapist and insisted that there was an organic difficulty with Maya. We were uncertain about how to proceed. From a CAMHS point of view we might have concluded that the family were not consenting to work with us and unable to engage. Yet, we were aware that the family may be uncertain about what our service was, and clearly they were seeking help. Titles such as 'psychotherapist' can be difficult for families, and perhaps even more so in community settings and when English is a second language.

We gained consent to join the general practitioner's next appointment with the family in order to introduce ourselves and see if Eva and Maya might be interested in working with us. This was quite a challenge, as instead of having a fifty-minute session, we had a ten-minute session and had to act quickly to link with the family. My (LO'D) assumption prior to meeting the family was that Maya would be a rather timid toddler who may be ill and clingy. In my process notes I wrote:

> *Maya was a red-cheeked robust two-year-old keen to explore the room. She ignored the toys that I had brought down, and instead reached for the medical equipment in the room. Eva tried to speak with the doctor about her vomiting, but Maya screeched and shoved a box of tissues under Eva's nose with increasing urgency. It felt difficult for anyone to talk. I commented that Maya did not want Eva to talk to anyone else. Eva said that Maya was always like this. Maya clawed at her mother's top possessively and glared at me and the general practitioner. I felt like an unwanted intruder. I commented that Eva was just for Maya. Eva added that she and her husband had not gone out together since Maya was born because Maya was always sick, and because Maya was not talking, a baby sitter would have difficulty knowing what Maya wanted. I commented that there seemed to be in Eva's mind, a Maya that was terribly needy and fragile, and yet there was also a Maya in the room that was quite assertive and very good at communicating. Eva laughed and acknowledged this as Maya banged loudly on the door.*

After this brief meeting with this family we wondered if there was something indigestible about a third person for Maya, which perhaps led to her vomiting, or wanting to leave the room. We were also interested in Eva's perception of Maya, as helpless and fragile. We wondered if Eva's perception of Maya's fragility was an unconscious confusion with something else, which prevented Eva from feeling she could help Maya to separate more easily. Eva and Maya agreed to meet with us again without the general practitioner. However, we thought that it was important to stay in one of the medical rooms in the practice, rather than the usual 'therapy' room, to respect the fact that for Eva, seeking help for Maya's projectile vomiting was a legitimate reason to seek help. We spoke with Eva about her sense that Maya was fragile, and Eva did not understand why she felt that Maya was fragile. Eva had said that she had wanted to go back to work when Maya was eight months, but because Maya had not settled with the nanny, Eva had decided not to return to work. This had been difficult for her as she enjoyed her work, but felt that Maya could not manage any form of childcare. At the end of the session, when I wondered about a further appointment, although Eva accepted, I had the feeling that Eva was doing me a favour by coming, as if I needed to have patients.

This made me wonder if 'neediness' was being projected onto me; similar to the way that separation difficulties seemed to be located in Maya.

> *I said that our time was coming to an end today. Eva looked at her watch and grabbed her coat and bag, and said to Maya, "Come on, Maya". Maya looked startled and frowned as mother removed the toy out of her hand. Maya started to protest, but Eva said, "Come on, coat on". Maya looked disorientated, and I commented that they seemed to be in a rush. Eva was already at the door and said, "Thank you. See you in two weeks" and was gone. I looked around the room and saw the toys still strewn on the floor and felt rather confused and abandoned.*

Eva had fled from the session, and there was little chance for Maya to say goodbye. I began to understand why Maya may have felt frightened about saying goodbye as there was a sense of abruptness. I took this up in the next session, and Eva was initially very matter of fact about this and said that she was used to goodbyes, her family were all abroad, and so she was always having to say goodbye. I wondered if some of her own more vulnerable feelings about loss had been projected onto Maya, so that Maya became the person for whom goodbyes were unbearable. This meant that Eva could avoid getting in touch with her own feelings of loss. In our work as child psychotherapists, we often see that unbearable feelings can be unconsciously projected onto other family members where they can be located rather than faced and felt. Making individuals aware of these feelings and making them bearable can free the other person from the projection and ultimately aid the relationship. In the case of this family when I spoke with Eva about what it was like coming to the UK when she was eighteen, she was much more able to get in touch with how overwhelming it had been. She spoke about how frightening it was to not understand the language properly and to find herself only able to see her family two or three times a year. She could then get in touch with Maya's experiences and think more generally about saying goodbye for them both. It also emerged that Eva's parents, who had separated when she was a child, were so preoccupied by their own animosity that they were out of touch with Eva's experience. Therefore, Eva did not have an experience of being helped to face separations. Eva's solution seemed to have been to leave home and turn to herself and a career in finance, which meant that she did not have to depend on anyone. As an economic migrant these qualities had been useful to her in developing her career and establishing a life for herself in the UK, but they were more problematic in relation to managing a dependant relationship with Maya. My understanding was that Eva's sense of autonomy made it easier to access help for Maya's projectile vomiting in a medical setting, than a therapeutic setting; however, Eva's fragility had also become unconsciously projected onto Maya, which made it difficult for Eva to help Maya to separate from her. We had to help Eva mourn some of these losses, in order for *her* to be able to separate from Maya.

REFLECTIONS

In this example, the work was mainly exploring the mother's internal world, as it related to Maya. The mother's loss in her own childhood had confused her perception of her daughter. As a consequence there was a great deal of confusion about what Maya could manage. A large clue about these difficulties arose in my own feelings about what I observed, that is to say, in my countertransference. I felt quickly pushed out by Maya and Eva. There seemed to be an idea around in both of their minds that a third person was not wanted. It was also important to reflect on Eva's cultural beliefs about separation, which were influenced by her Polish upbringing. She had come from a small town in Poland, where it was expected that many young people would leave as they finished school, and so separation at this stage was considered normal. Yet Eva also had to manage her feelings about her separation from her family and culture of origin. While this was a choice she had made, it remained painful for her. This needed to be thought about, so she could allow herself to process Maya's separations. In this case we felt that it might have been helpful to have involved Maya's father in the sessions too, as he may have been able to play a significant role in helping Maya and their toddler to 'separate' (Adamo & Magagna, 1998). However, despite offering several appointments he did not feel able to attend.

Keisha and Shanice

Keisha was a fifteen-month-old girl of Afro-Caribbean descent, who was referred to us (LO'D and LB) by the health visitor following concerns about her weight and development. Social services were involved, and Keisha was classed as a Child in Need[3]. The health visitor was responsible for weighing her weekly, and a paediatrician was monitoring her growth. Keisha lived with her sixteen-year-old mother Shanice, and her grandmother. The health visitor also felt that Shanice was depressed. We, ourselves, wondered if Shanice might find a clinic environment intimidating and stigmatising, and we therefore arranged with the health visitor for Shanice and Keisha to see us (LO'D and LB) during the baby clinic, which she was already attending. The first session was very difficult. These are our process notes:

> *We wondered what was on Shanice's mind. Shanice looked down into her lap and said, "Dunno". I (LO'D) felt pushed away. Keisha glanced up at us, but took a few shaky steps towards the door. We commented that maybe it was difficult being in a new room with new faces and new toys. Shanice called Keisha back and said sharply that there was no need to be silly about coming. Keisha sat on the sofa and snuggled up next to her mother and buried her head in her coat. LO'D said that perhaps they really were not very sure about coming here today, and perhaps they wondered why they were here. There was a pause. Shanice's expression did not change, although Keisha peeped*

her head out. LB said that Keisha was not so sure about exploring the toys in the room. Keisha looked at the toys, as if contemplating getting one, and LB asked her if she would like to see what was here. Shanice then sat back and took out her phone.

In this session, we felt painfully pushed away and rubbished by Shanice. In some ways her presentation was typical of many teenagers engaging in a therapeutic contact, the fact that she was isolated, has experienced racism, was a new mother, and had social service involved with her child perhaps further explained her cautious and withdrawn stance. We were also aware that we were two older middle-class women, who may have been perceived to be from the dominant cultural group. Lowe (2008) argues there is a power imbalance in such relationships, in which 'whiteness is equated with "power authority and control" and blackness with the opposite' (Lowe, 2008, p. 23). Shanice may have felt that she had little power or authority in the session. We felt the negative transference was so strong it needed to be voiced; otherwise we would not see this family again. We therefore had to address Shanice's wish not be seen. Shanice spoke quietly about being fed up having to attend so many appointments when Keisha was "fine now". We acknowledged this, although felt alarmed that the concern about Keisha had been split off into the professionals and that if we colluded with the idea that the annoyance was only with the other professionals it risked creating an unhelpful split in the network. We reflected that perhaps it was annoying to be sent to another place, and perhaps she felt that she was now going to be told what to do by two middle-class women, who were not Black. Shanice seemed surprised and nodded. We wondered how we could understand some of the things that she had been through and was currently experiencing. She responded to this, and we explored issues around her resentment about generally feeling "bossed around" and overlooked by adults, particularly White adults, because she is a Black teenager.

It emerged that Shanice had a difficult relationship with her mother, had never known her father, although was aware that he had been violent to her mother before she was born; Shanice had been sexually abused by a neighbour when she was fourteen. It was unsurprising then that she felt untrusting towards adults. We explained to Shanice that it was her choice to come and see us, and that we felt that this was particularly important given that she had had a history of being forced into situations by authority figures both in the form of abuse and in the name of statutory duty/'support', and we wanted her to feel that we trusted that she could make a decision as a parent. Yet at the same time, given the amount of abuse, loss and rejection she had experienced, it felt important for us to reach out to Shanice, rather than respond to her rejection of us by closing the case if she did not to engage. Rather than setting further sessions with her at the end of the first appointment, we reminded her that we would be at the clinic the following week, and that she could think about whether she would like further appointments.

When we later saw Shanice in the clinic, she barely acknowledged us. However, we approached her and said that we would be happy to see her again. She muttered that she would think about it. This pattern continued for a few weeks, but gradually as we briefly met in the clinic, we started to speak informally about Keisha.

We noticed that Keisha was walking around the table in the middle of the room more confidently, although her eyes remained fixed on Shanice. We commented on Keisha seeming more confident in her walking, and how much Keisha was looking at Shanice. Shanice blushed and seemed almost embarrassed. Shanice said that she had been practicing this with Keisha at home.

This was a simple observation that was not based on psychoanalytic theory. We were aware of Shanice having seen us talk to other families and it seemed to help Shanice to feel held in mind, and that we were interested in Keisha's development, which helped Shanice to get in touch with the parental part of herself. It also connected with Shanice's focus (for example, when she had previously described Keisha as "fine now") on what was going well for Keisha. Furthermore, she could see that we were available at the same time each week in the clinic, without having to take that risk in a therapeutic setting, which, given her life experiences of loss, abuse and prejudice, perhaps felt too risky and too intense. Shanice then voiced a concern about mealtimes being stressful, and we wondered if this was something she might want to discuss with us, to which she agreed. We arranged a limited number of fortnightly sessions. Shanice said that she often did not eat much herself, as her mother cooked traditional Caribbean food, which she did not always want. We spoke about Keisha and Shanice both finding it difficult to know what to 'take in', both in terms of food, but also emotionally. Shanice did not want her mother's Caribbean food, but she did not want our 'English' food either. Shanice was able to think about this, and it lead to a discussion about her confusion about her identity both as a Black British woman and a teenage mother. We linked this confusion with Keisha's anxiety about new experiences, particularly food. Shanice seemed genuinely surprised that her behaviour had such an impact on Keisha. She then began observing Keisha herself, and seemed to enjoy sharing with us what she had noticed.

REFLECTIONS

Goal setting and short-term work are controversial in psychoanalytic psychotherapy because if you are aiming to help an internal change take place, this cannot necessarily be quantified with goals and is unlikely to happen in the course of five sessions. However, in community work such as this, goal setting in the context of short-term work seemed to help Shanice think about our task and set a limit on it.

It also gave her some control and choice over our contact. Furthermore, in setting goals, we were asking her about her concerns about Keisha, as a mother; and she could then allow herself to voice them rather than having to defend herself against the concerns of everyone else and authority figures she did not feel understood her. Likewise, although it could have been helpful to involve Shanice's mother in sessions, we also wanted to respect her identity as a mother. The space and the neutrality that could be offered to Shanice in a psychotherapy setting allowed Shanice some space to think, which in a world of professionals who were 'doing' things to Keisha and Shanice, was important. Significantly, Shanice became increasingly able to integrate into the community by planning a return to college and placing Keisha in a nursery.

Conclusions

The parents who we have described in this chapter were all trying to develop their identity as new parents within multiple challenging contexts in relation to cultural, social, interpersonal and emotional issues. Aisha was mourning several traumatic losses in an alien culture. Eva lacked her family and also her substitute family, which had been her work, and Shanice was having to find an identity both as a Black teenager and as a mother in a racist world. Likewise as therapists in the community we were having to find our identity both as child psychotherapists, and within the new culture of the general practice. Becoming more integrated within the community setting we worked in, made it possible to find more flexible ways of engaging with the families in the community, while retaining a psychoanalytic framework and therefore, not becoming the same as the other community professionals, or as our colleagues in the multidisciplinary team. The families with whom we worked were largely displaced and unconnected with a community, and so it was important to think about flexible ways of working to reach out to them in ways that developed the beginnings of a sense of community for them.

Notes

1 We would like to thank Dilys Daws for letting us stand with her 'by the weighing scales' and introducing us to the work of child psychotherapy in a GP practice, and Louise Emanuel for her support and supervision and for so generously sharing her thoughts and experience.

2 Psychoanalytic theory describes projection as the way in which individuals states of mind are unconsciously either communicated to others or put onto the other, thus affecting them deeply and unconsciously. Aisha's projection onto Hani would affect their relationship and her sense of him.

3 'Child in Need' refers to a classification of risk in UK Social Services and indicates the need for some support services for this child and his or her family or carers.

References

Adamo, S. & Magagna, J. (1998). Oedipal anxieties, the birth of a second baby and the role of the observer. *Infant Observation: International Journal of Infant Observation and its Application,* 1(2), 5–25.

Andreou, C. (1999). Some intercultural issues in the therapeutic process. In: M. Lanyado & A. Horne (eds.), *The Handbook of Child and Adolescent Psychotherapy: Psychoanalytic Approaches.* (pp. 73–79). London, England: Routledge.

Baradon, T., Broughton, C., Gibbs, I., James, J., Joyce, A. & Woodhead, J. (2005). *The Practice of Psychoanalytic Parent-Infant Psychotherapy: Claiming the Baby.* London, England: Routledge.

Barrows, P. (1997). Parent-infant psychotherapy: A review article. *Journal of Child Psychotherapy,* 23(2), 255–64.

Daws, D. (1985). Two papers on work in a baby clinic: (i) Standing next to the weighing scales. *Journal of Child Psychotherapy,* 11(2), 77–85.

Emanuel, L. (2016). 'Border crossings': Reflections on undertaking brief psychoanalytic therapeutic work in community and primary care settings. In: T. Afuape & I-B. Krause (eds.), *Urban Child & Adolescent Mental Health Services. A Responsive Approach to Communities.* (pp. 66–80). London, England: Routledge.

Emanuel, L. & Bradley E. (2008). Introduction. In: L. Emanuel & E. Bradley (eds.), *What Can the Matter Be? Therapeutic Interventions with Parents, Infants and Young Children.* (pp. 1–14). London, England: Karnac.

Lieberman, A. (2004). Child-parent psychotherapy—a relationship based approach to the treatment of mental health disorders in infancy and early childhood. In: A. J. Sameroff, S. C. McDonough & K. L. Rosenblum (eds.), *Treating Parent Infant Relationship Problems. Strategies for Intervention.* (pp. 97–122). New York, NY: Guilford Press.

Lowe, F. (2008). Colonial object relations. Going underground black-white relationships. *British Journal of Psychotherapy,* 24(1), 20–33.

Miller, L. (2008). The relation of infant observation to clinical practice in an under-fives counselling service. In: L. Emanuel & E. Bradley (eds.), *What Can the Matter Be? Therapeutic Interventions with Parents, Infants and Young Children.* (pp. 38–53). London, England: Karnac.

Schmidt Neven, R. (2005). Under fives counselling—opportunities for growth, change and development for children and parents. *Journal of Child Psychotherapy,* 31(2), 189–208.

Stern, D. (2004). The motherhood constellation. Therapeutic approaches to early relational problems. In: A. J. Sameroff, S. C. McDonough & K. L. Rosenblum (eds.), *Treating Parent-Infant Relationship Problems. Strategies for Intervention.* (pp. 29–42). New York, NY: Guilford Press.

Williams, G. (2002). *Internal Landscapes and Foreign Bodies. Eating Disorders and Other Pathologies.* London, England: Karnac.

Part III

Prevention and accessibility in schools

Chapter 7

Child and adolescent mental health services in secondary schools

How systemic theory links to practice

Chris Glenn

Introduction

Whether or not it is recognised or openly acknowledged by mental health practitioners, and despite the emphasis on generic treatment in Child and Adolescent Mental Health Services (CAMHS), theory and practice inevitably inform each other. In this chapter, highlighting the influence of family systems theory on my therapeutic practice, I illustrate the challenges and complexities of working with secondary schools from a CAMHS perspective—an often unacknowledged specialist area. I am a systemic psychotherapist in a multidisciplinary CAMHS team that has a strong commitment to improved community access to our service. As part of this commitment I have worked in secondary schools for a number of years as well as maintained a clinic base where I often work with other team members.

London is characterised by even greater disparities in income, housing and economic status than the rest of the country (National Equality Panel, 2010). This is reflected in the pupil intake of its inner-city, non-fee-paying secondary schools, although not equally across the board. Many of those who can afford to, and some of those who can barely afford to, choose to send their children to private schools. It is by no means certain that children attending fee-paying schools achieve better outcomes (Higher Education Funding Council for England, 2014) and even within the non-fee-paying sector, disparities in intake may be further accentuated by the different types of schools which, whether openly or covertly, may be able to influence the make-up of their pupil intake. Additionally, the introduction of performance tables for each school has meant that carers of children may attempt to choose the 'better performing' schools and reject the 'failing' schools. This leads to some schools, often those with whom CAMHS practitioners regularly work, not being able to attract a 'comprehensive' intake but rather providing education for those pupils who may be thought or expected to be below average ability.

In this chapter I have included a number of case illustrations in which I have changed identifying information in order to ensure confidentiality. The pupils, carers and staff who inhabit these vignettes reflect the rich ethnic and cultural diversity of inner London secondary schools. However, to further protect confidentiality, unless it is directly pertinent to the points I am intending to illustrate, I have not provided these additional identifying features. I am myself a White European male who has for many years both lived and worked in inner-city London.

CAMHS practitioners in secondary schools and participants in multidisciplinary teams

There is a consistent evidence base supporting the view that young people wish to see a CAMHS that is accessible and includes outreach into schools (La Valle & Payne, 2012), that is flexible in terms of appointment times and offers the possibility of appointments away from school (Lavis & Hewson, 2011). A study commissioned by a teachers' trade union to ascertain teachers' views about the identification and management of pupils with mental health difficulties (National Association of Schoolmasters and Union of Women Teachers, 2006) concludes that their members would welcome CAMHS staff being based in schools to allow for easier access to services, enhanced communication, teacher awareness and greater joint working. This is particularly the case for pupils who are unlikely to access CAMHS through more traditional routes and/or before mental health problems escalate.

In the borough in which I work each secondary school receives an outreach CAMHS amounting to one clinician for one day a week during term time. Clinicians are also part of a clinic-based multidisciplinary team. Where necessary, this allows clinicians to move between managing CAMHS referrals as a solo professional based in the community and accessing the multidisciplinary expertise of team colleagues according to the clinical needs of the young person and his or her family. In what follows I give an example of this process.

A sixteen-year-old pupil who was achieving well in school, and did not present any concerns to staff, disclosed to her form tutor that she was self-harming, felt depressed and was developing symptoms of obsessive compulsive disorder (OCD). The school arranged to meet with the pupil's parents to inform them of this and gained consent for a CAMHS referral. I met with the girl in school and heard that following a series of family events her father had taken an overdose and her mother had begun drinking heavily. I arranged to meet with the student and her parents at the CAMHS clinic and asked a nurse on the team to join me. The nurse met with the sixteen-year-old to assess the extent of the mental health concerns while I met with the parents. Having been informed of their daughter's emerging mental health difficulties by the school, both parents, in the meeting with me, were quickly able to recognise the influence of their emotional distress upon their much-loved daughter. By addressing their own mental health needs and understanding that they had been neglecting their daughter's emotional well-being they were able to

*begin to re-establish a safe and secure home environment for their daughter.
I continued to meet with the girl fortnightly in school for six months, identifying what triggered the self-harming and OCD behaviours and jointly
developing strategies to manage these; at the same time I maintained regular contact with the parents. Both pupil and parents reported a significant
reduction in concerns during this time. The sixteen-year-old presented as
more confident and able again to focus on her studies, and we closed the
case agreeing that she, her parents or school staff could get back in touch if
concerns arose in the future.*

As I understand it my involvement with this family was successful because, as
the CAMHS school-based practitioner, I was able to respond swiftly to concerns that were raised with me. I was able to seek out and support the form tutor
immediately, to gather some assessment information before meeting with family
members, to provide a regular slot to see the pupil in school in order to reduce
the disruption to her education, and to gain regular qualitative and quantitative
information from a variety of sources, such as the pupil herself, her parents and
school staff. Information from these different sources enabled me to undertake
an on-going comprehensive assessment of the pupil's psychological wellbeing.
Additionally, I was able to use this case to affirm with the staff an appropriate response to pupils who present with mental health concerns, beginning with
school personnel themselves carrying out their duty to raise the worrying issues
with the responsible adults and also suggesting a referral to CAMHS. This helped
encourage positive management by the school of such situations in the future.

Theoretical ideas useful in school-based
mental health work

The systemic approach

In contrast to the psychoanalytic and behavioural therapeutic traditions, which
were developing by the beginning of the twentieth century, the systemic ideas
and interventions that inform this chapter first emerged as a coherent body of
ideas intended as a guide to practice in the 1950s (Hoffman, 1981). Early on in
its development, the systemic approach defined itself *against* these two other
great approaches—it may be argued this is a necessary stage for all emerging
movements—emphasising what made it different, rather than the commonalities.
As confidence in the value of the systemic approach grew, and as an evidence
base from research in systemic psychotherapy has developed (Carr, 2014), there
have been increasing moves to integrate into systemic ideas, key concepts from
these and other traditions.

Generally speaking systemic practitioners base their theory and practice on
three basic concepts, which distinguish them from mental health practitioners trained in other modalities. These are 'context', 'circularity' and 'curiosity'.

The systemic practitioner views the individual as existing within the multiple *contexts* of their relationships to family and other meaningful personal relationships, to wider systems such as schools and healthcare organisations, and to the structures and beliefs embedded within the wider society. While recognising the reality of inequality and oppression within society, and therefore the lived experience of each individual, systemic practitioners hope to emphasise *circular* patterns of communication and influence. Rather than viewing A (active) as causing B (passive), it is the recursive relationship between A and B (and indeed C, D, E and so on) which is of interest—even if these relationships may not be equal. Systemic practitioners place a great deal of emphasis on *curiosity* rather than, for example, interpretation. This means that questions about the beliefs that inform the behaviour patterns of all those within the network of relationships and about the beliefs and attitudes of others are routinely utilised, in order to open up for clients new ways of thinking about their problems. Each of these key concepts is centrally connected to the exploration of the relational aspects of individual resilience in the face of an often hostile, frightening and unfair world—the struggle to survive, to cope and to develop in the context of adversity. Two theories which have become increasingly integrated into the systemic approach and which have informed my practice with schools are joint systems approach and attachment theory.

The Joint Systems Approach

Joint systems approach, which was first developed in a book called *The Family and the School—a Joint Systems Approach to Problems with Children* (Dowling & Osborne, 2004) proposes that it is not helpful if home and school become polarised in a tug of war over the child—with one or other believing that they have a better understanding of the child's interests and needs. The authors suggest that the main protagonists who are trying unsuccessfully to solve the child's presenting problems are likely to take one of three positions:

1   The first position is that the child's carer believes that the school is managing their child incorrectly. Carers may express the view that the school is too strict or not strict enough or that their child is being unfairly picked on by staff. The carer may be viewed by the school as challenging the authority and role of the school staff and either siding with their child or excusing their child's behaviour.
2   The second position is that the school believes that the carer is managing the child incorrectly. Staff may believe that they are doing everything they can to work with the child but that they are not supported by the carers. They may express the view that it is not possible or desirable to work with the child's carers and that they have the child's best interests at heart more than the carers do. This may be experienced as the school undermining the parenting abilities of the child's carers.

3   The third position is that school staff and carers may unite in exasperation at their inability to achieve positive change for the child. It may be felt at this point that the child's issues are beyond the understanding of family or school and that it is necessary to enlist the expertise of a specialist. Of course, it may be helpful to utilise an educational psychologist if it is felt that the presenting problem may be explained by, for instance, identifying a learning difficulty, or to refer to a clinical psychologist or therapist if the child is believed to be suffering from past or ongoing trauma. However, the danger is that if the specialist referral is regarded as the only or major contribution to working with the child's issues, school and carers may then be viewed as powerless in the face of the child's challenges.

In contrast, a central tenet of a joint systems approach is that it is important for family and school to overcome their differences and work together, utilising their respective knowledges and resources in the best interests of the child. When successfully achieved, with the child now recognising the cooperation and benign authority of the significant adults in their life, this may lead to rapid positive change. From a CAMHS perspective, one important aspect of practice informed by joint systems approach is that practitioners give attention to the detail of how referrals are negotiated, trying to ensure that carers are invited to initially meet with school staff so that an open dialogue around the nature of the presenting problem can be encouraged from the outset and that the CAMHS role can be transparently explained. If it is not possible for the CAMHS practitioner to personally join such a meeting, it is good practice to contact the carer to introduce oneself and to discuss ongoing contact.

Attachment theory and school as a secure base

Attachment theory was developed by John Bowlby (1953) and others in the period following the Second World War. It proposes that an infant who grows up knowing that s/he is loved by her/his mother, is safe from outside threat, and is helped both to challenge boundaries and to recognise the limitations of acceptable behaviour, will grow up to explore her/his own potential in relation to the world around her/him—secure in the knowledge that appropriate risk taking and experimentation will lead to new and life enhancing experiences. Rutter (1986) and others such as Byng-Hall (1996), partly in response to critiques from feminist and non-Western perspectives, later developed the theory beyond the mother-infant dyad to include other members of the family and community. *A secure base* described the ways in which the young child, having experienced a stable, nurturing and emotionally warm first few years, is able to gradually explore the possibilities of the world around them. Crucially the child is able to form appropriate relationships with others and negotiate new opportunities. Bowlby is increasingly recognised as a key influence on the early development of family therapy whilst Byng-Hall, his successor as consultant psychiatrist at the Tavistock Clinic and a trained systemic family therapist, continued to develop these ideas within systemic theory and practice (Hills, 2013).

In the school context, there will always be a proportion of pupils who experience aspects of family life as distressing. School staff and CAMHS practitioners are all familiar with children and young people who have been brought up, for instance, within a context of violence, abuse and parental addiction and mental ill-health. To the list of negative childhood experiences may be added bitter and poorly managed family breakups, the illness or death of a loved one or exposure to unexpected catastrophic events. Such children may view school as a safe haven where they can begin to relax away from the anxiety and insecurity of their difficult home lives and take advantage of the positive experiences school has to offer, secure in the knowledge that there are other responsible adults who can support their emotional well-being. On one level, the additional pastoral commitment that teachers and school support staff give to such pupils may be viewed as taking the focus away from the core responsibility of the school to maximise the educational potential of their pupils. However, many schools now recognise that the greater the effort that is focused on helping children to mitigate the impact of adverse life experiences, by providing a secure base, the greater is the chance of the child maximising their potential. There is, though, a paradox at the heart of attachment theory. It seems logical that if all pupils are valued by a school—they are treated with kindness and respect, they are taught about the boundaries of acceptable and unacceptable behaviour, their work is praised and so on—they should settle more easily into the educational institution with all its expectations, rules and responsibilities. However, when working with pupils who have had very distressing lives, many school staff have had a different experience, in that being caring and committed to a pupil may lead to an abusive response or an escalation of poor behaviour. If they praise the pupil's efforts they may witness the pupil destroying a recently completed piece of work. Despite the apparent paradox, attachment theory is helpful in understanding such patterns. If a child experiences a warm, nurturing environment in school, this may contrast with a family life characterised by separation, loss and even more damaging experiences and, in turn, provide the child with a context in which he or she may be able to communicate difficult feelings and frustrations not acceptable at home. Working with such children may then, in turn, become an abusive experience for school staff.

Due to the structure of teacher training in the UK, teachers have very little, if any, training in the emotional aspects of a child's development. I have found it helpful to describe the basics of attachment theory to staff to help them understand a pupil's rejections of their best efforts. One technique I may suggest to teachers is that rather than lavishing praise upon a pupil—risking heightening the contrast between home and school experiences—it may be more helpful to be *curious* about different aspects of their work or how they managed a difficult situation differently. Using questions that enquire about how the pupil approached and planned a piece of work—*What made you think to do it this way? How did you choose to use this particular approach?*—may foster a dialogue which positions the pupil as an active participant in the creative process, rather than a passive recipient of positive comments (Cecchin, 1987). These systemic ideas may be offered up in a number of different school situations, in order to support, join and engage with school staff.

Joining and engaging with school staff

There are, of course, some similarities between families and schools. Just as with families each school is unique, having its own strengths and weaknesses informed by each individual member's contribution to the system. Just as with families, it is necessary to engage with the responsible adults in the best interests of the child. Finally both families and schools, influenced by the lived experience of participants, develop and change their structures and beliefs through time.

I was asked to work with a school that had experienced difficulties in working positively with some outside professionals. Some key staff felt their experience and expertise had not been acknowledged by previous specialist staff, who came into school to consult with them and work with pupils; whereas the outside professionals felt that inappropriate referrals were being made. I requested a ten-minute slot at a meeting with Heads of Year and a member of the school management team to introduce myself and explain how I saw the CAMHS role. I began by stating: "The first thing I would like to say is that in my experience staff in your position have provided pastoral support to many pupils with a wide range of difficulties over the years. Most of the time you get on with this work and do not need to involve CAMHS. I assume that when you think about asking me to be involved you are making a judgement based upon your experience that my involvement could be helpful". One Head of Year responded: "I'm glad you said that as we don't take the decision lightly to involve other professionals". I was then in a position to be able to demonstrate to key staff that I wished to work in partnership with them rather than become involved in a battle over who had a better idea about what was likely to be in the pupils' best interests.

Respecting the hierarchy

Family systems theorists stress the importance of 'respecting the hierarchy' within organisations (Selvini Palazzoli, 1984). Just as it is usually not productive for the practitioner to ally with a child against a parent (the partial exception being when there are child protection issues), it is generally not helpful to side with a pupil or family *against* a school. In professional contact with schools, the price for doing so is likely to be mutual distrust, poor communication and the eventual exclusion of the outside professional. In the terms of Gregory Bateson (the English anthropologist, social scientist, linguist and cyberneticist who influenced systems theory), rather than practitioners introducing 'the difference that makes a difference' (Bateson, 1979, p. 110) that is required to develop positive relationships with school staff based upon mutual respect of each distinctive professional role, aligning oneself with one side or other of a hierarchy heightens the possibility that partnership working may be destroyed.

> *A newly qualified team colleague and I met with school staff in a neigh-bouring borough to review our work with a year-seven pupil and her family. The pupil and her mother, who was supportive of the school, were also in attendance. The school had a system of positive and negative points—when pupils reached thirty negative points in an academic year they spent a day in 'isolation' in school—an internal exclusion; when they reached forty points they received a one-day external exclusion. Neither my colleague nor I had previously come across this system of sanctions, and it seemed to us rather arbitrary and rigid. In her individual work with my colleague, the pupil had voiced her criticisms of this system. It did not seem to fit the needs of the pupil we were working with, whose family background included exposure to domestic violence and a sibling with complex special needs who attended a special school. In the meeting, my colleague began to question the points system. I decided to intervene, stating that I imagined this system had worked well for the school and that it was important that we all worked together to try to ensure that the pupil could keep her negative points to a minimum and increase her positive points. We were then able to move on to think about how we—school, parent, CAMHS—could work together in the pupil's best interests.*

This example illustrates that a skill required of CAMHS practitioners working with schools is to be able to assess at which level of the school system it is use-ful to make an intervention. In this case there was no possibility of two CAMHS practitioners from a neighbouring borough being able to influence the policy and organisation of a large secondary school.

Respecting the hierarchy and demonstrating anti-discriminatory practice

Within the school system, teachers have the power to exclude pupils, while pupils cannot exclude teachers; teachers may at times be sarcastic to or shout at pupils, but unless this becomes an established abusive practice there is little risk of sanction; if pupils act in this way towards teachers there is a real likelihood of punishment. Within families, parents are able to withhold pocket money, take away laptops and mobile phones or ground their children; children do not have the same power over their parents or carers. Whether the greater power of teachers and parents over children is utilised with benign or malign intent it nevertheless remains the case that the relationships are unequal. In order to address these ine-qualities and power imbalances, mental health and social care professionals are increasingly expected to demonstrate in their practice that they are aware of the realities of inequalities and discrimination within society (Thompson, 2003, 2012).

This area of work is also emphasised within a systemic approach (Gorell Barnes, 2004; McGoldrick & Hardy, 2008). On the surface it may seem as though it is impossible to practice in such a way that respects both the hierarchy and also openly acknowledges inequality and discrimination. The following example, informed by the systemic ideas of both/and acknowledgement of different beliefs rather than taking either/or mutually exclusive positions (Papp, 1983), suggests a way of respecting the hierarchy while at the same time practising in an anti-discriminatory way that benefits the pupil.

I was asked to meet with a year-eight pupil of African-Caribbean origin, who had already received a number of fixed-term exclusions and was now close to being placed in a pupil-referral unit, and his single-parent mother. The mother felt that the school was unfairly picking on her child and announced her intention to try to overturn the latest five-day exclusion. I asked the pupil to leave the room so that I could talk with his mother alone. I began by saying that I was very aware of the concerns within the African-Caribbean community about the high levels of exclusion of Black boys and that this was in my view a justified concern. I empathised with the mother's position as the only consistent protector of her son in the face of an unfair and discriminatory society. I then described an example of her son's very challenging classroom behaviour. When told off by the teacher, the boy had replied that the teacher would be hearing from his mother. It was clear that the mother and her son had taken a position against the school. I stated that in my experience when a parent decides to engage in battle with a school, the school usually wins and that it is the young person who suffers by getting caught in the crossfire (I consciously used this metaphor as I was confident that it would connect with the mother's wish to protect her son from becoming a victim of gang culture). When, shortly after, the mother and her son attended his reintegration meeting, the boy began to disrespectfully challenge his Head of Year fully expecting that he would be supported by his mother. The mother forcefully intervened to admonish her son and instruct him to show respect to the school staff. From this point in time the pupil's behaviour improved immeasurably. He received no further exclusions and staff commented that the angry look that he often wore had been replaced by a cheerful face.

Respectfully challenging the hierarchy

It is not at all unusual for CAMHS professionals entering into the secondary school system to be presented with the challenge of working with pupils with whom nobody else has managed to achieve positive change. The professional may be pessimistic about the prospects of them being able to make a difference, and yet a refusal to accept such referrals may lead to anger and frustration from school staff towards the CAMHS practitioner at an early stage of the developing professional relationship. The following example illustrates how tactically it may be more possible to influence the school system's relationship to the CAMHS practitioner by initially accepting problematic referrals rather than refusing to accept work from hard-pressed school staff.

> *Early on in my work with one secondary school I accepted a referral of a pupil who was at imminent risk of being transferred to a Pupil Referral Unit (PRU). I let staff know that I would "give it my best shot" but that I was not sure I had any greater chance of success than the school staff, who had made real efforts to maintain the pupil in school. After three weeks, during which time I had met the pupil twice and his carer once (a level of engagement the school was impressed with) he was indeed placed in the PRU. As I had begun my therapeutic engagement and while the pupil remained on the school roll possibly returning if the PRU managed to work successfully with him, I arranged to meet with him at the PRU six times over as many weeks. This meant having to leave the school for two hours on each occasion. The pupil did not return to the school, and my involvement ended. I was then able to open up a dialogue with key staff around the best use of my limited resources and the identification of pupils who might benefit from earlier CAMHS involvement.*

Many carers of secondary school pupils have shared with me how they feel humiliated and criticised in their parenting when receiving yet another phone call from school concerning their child's poor behaviour. Sometimes they might be called several times a week by different members of staff. They may then decide to withdraw approval and affection and impose draconian sanctions on their child in an attempt to demonstrate that they are responsible parents. A pattern develops whereby the school (more powerful) is perceived as criticising the parent (less powerful). The parent (more powerful) responds by punishing the child (less powerful). At times such an approach may help the pupil to understand that the authority figures in his or her life are working together and behaviour in school may change for the better. However, on other occasions it may lead the child to experience a deprived environment in both settings. It is often unbearable for a child to feel criticised and humiliated in both school and home environments and this may lead to a depressed state or outbursts of delinquent behaviour. The CAMHS practitioner based in school is in an optimum position to intervene both at the level of the school and the family to alter this pattern of interactions. I have found that school staff are often receptive to the suggestion of a weekly phone call home from one member of staff that summarises both positive and negative events. This may then facilitate a creative dialogue between, for instance a form tutor, who comes increasingly to be seen as a trusted ally by the embattled carer. Additionally, having empathised with the carer in their plight, the CAMHS practitioner is then well placed to suggest that instead of, for instance, withholding pocket money or stripping their child's bedroom of television, games console and computer for several weeks a more helpful response may be to apply rewards and sanctions on a day-to-day basis in response to feedback from school.

Alternatively, it can be suggested to a parent that the school can be left to apply a specific sanction in response to the difficulties they are experiencing in school. It can be a huge relief to both carer and child if the carer is given permission by the CAMHS practitioner to not punish their child in response to school misdemeanours. The parent can be seen to be supporting the school by calmly telling their child that they are disappointed with their behaviour and hoping that tomorrow is a better day at school and showing a sign of affection towards their child.

Challenges to the role of the child and adolescent mental health practitioner

My experience of working with schools is that often in the first few weeks a challenging situation arises that can serve to define the nature of the future CAMHS role. One school I worked with was known in the borough for its tremendous commitment to its pupils, who often came from disadvantaged ethnically diverse backgrounds. At the same time there was a concern that in fighting for their pupils to receive what the school felt was the best intervention, parents were not always involved in working in equal partnership.

Early on in my involvement with the school, a member of the school management team asked me to attend a meeting he had arranged with a parent whose child was in the second term of year seven. The member of staff introduced me to the parent and then went on to outline his concerns about the pupil and how he thought I could help. The parent angrily responded that they had not been informed that I would be present at the meeting and that she felt that she should have been informed. Furthermore she did not feel that there were any concerns with her child that warranted such a meeting. I wondered how I could manage this tricky situation without damaging my emerging working relationship with the school at the same time acknowledging the parent's right to be informed of who the school would like to be present at such meetings. I responded to the parent that she did have a right to be informed that the school wished to ask me to be present at the meeting. Furthermore I imagined that if I was in her position I might feel annoyed and worried about the presence of a CAMHS practitioner. I then quickly went on to say that in my experience school staff usually only ask me to become involved if they are genuinely concerned about how a young person is managing in school and that I had heard that there had been previous CAMHS involvement at primary school. I hoped that the parent would agree to me being part of the discussion about her child's well-being today and that she could then decide if my further involvement might be useful. The parent agreed to my remaining in the meeting. After hearing about the school's concerns, the parent acknowledged that there had been some very worrying concerns about her child's emotional well-being at primary school. However, the transition to secondary school had gone far more smoothly than she had expected. Her child was much happier than at primary school. On this basis I suggested that there was not currently a role for me but that I was available should she or the school have any concerns in the future. After the meeting I then spent some time with the member of school staff and affirmed both my support for the school in calling the meeting to share their concerns and the need for parental consent for CAMHS involvement if a positive working relationship was to be developed with pupils and families.

Spreading the news

CAMHS practitioners are bound by a commitment to their clients of maintaining confidentiality. Conversely, school staff are accustomed to sharing information within the school system about pupils and their circumstances. This may lead to difficulties in the CAMHS-school working relationship if staff take the position that they have a day-to-day duty of care for their pupils and that withholding information from them about a pupil's well-being is unhelpful. It seems to me that some of the concern about the reluctance of CAMHS practitioners to share information is justified. For instance CAMHS staff may not routinely let the school know who they are meeting with. At the end of each school visit I compose an email, which I send to key staff. This may consist only of a one liner stating who I have met with and when we have agreed to meet again. I may add a little more information. It seems important to me to share information with key staff when this may be useful to the pupil. I have also found that I am increasingly negotiating with pupils about what it could be useful to share. The following gives some examples of how I may approach information sharing with a young person him or herself.

> *I saw a young carer who after our fourth meeting told me that he was much happier as his parent was also much happier. We agreed to meet again a few weeks into the new term to review and decide if we needed to continue to meet. With his permission, I passed this information on to his Head of Year.*

> *I met with a pupil who was on his last warning prior to permanent exclusion. Two adults in his family home had been diagnosed with serious medical conditions. He was one of four siblings in the school and had the worst behaviour record of them all. He told me that unlike his brothers he had made a conscious decision to take on a significant caring role in the family. The contrast between being the 'worst behaved' of the siblings in school but the most caring at home seemed important. I wondered if it would be helpful for his subject teachers, with whom he was having regular confrontations, to know about his home circumstances. He immediately agreed to this as he felt it might help staff to see him in a different light. When I saw him two weeks later I asked him if the email I had sent had made any difference. He told me that his Head of Year had taken him into his office and told him how proud he*

was of him. Additionally, a class teacher had sent him out of her lesson and had a sympathetic word with him outside of the classroom to let him know that she was aware of his home situation. This had helped him to calm down and return to the lesson.

Another year-ten pupil on the verge of exclusion met with me for the first time. He told me in our first meeting that he had spent his time at the school blaming teachers whenever he got into trouble but now he realised he was at fault. Most of the people that he hung around with had been excluded, and he had decided now to distance himself from them. He was spending more time at home and had given up smoking skunk. We agreed to share this information with his subject teachers. I received a number of emails back from his teachers noting the positive efforts that he had made to focus in class, which I then shared at our next meeting. However, between our first and second meetings the pupil had been involved in a serious altercation with another boy which again pushed the tolerance of the head teacher to the limit. However, in light of the pupil's noted efforts in lessons in recent weeks this was viewed as an unfortunate blip rather than a continuation of the old pattern of negative behaviour and he was not permanently excluded.

I met throughout an academic year with a pupil whom it had been predicted would not manage the transition from primary to secondary school. When he had settled into his second year at the secondary school, we arranged to write a letter to his primary school head teacher updating her on how he was managing.

Conclusion

In this chapter I have sought to highlight the complexities of working with pupils, their carers and schools within the context of a results-driven education system that is also expected to maximise the potential of all young people. On the level of personal beliefs, I am informed by a political outlook that asserts the objective reality of an unequal and discriminatory society as it is experienced by those with whom I work. Within this I also hold the view that neither I nor those with whom I work are powerless victims of overwhelming social forces. To paraphrase Karl Marx—people make their own histories but not in circumstances of their own choosing (Marx, 1978). This connects with the value I attach to the therapeutic stance of systemic family therapy. Within systemic theory there is recognition both of the realities of social disadvantage and of the sense of agency that each individual or organisation possesses even in the most unequal of situations. As a White, English-born, well-educated and articulate male I find this stance particularly helpful in allowing me to try to locate a position for myself that both articulates the nature of inequalities and tries not to speak on behalf of others, in this case children and young persons, in a way that may silence or disempower them. I have aimed to draw out at what level of the system, which includes secondary schools, families and mental health services, it may be most opportune to intervene. Systemic theory suggests that a richer understanding of each person or collection of persons is gained by viewing them within the context of their meaningful relationships to each other and that these are influenced by the structures and discourses of the society we live in.

At what level might a systemic practitioner meaningfully intervene? Fortunately it is possible to move between levels of the system. Therefore the systemic practitioner is able, for example, to work with individual pupils while also keeping communication open with their carers and developing dialogue with school staff, showing appreciation for the efforts each are making in difficult circumstances. On a more personal note I consider that there is an implicit challenge in systemic theory, to practitioners, to contribute in their professional practice, their workplace and the society in which they themselves live, towards a more just world with equal access and opportunities for all.

References

Bateson, G. (1979). *Mind and Nature—a Necessary Unity*. New York, NY: Hampton Press.

Bowlby, J. (1953). *Childcare and the Growth of Love*. London, England: Penguin.

Byng-Hall, J. (1996). *Rewriting Family Scripts: Improvisation and Systems Change*. New York, NY: Guilford.

Carr, A. (2014). The evidence base for family therapy and systemic interventions for child-focused problems. *Journal of Family Therapy,* 36(2), 107–57.

Cecchin, G. (1987). Hypothesising, circularity and neutrality revisited: An invitation to curiosity. *Family Process,* 26(4), 405–13.

Dowling, E. & Osborne, E. (2004). *The Family and the School: A Joint Systems Approach to Problems with Children*. London, England: Karnac.

Gorell Barnes, G. (2004). *Family Therapy in Changing Times*. Basingstoke, England: Palgrave.

Higher Education Funding Council for England (2014). *Differences in Degree Outcomes: Key Findings*. London, England: Higher Education Funding Council for England.

Hills, J. (2013). *An Introduction to Systemic and Family Therapy*. Basingstoke, England: Palgrave.

Hoffman, L. (1981). *Foundations of Family Therapy: A Conceptual Framework for Systems Change*. New York, NY: Basic Books.

La Valle, I. & Payne, L. (2012). *Listening to Children's Views on Health Provision*. London, England: National Children's Bureau.

Lavis, P. & Hewson, L. (2011). *'How Many Times Do We Have to Tell You?' A Briefing from the National Advisory Council about What Young People Think about Mental Health and Mental Health Services*. London, England: National Advisory Council for Children's Mental Health and Psychological Wellbeing.

Marx, K. (1978). *The Eighteenth Brumaire of Louis Bonaparte*. Peking, China: Foreign Languages Press (first published 1852).

McGoldrick, M. & Hardy, K. (eds.) (2008). *Re-Visioning Family Therapy*. New York, NY: Guilford.

National Association of Schoolmasters and Union of Women Teachers (2006). *Identification and Management of Pupils with Mental Health Difficulties: A Study of UK Teachers' Experience and Views*. Birmingham, England: NASUWT.

National Equality Panel (2010). *An Anatomy of Inequality in the UK*. London, England: Government Equalities Office.

Papp, P. (1983). *The Process of Change*. New York, NY: Guilford.

Rutter, J. (1986). *Maternal Deprivation Reassessed*. London, England: Penguin.

Selvini Palazzoli, M. (1984). Behind the scenes of the organization: Some guidelines for the expert in human relations. *Journal of Family Therapy*, 6(3), 299–307.

Thompson, N. (2003). *Promoting Equality: Challenging Discrimination and Oppression*. Basingstoke, England: Palgrave.

Thompson, N. (2012). *Anti-Discriminatory Practice*. Basingstoke, England: Palgrave.

Chapter 8

Young men in the eye of the storm

Group intervention with young men in schools

Zoe Dale

Introduction

Using the example of therapeutic group work run within a secondary school, I will explore some of the cross-cultural, social and emotional challenges faced in a disadvantaged inner-city by teenage boys and their families from South Asian communities. I aim to explore both the benefits and challenges of school-based group work with young people and their families who may not have been able to access mainstream child and adolescent mental health interventions. In addition to potential exclusion from services, these boys described feeling marginalised by wider British society and distanced from the cultural and ethnic values of their parents.

The group was specifically set up for boys at risk of school and social exclusion; these young men increasingly challenged the authority of both the school and their parents. Their emotional outlook and struggles reflected wider social and cultural concerns for their families and community. In particular, inspired by the anthropological concepts of transitions and rites of passage, I will explore the profound impact of discrimination and social marginalisation on the development of their identity. The narratives emerging from the group focussed on the boys' experience of conflict, within themselves, with their peers, families and cultural identity.

The group, and concurrent family review meetings, were facilitated by a White Italian male and a White British female therapist (ZD) from social work and occupational therapy backgrounds, respectively. The group consisted of six boys from years eight and nine (that is twelve- and thirteen-year-olds) over two academic years. Drawing on reflective art activities our approach was both psychodynamic and socio-centric (Krause, 1998) in outlook, in order to effectively address the boys' complex emotional needs and relational difficulties within the context of their lives. This will be further explained later in the chapter. Creative art activities provided a fundamental structure to the group. We provided good-quality paper, coloured pens and pencils, acrylic pastels and each member had their own art folder. A careful balance was maintained between shared materials and those for personal use only. This was important in the early days of the group when sharing was a continual challenge. Even the simplest art task facilitated discussion about the boys' day-to-day experience; for example, creating a label for their art folders led to a detailed narrative about the lack of personal space in their chronically overcrowded family homes. These reflective art activities, with an open-ended focus such as, "what might your dream super-powers be?", opened up discussions about masculine identity and fear, which may not otherwise have been tolerated.

Our aim for the group was to support the boys in developing alternatives to acting out their frustrations and seeking out sources of self-esteem through, for example, joining a gang. In our inner-city, gang membership and the quick grati-fication of 'easy money' from gang connections at times represent a tantalising alternative to social isolation, poverty and struggles to attain academically. The group facilitated the unfolding of an important drama, which included dominant and alternative narratives, featuring both hope and tragedy for the boys, their families and the local community.

Context proved crucial to understanding the internal and external experience the boys described in the group. To explore the socio-centric perspectives in this chapter, I will describe some of the themes emerging from work with school staff and parents before going on to describe in more detail themes emerging from the adolescent group work.

My context

I am an occupational therapist and my current clinical role in a Child and Adolescent Mental Health Service (CAMHS) is based in an inner-city secondary school in a socially deprived area. In my clinical approach I draw on psychodynamic and socio-centric perspectives (Krause, 1998). Communities from deprived areas of the UK, as well as communities from minority ethnic backgrounds, are often subject to the greatest exclusion from mental health services (Fernando, 2002). The importance of working within educational set-tings is highlighted in the latest implementation strategy for mental health: 'No Health Without Mental Health' (HM Government, 2011), which also highlights the public-sector duty to improve access to mental health services for ethnic minority communities. Though the primary task of schools is to educate young people, increasingly educationalists are expected to play a key role in identifying the mental health and safeguarding needs of children and young people. Govern-ment policy, at the time of writing this chapter, defined child mental health as being 'everybody's business' for those who work with children, young people and their families. This additional responsibility can present many challenges for schools and their staff. Despite these challenges, in my experience, being school based allows for the greatest potential to reach the most excluded fami-lies. Many families from ethnic minority communities are more likely to engage with a known CAMHS professional based in a school than a separate Child and Adolescent Mental Health Team.

The school context

A therapeutic group was set up for young men of South Asian origin at risk of school and social exclusion. All the boys were Muslim. They lived on the estates surrounding the school. The group aimed to be a preventative intervention for these young men teetering on the edge of antisocial behaviour and reportedly at risk of exclusion and gang involvement. In fact, the older boys in the group would repeatedly describe the local gang activity they had witnessed, such as drug deals and fights with rival gang members. The school itself reflected the wider community, with sixty per cent of pupils being of Bangladeshi origin, twenty per cent Somali, Afghani and other South Asian backgrounds and twenty per cent White and Black British pupils. The school seemed to be a microcosm reflecting the ways in which culture and faith can both build bridges and create tensions. For example, the fights within school often represented wider community and gang tensions in the area.

The family context

Local families were often reluctant to engage with the local CAMHS, even though they were geographically close. Parents seemed at times to be fearful of CAMHS and Children's Services, and these fears often reflected their knowledge of mental health care and social work within their country of origin, as well as resulting from experiencing such services in the UK as irrelevant, culturally incompatible or pathologising. Parents often described the emotional distress and mental health needs of their children as being the family's responsibility to manage. Our services were at times viewed as not being culturally sensitive to how 'mental health' is understood and described within different ethnic minority communities. As a trusting relationship began to develop with these parents, through family review meetings, several parents described experiences of discrimination by local services towards them, and their wider family.

Setting up the group

Early negotiations with senior school staff concerning additional funding from the 'Targeted Mental Health in School' (TaMHS) project (Department for Children, Schools and Families, 2008) enabled the development of preventative clinical approaches, alongside the existing CAMHS provision for young people experiencing acute distress. Previously, staff had been deeply concerned that young people with complex mental health needs would lose out to those perceived as less in need; as a result the group was set up to address major concerns for the school, specifically the growing rate of school and social exclusion of young men of South Asian origin. As schools become increasingly monitored for their exclusion rates, it is important that CAMHS consider their role in both addressing and taking a preventative approach to the emotional needs that contribute significantly to school exclusion. Thus, French and Klein (2012) note in their work on school-based therapy services, 'It is the school that moulds the context for the work' (French & Klein, 2012, p. 55). From the outset the primary task of the group was to engage these disaffected boys as well as school staff, in a more hopeful narrative, with respect to the potential of these young men rather than just the concerns that surrounded them.

The presence of child mental health professionals within any school conveys a powerful message that staff want at some level to think about the distress that young people may experience (French & Klein, 2012). However, a school community may have ambivalent feelings about entering into the mental health arena, and staff and pupils may have personal feelings of their own to address. Effectively addressing emotional distress and emerging mental health needs takes time and requires a culture that, supports collaboration, can tolerate psychological intervention and has clear communication (Wilson, 2004). Learning takes place within the context of relationships, and in our case the group provided a 'secure base'—a containing place where emotional and attachment needs could be addressed—for reflection on current patterns of behaviour, and for exploring new and less conflicting ways of relating. As such, 'Learning involves putting ideas together, holding things in mind, challenging what has gone before and coming up with new ways of thinking' (French & Klein, 2012, p. 54).

The group was given clear validation by a senior teacher who championed the idea with his colleagues, ensuring we had dedicated and protected room space. This was important as meeting room space in the school was limited throughout the life of the group. The group ran on a weekly basis within the school day. Reciprocal to this process was our respect as therapists for the school's behaviour and learning policy. Though we chose not to rank the boys' behaviour when they were on report, the boys were aware that we had regular liaison with senior school staff responsible for their pastoral care. As the life of the group progressed, the boys often debated in detail what should, or should not be shared outside the group. An area of greatest contention was whether or not the glimpses of challenging behaviour that took place in the playground just prior to the group should be shared with school staff. Our respect and maintenance of the school rules, both in the group and while moving to and from it, provided fundamental emotional containment. For example, as group therapists we respected the school ethos, but were able to notice and explore important differences between staff and the young people's approach to authority and parental expectations.

Our intervention was three-fold: An assessment process with the families, the school and CAMHS in initial meetings; the adolescents' group (set up as a result of these meetings); and termly family review meetings. Our intervention model combined psychodynamic group work and family-focussed approaches that considered the nature, quality and function of relationships, both at home and at school and within a wider social context. In addition, we drew on the support of home-school link workers and interpreters to support parental engagement. The regular family review meetings provided sensitive cross-cultural support and continuity within the school system, by providing the parents of the adolescent boys in the group, a space to also talk about their experiences.

The emotional and relational challenges of adolescence

It was striking that the older boys had significant issues with authority and relating to others, challenging staff in school and their parents and attempting to dominate peer relationships. The two younger boys were more quietly challenging of authority and often appeared on the periphery of friendship groups. Staff feared that these boys would become disaffected as a way of managing their social isolation while, in turn, the boys shared their experiences of perceived prejudice and unfairness in school, often experiencing staff authority as being a direct challenge to their identity and social status.

From a psychoanalytic perspective adolescence (as experienced in the West) has been likened to the early stages of pregnancy, a 'deeply primitive state' where the young person can neither be controlled by others nor entirely be 'in control' themselves (Waddell, 2002). This psychoanalytic perspective on adolescence acknowledges that, as part of an acceleration of intellectual growth, great changes in brain development take place, which renders egocentricity characteristic of adolescent behaviour. This intellectual growth prioritises abstract thinking, which becomes the dominant modus operandi, while a comparable reduction in the capacity to be self-reflective and develop moral awareness takes place. The wall of noise, the physical energy and the barging into personal space, experienced when walking down a secondary-school corridor seems to convey the tension for many young people trying to contain the maelstrom within, while struggling with the external world, which might include experiences of discrimination and social marginalisation.

As the course of adolescence progresses, peers and social networks increasingly provide a set of alternative values to parental ones, providing the opportunity to both explore who they are and challenge the status quo. Waddell (2002) writes about how the process of rejecting parental values may in turn, be the first step in exploring and then accepting the family ethos. Although these processes may be thought of as universal in all cultures, we may expect specific variations and divergence in different cultural settings, as different cultures view the notion of 'self' differently (Heelas & Lock, 1982). In some cases, this process is further complicated by fathers having had a very different experience of adolescence from that of their sons in the UK. In turn their sons often feared what would be expected of them by their fathers. Several fathers, in the parallel family review meetings, movingly described how when they were their son's age they were expected to hold the responsibilities of a man. These expectations placed the need to work before their own wishes to complete their education. These expectations were very different from those of their sons in a UK inner-city comprehensive school.

All of these issues are intensified by our society's current preoccupation with the risks and dangers that young people face. For many young men in inner-cities there are limited opportunities for exploring physical risk in more ordinary ways, hence the increasing immersion in online games and the attraction of gang culture as alternatives to the feelings of denigration linked to discrimination and social marginalisation. While many of the young people in the group described their upset and anger about adults assuming they were gang members, frequently crossing the street away from them or being stopped by the police, they also acknowledged that hanging out on the street was a risk in itself. In her anthropological study of the experiences of young Turkish men in Berlin, Ewing (2008) notes how such risk is further exacerbated by marginalisation and poor job prospects leading young men to 'seek other sources of self-esteem', such as might be provided by peer-led groups—or those we term 'gangs' (Ewing, 2008, p. 56).

Strengthening the school community—building links between parents and teachers

In the struggle to address these serious issues, staff risked drawing on cultural stereotypes and assumptions that exacerbated miscommunication between parents and school; for example, some staff members held the idea that parents were increasingly unwilling to challenge the behaviour of their sons. In contrast, many parents, in the parallel family review meetings, shared the school's fears for the profound disrespect the young men were showing to both the family and wider community alongside the feeling that whatever they did to challenge the lure of the gang was not enough.

The tripartite structure of our intervention involving the family, the school and CAMHS was critical in enabling new perspectives on the challenges the boys faced. In particular all the meetings centralised the voices of the young men themselves and provided a framework for sharing the difficulties they faced. Combining group work and family approaches in our interventions enabled the issues raised to be explored from differing perspectives, making links between the challenges in school, experiences at home and social disadvantages within the local community. The success of this approach centred on the group being run concurrently with regular family review meetings that addressed issues of concern as they arose and supported engagement in narratives linked to change and hope, rather than frustration and despair. A striking, and for us valuable, outcome of the tripartite assessment process was how the concerns of the school and the parents became aligned, with both highlighting the need for greater respect towards adults. In addition, the school staff and parents were better able to understand the experiences and views of the young group members.

The impact of migration on the families—transition and trauma

A significant context, named by all of the parents we worked with, was the process of migration to the UK and the stress this had placed on their families. It is important to note that the profile of migration to the UK from South Asian countries has shifted from women to men with a profound impact on wider family dynamics. At the beginning of the 1960s and 1970s South Asian men were recruited to work in the UK. Many aimed to return but were eventually joined by their wives and children. This set up a relationship between the UK and certain areas in Bangladesh, the Punjab and Pakistan, in which remittances were transferred overseas for support, the building of houses and the buying of land. The relationship between the two areas was cemented through marriages between the UK minority communities and those back home, and family reunions in either direction have kept these relationships alive. However, more recently immigration laws have restricted the eligibility of persons able to enter the UK; it is now only possible for spouses. This has meant that recent immigration has been dominated by men who come to Britain as the spouses of British Asian women, whose parents are keen to keep the relationship with their place of origin (Gardner, 2008).

This context constitutes the background to the phenomenon of 'stolen honour' (Ewing, 2008), which seemed a useful concept to understand some of the issues facing the adolescent boys and the families we worked with. Stolen honour refers to the loss of the sense of honour and status described by some young men from ethnic minorities. The parents of the young men in the group settled in the UK during the 1980s and 1990s. Within the group there was a mix of either both parents migrating, women marrying men already based in the UK, and mothers who grew up in the UK having had arranged marriages with men from 'back home'. Mothers who married men from 'back home' described their husbands as less at home with the English language, institutions and dominant culture, than themselves. In the context of the difficult economic situation leading to high unemployment, many South Asian men struggle to maintain full employment, as conveyed in the narratives of the fathers in the family review meetings, who described a sense of angry desperation, stigmatisation and worthlessness, which manifested itself in oscillations between giving up completely and angrily trying to control their sons.

Parents described how in their tradition their "honour" was expected to be a vital part of their personhood, but they felt that the possibility of exercising this had been removed by the expectations of the dominant culture, with disastrous implications for their sons. Similarly, Ewing (2008) describes, when parents 'clamp down' on their children's activities to protect them from wider cultural influences, the result may be rebellion against those values, rather than an acceptance of them (Ewing, 2008). This was most acute for those boys whose fathers experienced long-term unemployment and desperately wanted a different experience for their sons. These boys expressed feeling torn between the wish to fulfil their fathers' dreams, while being acutely aware of the challenges of their present social context. Such intense frustration and issues of 'disrespect' between young men and their fathers were frequently at the centre of tensions within the families. These were also the young men most likely to seek out the 'gang' as a refuge from the difficulties arising from school, family and social expectations. Often they would openly challenge the family expectation that they should achieve greater things than their father, and in particular, help ensure economic security for the family. Their parents, for their part expressed fear that the group in school would contribute to their sons losing contact with their culture and faith entirely.

Our role as therapists

The boys were very curious about our experiences of migration and status as staff within the school. Despite the cultural differences between us as White European therapists and them as young Asian British men, we felt that this male-female combination mirrored the heterosexual parental make-up of the families we worked with. For the fathers, the presence of a male therapist supported their engagement, and they were curious about the therapist's own experience of migration to the UK. For the boys, the male therapist served a powerful function of providing a different male narrative to that of unemployment or the gang. As the female therapist, I held the group within the wider school context and in time was seen as the maternal provider and negotiator on behalf of the boys. In the room we approached the group dynamics in a multi-faceted way, considering the social experience of the boys outside of the group with respect to gender, ethnicity and class, relationships between the boys within the group, the impact of parental hopes and life experiences, alongside the assumptions and expectations of school staff. The young men were highly attuned to all these dynamics, but inevitably the themes that emerged within the group were mainly about their peer relationships, both in the external world and in their internal emotional lives. From the outset it was clear that how the boys related to both their parents and teachers had a profound impact on their capacity to relate interpersonally and socially and their interpersonal and social experiences likewise influenced how they related to their parents and school staff.

In the termly family review meetings throughout the life of the group the discussion would return to the progress the boys were making in relation to the concerns that precipitated the referral to the group. In time the regular and pre-planned nature of these meetings formed an important and positive connection between the group, school and home, which was not triggered by a crisis. This modelled a socio-centric perspective (Krause, 1998), in which connections between first and second generations within the boys' families would be paramount and supported parents to support their sons through adolescence, without resorting to rejection or overt control. In some cases additional support was offered in the form of a regular reflective space for the young men with their parents, to explore social, cultural and emotional issues of concern. Maintaining the confidentiality of the group, while continually exploring what might need to be shared with staff regarding risk or safeguarding issues, supported the development of a 'secure base' within the school environment. Throughout the two years it ran, the group, as well as the regular family review meetings, enabled the school to remain a significant attachment figure for the young men and their families, though this was at times significantly challenged by the complex needs of the most vulnerable boys in the group.

The group journey

Conflict, containment and rites of passage

When we were discussing which therapeutic approach to use we were immediately drawn to the potential of therapeutic group work for two reasons: first, these boys seemed to need a framework to support their understanding of themselves and their emotional responses, and second, they needed to experience ways of being with and understanding others. A key part of this process was supporting the boys in creating the rules for their group themselves, and this set the scene for an ongoing ritual at the start of each session, in which the boys insisted on revisiting and challenging these rules. This ritual provided an important reflective function for the young men who struggled to reflect on the impact of their behaviour on themselves and others and who in life often had been reduced to fight-or-flight responses, seeking to avoid both responsibility and retribution for their actions. Initially all of the members displayed ambivalence towards the group, fearing being labelled a failure by the school and as 'mad' by us. This perception was quite accurate as from the school's perspective these were pupils who were frequently in 'trouble', skilled in provoking staff and in becoming disaffected with learning. However, as the group progressed, the boys began to explore what they could do, rather than the focus being on what they had trouble with. The importance of culture and migration also remained live issues throughout the intervention, with fantasies about visiting 'home' being a source of hope for parents in the review meetings, and the boys in the group.

All of the boys experienced intense performance anxiety when beginning any art activity. At the start of each group session they were given a general theme to explore, with free use of a range of art materials. They were then encouraged to share something about their work. Early on in the group, they often destroyed their drawings before anyone could see it, as though afraid of how it would be judged. In these moments, their needs felt more akin to the needs of anxious pre-schoolers, rather than teenagers. Some of the boys had an emerging awareness of the risk of exploitation and grooming for crime, while for the more vulnerable boys the older gang members represented a seductive alternative paternal figure, one that could make them a man, rather than keeping them a child.

Adolescence, in the West, is seen as a time where young people form their own identities, involving separation and autonomy from their family and a rise in the importance of the peer group (Erikson, 1995). In Western culture it can be difficult for young men to find safe outlets for the rebellious and risk-taking impulses that define adolescence. It seems that, as a consequence of this, as well as the other emotional, cultural and economic issues previously mentioned, an array of alternative initiations involving taking physical risks have developed, including the use of drugs and alcohol, and self-harm. It seems as though it is increasingly hard for young people to be able to find initiations, which are both acceptable and outside the world of adults enough to perform these functions.

Adolescence forms a precarious bridge between childhood and adulthood and raises many complex questions as to the nature of childhood and the meaning of social maturity, particularly across historical, political and cultural contexts (Montgomery, 2009). In his work with young people Nicolson (2010) describes rites of passage and ritual as powerful tools for social integration and reminds us of the need to allow risk-taking in moderation as part of an adaptive process, allowing exploration of autonomy, boundaries and emotional independence. However, the more troubled one's early childhood experience, the more the initiation behaviour is at risk of being distorted, extreme and difficult to tolerate by others. We hoped that the group could act a bit like a safe rite of passage (van Gennep, 2004) providing a setting for the boys in which social status and the social and psychological aspects of transition to manhood could be experienced and thought about, rather than acted out as within a gang. It was our assumption, based on our cultural background and training, that growing up requires separation, in this case to enable the boys to establish their own emerging masculine identities (Chodorow, 1978). This assumption was mirrored by what was said by the boys in the group and family review meetings. For the boys in the group, this process was complex, as they straddled the different cultural expectations of their UK peers, alongside those of their South Asian parents, in the context of disadvantage and prejudice. Montgomery (2009) suggests that this places them at further risk of the most intense rebellion, as they experience the potentially conflictual messages of different cultural narratives.

Forming relationships—fragile beginnings

At the beginning of the group the boys appeared at sea in the maelstrom of secondary school life. Their narratives frequently described both fearing and being tantalised by the power of the elder boys in the school. They shared tentative descriptions of fights in school, their connection to gang violence outside, and their struggle to have a sense of the world as safe. If one group member appeared to have more than another, for example more attention or more art materials, the fragile peace of the group would collapse and the boys would resort to attempting to cancel each other out, by talking over them, denigrating their art or when most vexed, walking out of the group. We found ourselves searching for a 'safe' topic which would enable the group to momentarily step away from conflict and an alarm-led response (Howe, 2005). This topic emerged in the form of the boys shared passion for online gaming. Animated discussions would ensue about what violent acts and level of play had been achieved in online gaming. When we suggested that these games were not appropriate for young people, we were met with open derision. The boys shared a repeated narrative about this exciting online world where they could exert power and control, safe from 'reality'. Fragile social connections gradually emerged through the discussions about gaming technique, which had the additional effect of excluding us as adults from group interactions.

As tentative trust gradually emerged the boys shared in more detail their frustrations with school, fears of being scape-goats, and especially boys being blamed for things that girls did. This could lead to challenges towards staff and the boys feared the escalating consequences. This was also the period when the boys began to get in touch with raw feelings and could easily become acutely angry or upset. The acute difficulties the boys experienced in school were now fully enacted in the group. Our capacity as therapists to tolerate anxiety and uncertainty was being pushed to the limit. Central to containing these dynamics within the group were our discussions with school staff and when appropriate, with parents, to address concerns. The boys were keen that we would share their side of the story. In this initial search for commonality the boys began to explore and become more aware of their own feelings, such as the roots of their anger and insecurity. They shared experiences of poverty, social exclusion and (literal) hunger, bringing attention to what Copley (1993) terms 'double deprivation', experienced within the external and internal worlds of the boys. This process marked a turning point for the group, and the focus increasingly became the boys' day-to-day experience of life, expressed through group discussion, acting out in the group and via their art. For example, whatever art theme we chose, it somehow became an opportunity to pretend to smoke, roll pretend joints, make fantastical weapons, and talk about gangs and drug use. At this time members of the group acquired a powerful valency for flight or fight (Bion, 1962) with the boys both excited and terrified by what they were on the edge of.

As the group developed, the conscious and unconscious preoccupation of the boys with their fathers became more overtly expressed and the relationships in the group became more familial and intimate. For instance, the boys expressed concern for a particular boy in the group, for whom a gang had become an alternative family. For this group member, the only option was to care for himself. As he would tell us repeatedly in the group, he could only be 'casual', as though feeling would get in the way of 'surviving'. This serious situation triggered careful discussions about the nature of safety and when adults might need to intervene to protect young people. For this young man a safeguarding referral was made in discussion with his family. The sense of maleness in the group at this time was hard and linked to violence, violent language and aggressive enactments in art and group discussion and members of the group felt very connected to the culture of the gang, which mirrored the increasing gang violence taking place locally and nationally. Other boys expressed open despair at the experiences of their fathers, the poor pay, lack of job security and status in their work; worse still, their families being dependant on benefits, with the family 'back home' still needing financial support. The boys feared this becoming their experience and described an intense desire to be different from their fathers.

Struggling towards integration

The group process became shocked into working towards a sense of reintegration by the arrest of a peer. It seemed as though, what they feared in themselves, their aggressive impulses getting out of control, had happened too close to home.

Rather than the excitement of pretending to make and smoke a paper 'joint', the group began to discuss how they might avoid this fate for themselves. Finding the common ground between them took on increasing importance. Discussions began to focus on the meaning of 'home' and what this was. For all the boys, 'home' was represented by their parents' country of origin, rather than the UK where they were born. 'Home' was symbolised by a house being built in their parents' mythical homeland; a place, bigger and better than their current cramped social housing. The boys were caught up in the 'myth of return' of their parents; that is, for their fathers to be able to return home with honour and regain the status of the traditional man (Ewing, 2008). *Where is home?* remained a powerful and complex question for the boys. The shared desire to explore 'home' supported the boys in exploring other aspects of common ground such as, their hopes for friendships and an acceptance of the need to achieve in General Certificate of Secondary Education (GCSE), which for some required support with learning.

Ewing (2008) proposes the process of hybridisation, the fusion of two distinct cultures into a new dynamic form, rather than young people choosing between cultures (Ewing, 2008). For example, elements of youth culture may bring together attachment to homeland, religion and ethnicity with hip hop style music. Nicolson (2010) notes that once young people begin to feel more secure in their separate identity they are able to re-join society as individuals in their own right. As the group neared its close, after two academic years, the boys began to develop a sense of self which enabled them to acknowledge the different responses to their struggles and celebrate aspects of both their British and South Asian identities.

Conclusions

The group represented a rite of passage for us all; an important journey into understanding the nature of male adolescence for the boys who attended this group in an inner-city school. The impact of the group was striking, with all boys becoming more aware and vocal about their thoughts and feelings. Initially this greater emotional awareness was more demanding on school staff, with the boys asserting their feelings and needs in a more constructive, but still challenging way. At times the boys were impatient for the changes in their behaviour to be acknowledged, and a key aspect of the group was containing the frustration of having a 'reputation' in school. They furiously debated the challenge of a reputation being quick to gain and hard to lose. They also seemed to have a growing awareness that for their abilities to thrive, the changes that they had made needed to be seen and acknowledged by significant members of school staff. As the link strengthened between home and school, staff became more aware of the boys' home and social circumstances and made active links between behaviour in school and struggles at home and found that their discussions with the boys integrated these experiences, rather than locating difficulties within the boys themselves.

Four of the boys in the group fared better than two of their peers. They were able to reflect on their feelings and make links between their behaviour and the reactions of both peers and staff in school, deriving a greater sense of achievement from learning, and from friendship groups separate from gang alliances as well as positive relationships with core staff. The commitment of their parents to attending review meetings and acknowledging the achievements of their sons was also important in conveying a sense of hope for their sons' futures. In contrast, the two vulnerable boys in the group seemed to struggle to find meaning in the process of maturation. When these two boys became at high risk of school exclusion, the group structure supported school staff in continuing to offer pastoral support during this time of crisis. This ongoing support from staff was key in supporting the boys to maintain a belief that some adults could be trusted, rather than retreating back into antisocial behaviour. It was striking to note that though these two boys did become isolated and disaffected for a significant period, they were able to actively engage with local services and continue their education.

On reflection we believe that the most important outcomes of the group were to strengthen parent-child relationships, demystify the lure of the gang and explore alternative narratives about manhood. The group reminded us that the family remains fundamental to this process, for it is our belief that without basic emotional security these young men remained vulnerable to seeking out unhelpful alternatives. For example, many of the fathers became more acknowledging of their sons' achievements and held, what the boys described as, more realistic expectations of them. The boys were more respectful of their parents' cultural values and began to voice pride in being Muslim. It seemed as though both the fathers and sons had regained a sense of honour in their masculinity and their community. Though at the beginning the boys had ambivalent feelings about the group, by the end of the process, the boys and their parents described the importance of the group. Both parents and the school agreed that the boys were more engaged and less drawn into conflict. Staff narratives became less based on stereotypes and prejudice and more focused on the positive potential of the boys. The boys were so aware of this difference in approach, that some requested remaining on positive report, to ensure their achievements were noticed. This was a striking contrast to the avoidant and conflicting relationships with authority at the start of the group. The boys seemed to have gone from avoiding and challenging school staff, to wanting to be acknowledged by them, not as problems to be managed, but as resourceful young people with the potential to achieve. As therapists we experienced our own powerful journey, steering the group through waves of concern and towards hope that these boys will be able to find a constructive future in an inner-city world.

References

Bion, W. (1962). *Experiences in Groups.* London, England: Routledge.

Chodorow, N. (1978). *The Reproduction of Mothering. Psychoanalysis and the Sociology of Gender.* Berkeley, CA: University of California Press.

Copley, B. (1993). *The World of Adolescence: Literature, Society and Psychoanalytic Psychotherapy.* London, England: Karnac.

Department for Children, Schools and Families (2008). *Targeted Mental Health in Schools (TaMHS) Project: Using the Evidence to Inform Your Approach: A Practical Guide for Headteachers and Commissioners.* Available online at http://www.chimat.org.uk/camhs/tamhs/policy.

Erikson, E. H. (1995). *Childhood and Society.* London, England: Vintage (first published in 1950).

Ewing, K. P. (2008). *Stolen Honour—Stigmatising Muslim Men in Berlin.* Stanford, CA: Stanford University Press.

Fernando, S. (2002). *Mental Health in a Multi-ethnic Society.* Hove, England: Brunner-Routledge.

French, L. & Klein, R. (2012). *Therapeutic Practice in Schools. Working with the Child Within: A Clinical Workbook for Counsellors, Psychotherapists and Arts Therapists.* Hove, England: Routledge.

Gardner, K. (2008). Keeping connected: Security, place and social capital in a 'Londoni' village in Sylhet. *Journal of the Royal Anthropological Institute, 14*(3), 477–95.

Heelas, P. & Lock, A. (1982). *Indigenous Concepts of the Self.* London, England: Academic Press.

HM Government (2011). *No Health Without Mental Health: A Cross-government Mental Health Outcomes Strategy for People Of All Ages.* Available online at https://www.gov.uk/government/uploads/system/uploads/attachment_data/file/213761/dh_124058.pdf.

Howe, D. (2005). *Child Abuse and Neglect: Attachment, Development and Intervention.* London, England: Palgrave.

Krause, I-B. (1998). *Therapy Across Culture.* London, England: Sage.

Montgomery, H. (2009). *An Introduction to Childhood Anthropological Perspectives in Children's Lives.* Oxford, England: Wiley-Blackwell.

Nicholson, C., Irwin, M., & Dwivedi, K. (eds.) (2010). Children and adolescents in trauma: Creative therapeutic approaches. London, England: Jessica Kingsley.

van Gennep, A. (2004). *The Rites of Passage.* Anthropology and Ethnography series. London, England: Routledge (first published 1960).

Waddell, M. (2002). *Inside Lives: Psychoanalysis and the Growth of the Personality.* London, England: The Tavistock Clinic Series.

Wilson, P. (2004). *Young Minds in our Schools.* London, England: Young Minds.

Chapter 9

Does community CAMHS miss a trick? A F.A.S.T approach to preventative work in the community

Esther Usiskin-Cohen

Introduction

In this chapter I aim to challenge the prevailing reactive and treatment-based approach usually adopted by Child and Adolescent Mental Health Service (CAMHS) teams. I do this in order to begin to wonder how CAMHS clinicians could be more proactive in strengthening the mental health and emotional well-being of children, young people and their families. It seems to me that a 'lighter touch' earlier can save much heartache and cash. I want to outline an approach that frees up clinicians to move away from an expert 'treating' position, in order to embed themselves in 'not knowing', 'collaboration', 'transparency' and 'empowerment'. The approach I describe is called FAST (Families and Schools Together), which although manualised and developed in another cultural context, has offered me some interesting insights into ways of being more preventative and responsive to the communities we serve. I go on to describe FAST, and how families who may have been termed 'hard to help' in CAMHS engaged with the programme against my expectations. I will touch on some of the underpinning values of the programme, which CAMHS clinicians could learn from, and how these values mirror my own ethics. I will offer some (anonymised) clinical vignettes and some critiques of the programme. Finally, I will pose some questions about how some of what I learned might be used by other CAMHS clinicians.

The FAST programme

History, development and aims

FAST was founded by Professor Lynn McDonald (social worker and family therapist at Middlesex University) as a programme which could be implemented by parents working alongside professionals to increase child well-being, parent involvement in school and social capital. It is predicated on the belief that all parents and carers aspire to support their child to succeed in the school and community, and in the right context and if given the right support, can achieve this aim. The idea is that by attending a FAST programme for eight weeks, relationships are strengthened within families, between families, between families and the school and within the local community—a simple idea which fortifies resilience. It is a manualised programme based on systemic, behavioural and cognitive theories as well as community building principles. It has an impressive record for its ability to engage parents. At least eighty percent of parents that come to the programme once stay for six out of the eight evenings, 'graduate' and go on to run their own monthly meetings (McDonald et al, 2012). In particular, it has a good track record of being able to engage socially marginalised families, with only twenty per cent (the numbers have been much lower in the UK) dropping-out. This has confirmed my view that families might often find *us* clinicians and our services *hard to engage* and *hard to reach*.

How it works

My prejudices about manualised programmes were challenged by FAST. My previous experience was that families can find them somewhat patronising and I also considered (perhaps with some arrogance) that as an experienced clinician formulaic approaches limited my therapeutic creativity. When I participated as a team member in the first FAST team it was with some cynicism. Yet, it was an experience that seemed surprisingly helpful in facilitating sustaining relationships. There was something about the experiential nature of the programme and the inclusion of a variety of team members that did not stigmatise families that had been defined elsewhere as 'hard to engage'. So what does the FAST programme look like, and what ideas might be borrowed to embed into a community CAMHS setting?

The programme works in the following way: parents of children in a primary school class or year group are invited to attend FAST with their family. Attendance is completely voluntary and recruitment is via peer recommendations. The core value of the programme being offered universally to a year group means that families are less likely to feel targeted or stigmatised. Up to forty families may attend eight weekly sessions in which children and parents take part in structured activities together in groups of up to twelve. Families are grouped together into 'hubs' that have some shared activities together. The team is made up of local people, and must include at least one parent from the school (but not from the year group to whom the programme is being offered to, and usually a previous participant of FAST), a member of the school staff (for example, a teacher, special educational needs coordinator (SENCO), a catering assistant, or receptionist), a member of the local community (a priest, an imam, a lollipop person from the school gates, a local youth club worker, café owner/worker) and a professional person who has some mental health experience.

Each family is warmly welcomed by the team and invited to choose a table to sit at. They eat together, sing songs—guaranteed in my experience to invite a grimace from (British) team members when they learn they are going to have to enable group singing, but which quickly becomes a hugely pleasurable experience for all—and parents direct the table-based activities, essentially communication games, which help families practice talking about emotions and experiences, experience cohesion through a lot of laughter and feel listened to, safe and connected. During this *family time*, which lasts for one hour, parents are empowered through gentle coaching by the team in a way that children cannot hear. Although being part of multi-family groups can implicitly discourage family conflict, the team is also there to monitor overt and convert conflict and support families to dispel it.

Following *family time* and once basic needs have been met through food and settling in, the children separate for an hour of *peer play time*, and the parents have an hour of *adult time* (fifteen minutes for parents/carers from one family to meet, then forty-five minutes where parents across families form small groups, which seems valuable in generating mutual aid and support). Following this, one parent provides the focal child (the child in the family that is in the school year that has been targeted) with '*special time*', fifteen minutes of uninterrupted attention with non-judgmental, non-directed play, taking the child's lead. The parents are themselves gently supported by the trained team members who coach and encourage them through the process. Everyone gathers after this for the 'lottery', which is fixed so that the family who seems the most stressed (or the least likely to return) is given a prize. The family that wins agree to bring meal-time food for all the families the following week. There is usually a great celebration and everyone ends with a calming and restoring closing circle ritual (making a kind of rainstorm sound – which I have since used in various training events). There is a *special session* in week five in which parents can decide who they want to invite in to the programme to offer advice and/or information that can lead to their increased social capital. In a graduation ceremony in week eight, 'affirmations' (written appreciative reflections prepared by team members about each member of the parents' group) are read out in the parents' group. This safe but public noticing and highlighting of resilience promotes a sense of achievement and agency. The supportive witnessing by the group enforces this. Despite the repetition of activities every week, families report that they have fun and do not feel that they are being 'therapised'. After the eight-week programme, families are invited to attend for the following two years in FASTWORKS (World's Opportunity to Raise Kids Successfully), monthly meetings run by graduated FAST families. Delivering the programme was part of the clinical outreach service I provided as a systemic psychotherapist in an urban CAMHS.

Schools and community

Outreach work in schools is fascinating as we can view schools as being at the heart of the future of the community (Lang & McAdam, 1996). It is in schools that children grow in knowledge, morality and their abilities to relate to others. Their concepts of community and the ability to live life to their potential are fostered and cultivated in schools. It could be argued that it is in schools that the future gains formation and direction, and therefore school-based work represents a cradling of the future, given the enormous influence schools have in children's lives. The FAST programme itself seemed to draw on the sense of community that schools can potentially foster as a resource that benefitted both the school and the families that attended. For instance, research (McDonald & Fitzroy, 2010) indicates that, four years after the programme, parents are still in touch with friends they made through FAST. In addition, children and teachers report that children are happier at home and at school and more engaged in learning, parent-child bonds improve, family conflicts decrease, parents' involvement in school increases and crucially that social support networks develop between parents.

A case example

To provide an example of the positive impact of this programme on families, I present two vignettes below from a FAST programme that I trained a team to deliver in a local primary school, based on talking with parents and school staff who attended about their experience. In both cases, the families gave explicit permission for their stories to be shared but names and identifying details have been changed.

Amy and her four sons were a lone-parent, White/UK family. All four boys were considered to have learning difficulties and their educational progress was a concern for the school. The family had been on the child protection (CP) register, and Amy was very suspicious about "being watched" by professionals. Jack, the youngest son, was seen individually in school for fine motor skills work and the two middle boys, Davey and Richie, were considered by the school to have undiagnosed ADHD, given 'challenging behaviour in the classroom'. The eldest son, Jamie, at secondary school, had many periods of non-school attendance and at the time of the programme was not in school. The entire family felt misunderstood and negatively judged. They were invited by another parent to attend a coffee morning at school where I gave a presentation on FAST, and it was clarified that the youngest son was in the 'target year group' being invited into the programme. Amy felt able to consider attending to 'try it once' with no obligation. She attended the first week with her two youngest sons, her sister and niece. Amy challenged FAST team members and was perceived by them as both defensive and aggressive. She circulated ideas that FAST team members were 'spies for social services' and that their task was really to 'judge' parents. However, despite giving several reasons why she would not be able to attend again, she returned for the second week voluntarily having 'won' the weekly lottery prize, and provided the hub meal. By week three it seemed that the underlying values of FAST, particularly parent empowerment, enabled her to begin to consider that rather than being judged, she was being supported. FAST team members noticed a vastly improved engagement with her son during their 'special play', which had been a challenge for both previously. At week four, Amy brought her mother and eldest son to FAST. He was given a task to help in the programme.

Overall Amy attended seven out of the eight sessions (missing one week to support her middle son at a school event). She attended graduation with her mother, sister and eldest son and brought in food for the communal party. She became a stalwart supporter in the continuing monthly group run by FASTWORKS. In addition, school staff noticed that she was attending the parents' coffee mornings every week promoting FAST, was offering support on school movie nights and there was a significant improvement in both boys' engagement with learning and socialising with peers. In particular Jack was said to have made "remarkable progress in the classroom". Somehow the difficulties that had defined this family had lessened. Amy appeared prouder, appearing to walk taller, with a newfound sense of herself as capable and a connection with others. This connection with others was the most significant outcome for Vanda too.

Vanda, a lone parent, of Greek/Cypriot origin was an ex-drug user with previous social services involvement, and came to FAST with her three daughters. All three girls were reported as being behind academically by the school. Vanda had been offered a variety of support packages by the school but had been resistant to them all. School staff were amazed that she attended FAST. It seemed the horizontal recruitment process, parent to parent, enabled her to agree to attend. School staff thought that she might be challenging and cause some difficulties in the group. She seemed withdrawn (perhaps suspicious) at first, but by the third week, after having 'won' the weekly lottery prize and preparing the hub meal the following week, she noticeably grew in confidence and attended seven out of the eight sessions, missing only one when her youngest son was ill. She developed an ability to engage well with other parents in 'parent time' which led to supportive friendships; at the end of the programme she gave effusive, wonderful feedback about FAST and to this day remains involved in FASTWORKS.

So what can we learn from this programme about how CAMHS workers might work with schools and families together in order to build and foster a sense of community, leading to improved well-being for the whole family system?

The essence of community development work

My aims in writing this chapter are to highlight the ways traditional CAMHS may miss a trick and tease out the learning that CAMHS teams might gain from preventative community-oriented programmes, in order to use a focus on social connection, resources and abilities to foster well-being in families and communities. Before I do that it seems important to tell the reader something about who I am and why I am drawn to community development work.

The context to my focus on community

I am a White, middle-aged and middle-class, heterosexual, Jewish, married woman with three children. I grew up in a family where 'community' mattered. What does that really mean? I had largely immigrant grandparents and my parents were involved in voluntary youth work and established charities for both domestic violence (*Jewish Women's Aid*, for which my mother received an MBE) and AIDS (*Jewish AIDS Trust*, now known as JAT—*Jewish Action and Training for sexual health*), within the North London Jewish community in which I grew up. I saw myself as located in a community network, which although perhaps competitive with each other, also enjoyed each other's successes, and commiserated and supported each other through difficult times. Not surprisingly perhaps, I and my two sisters ended up in the 'caring professions'. As an idealistic, politically aware and perhaps somewhat naive graduate of social anthropology, sociology and comparative religion, in the early 1980s, I wanted to make a difference in people's lives, specifically those who seemed disadvantaged in some way, and marginalised in society. I began work first in residential social work with, those who were in those days termed 'emotionally disturbed adolescents', and then moved to an assistant probation officer post in East London. After completing a Masters in Social Work, as a home office—sponsored student (those were the days!) and working for many years in East London as a probation officer, I moved (with the demise of the therapeutic element of probation in the mid-1990s) into family court welfare work. I then transformed into a Children's Guardian, working in the High Courts in central London, in private law cases with separated parents in conflict over contact and also in public law representing the child's best interest in Local Authority Care applications. I began my training as a systemic therapist while in the probation service in 1996 and finished over ten years later. Taking it slowly, while working, helped me to practice my skills, embed theory and begin to authentically own the ethical stance I was developing. Throughout this time my belief grew stronger that, what was far more important than the relationship *I* could make with people in distress was the links that people made with each other, in their families, friendships and communities.

Reconnecting through FAST with some of the ideals that brought me into community work has made me curious about why, within the health service, there is an implicit and explicit orientation towards problematising-treatment as opposed to prevention, and the 'othering' of clients that can happen as a result of this. Working in the community and training teams to deliver FAST in schools was a way for me to practice what Shotter (2004) calls 'withness' (a dynamic form of reflective interaction that involves coming into contact with another's living being, as opposed to 'aboutness' thinking which turns the other person into an object, without a soul, or desires or capability) and promote voices to be heard that may have previously been stifled.

Ethical stance within therapy

My significant and lengthy experience in public service, and as a court 'expert', developed my therapeutic orientation and ethical stance towards spotting resilience, strengths, resources and skills when working with individuals, couples, families and communities in order to harness hope. I have found this a more productive outlook for change. Rather than having a focus on fixing or compensating for deficits, my experience has been that a focus on abilities, achievements and interests, and on the client as expert in their own life, makes therapeutic intervention more potent, useful and productive. In my experience, therapy with a lighter, more respectful touch seems to conversely bring about deeper, quicker and most importantly, more sustainable change. With respect to Jim Wilson's continuum, with 'passionate conviction' at one end and 'systemic humility' at the other (Wilson, 2007), I try to balance my 'humility' in clinical practice with my 'passion' for the systemic concern with context, relationships and circularity. I have found that taking a strength-based orientation to my work can create a tension between the expectations on me as a clinician, (to devise formulations and intervention plans informed by the medical model that enquire about deficits), and what feels most responsive and useful to families and communities (a focus on previous successes and hope). Although there are imaginative ways around this, rather than only testing our creativity within the limited treatment-focused paradigms mostly available within CAMHS, I wonder whether it is time for some of us working in the community to think about other ways we can help people in distress go on to live rewarding and joyful lives.

Despite my negative experience of manualised programmes previously, the FAST programme seemed to me to be able to address the political aspects of the lives of families in interventions that go beyond 'therapy', towards creating community; that is, being responsive to the needs of local families and communities, prioritising prevention and empowering parents by bringing them together. While I do not advocate FAST as a panacea, clearly some lessons can be learned from the principles embedded within it.

Beyond therapy—learning from FAST

At the time of writing of this chapter, there is much in the political discourse that refers to 'problem families' and 'hard to reach' communities, particularly in the urban context. Namely, there is the 'Troubled Families' agenda, being piloted in several inner London boroughs, by the Department for Communities and Local Government (DCLG) (2012). This programme describes these families as having 'serious problems', including parents on benefits and not working, serious mental health problems, children not in school, and young people engaging in crime and anti-social behaviour. Most strikingly, these 'troubled families' are described as facing multiple problems *and* being the cause of multiple problems for others. This type of rhetoric, based on the psychologisation of poverty and marginalisation, can easily problematise families and communities in urban contexts, leading to a 'treatment' approach to social problems.

Recent cuts in benefits and services have made it even more urgent for us to develop new ways of working that directly address social issues in social/relational, rather than purely individualistic/intrapsychic, ways. While community interventions cannot eradicate poverty and poor housing, given that social isolation compounds stress, having a network of relationships can give an individual a sense of worth and support well-being. None of these banal observations are new, but as more and more distress emerges in communities, perhaps now is the time to think about designing CAMH services that can think about prevention in the same way it thinks about treatment.

Reflecting back on the benefits I saw as a probation officer of running community groups for families of ex-offenders, I still regard groups in the community as a potent way of enabling links to forge that sustain any success seeded in a therapeutic relationship. It seemed to be those relationships that group members made with each other that protected them against, or supported them during, any relapse into drug and alcohol abuse and/or offending behaviour for example. Those relationships provided a non-stigmatising route out of depression, the daily stresses of parenting or managing poverty and the shame and isolation that can result from those difficulties. Rather than just a therapist or therapy team spotting resilience in clients, creating space for clients to notice and validate each other's strengths can create extended webs of connectedness and support in a family's community. Although I acknowledge that community can also be abusive at times, the transformation from 'someone of concern' to 'someone that has something to offer others' de-centres me as a therapist and is humbling for me to witness. As a community CAMHS clinician, I am often deeply moved by the sense of shame, blame and social isolation a family or parent describes, compounding whatever difficulty they may have. I often wonder how much more valuable a connection to others in their community would be—in order to share some of the load with, to have fun with and to feel connected to, others. There are times when this need not be a clinician. To illustrate this point I will offer an example based on a typical CAMHS case.

Lule from Albania had suffered from severe domestic violence. She lived without her ex-partner and with their two sons Agim (aged ten, referred to CAMHS by their GP) and Behar, (aged four). Agim had been excluded from school, had angry outbursts at school and home and his mother was very concerned that he was biting his nails to the extent that he made the tips of his fingers bleed such that holding a pen was difficult for him. Behar was very quiet and watchful in sessions but was reported to be a "tyrant" at home, often keeping Lule and Agim up all night with his demands. Nursery also raised concerns about Behar's 'selective mutism'. Lule was a hairdresser in Albania and wanted to work in the UK. Lule described herself as having 'no friends', as she was 'too shy' and lacked confidence after escaping a domestically violent relationship to converse with other mothers at the school gates. As part of our CAMHS intervention, I connected her to a local domestic violence (DV) organisation, offered treatment for post-traumatic stress disorder (PTSD), and explored positive aspects of the family's cultural heritage with the boys via a genogram (Hardy & Laszloffy, 1995) and the Tree of Life (Ncube, 2006). In many ways this was a rewarding piece of clinical work, as Lule described how important her relationship with me was; how it empowered her to make friends at the boys' nursery and school, which gave her the confidence to attend college herself. While I do not want to diminish what I offered and what she gained from my relationship with her, in the absence of her family who were in Albania, it was the delicate relationship building in her community that made the most difference to her.

For a practitioner, holding, having, and generating hope is crucial in guiding others through demoralisation, creating and giving life to new ideas. However, as Paulo Freire (1992) suggested, hope needs anchoring in practice. So how might CAMHS provide an anchoring experience of hope for the children, young people and families we work with? It seems to me it can do this by building sustainable and generative relationships (that is, 'community'), based on the proverb from Africa, that "It takes a village to raise a child".

Two further underpinning FAST values, which could be centralised in CAMHS more are:

1   Shared governance (highlighted by the phrase, "nothing about us without us")
2   Reciprocity (so nothing is given without an expectation that parents can and will 'give back'). For instance, in the FAST programme parents are asked to cook at least once for everyone in their hub, (the money is given to them the week before). It is staggering that while this could be a daunting task for anyone, I have seen even the most unlikely family rise to the occasion, and children taking pride in their parent's/carer's offerings to all. In addition, parents plan the 'graduation' party, inviting who they want to attend, and then take over the running of the family groups called FASTWORKS, that continue for two years.

Sam and Vid had five children, aged ten, eight, six, four and two, who all had previously been on CP plans. When I asked what had drawn them to this programme, despite their suspicion of services, Sam replied that it was because it had been offered to every family with a child in Years one, two and three in the school (so they did not feel targeted or further stigmatised), it looked like fun, it would mean that all family members would get a free hot meal on the night they attended, and there was the opportunity of winning a prize. The family completed the eight-week programme. They were noticeable (out of the other twenty-plus families) as there were so many children, who were very noisy and a challenge initially for the parents to manage around the family table in the programme. They were one of the first families to 'win' the prize—a basket of games, one each for the children, some drawing materials, a silk scarf and scented candle for Sam and some socks and a small do-it-yourself (DIY) kit for Vid (who had already shown his ability to fix a table broken by his four-year-old son) along with a huge wok and baking tray (to symbolise the obligation to return the following week and provide food for all the families in the hub). By week three, the team's coaching had enabled and empowered the parents to maintain a better level of control and all were engaging in the games and activities at the table.

When I returned to the school two years later, Sam was a member of the team delivering the programme to a new cohort. Her eldest had successfully transferred to secondary school and was doing OK. All services had withdrawn. I was moved by her heartfelt commitment to the team and families and impressed by her ability to capably manage potential rifts and difficulties in the group. Sam had transformed into an inspirational team leader, successfully running a team of four to deliver FAST to twelve families. She had become involved in the Parent-Teacher Association (PTA) at school and had started a small baking and jewellery-making business (partly as a result of the parents in the group that her family had participated in two years earlier inviting in experts in craft activities for the special session in week five).

Centralising the importance of 'community'

As a systemic therapist I connect with the ethical and political concept that everyone is located in multiple levels of contexts. I have shared this idea with school staff using a *Baboushka*—the nickname for the Russian dolls within dolls or 'nesting' dolls—to demonstrate that a child is located within its family/with carers, who are located in a wider community based on neighbourhood, environment, religious belief systems, educational institutions, employment, housing and so on, who are located within wider social and political contexts. This can have a powerful effect of neutralising the potential for blaming the individual child, parent or family system and it makes it easier to develop interventions that draw on a variety of 'others' within the community to support families. In the FAST programme school staff, parents, CAMHS professionals and local people from youth work, library, sport or religious settings, all work together, which makes these community settings more approachable and inviting for families. By drawing on community, resilience is strengthened through enabling friendships and sharing activities, and parents/carers are better able to focus on their children. Because the programme is not delivered in a stiff or formal manner, and there is no didactic teaching or preaching, just creative support, I have found there to be lots of banter and laughter between team members and families. In many cases children like the activities so much they persuade their parents to return.

The significance of community to well-being is also supported by research. For example, Hill's family research after the Great Depression in the US (Hill, 1949; Boss, 2002) suggested that with loss of economic security families were at risk of crisis (ill-health, separation, domestic violence, depression, alcoholism and so on), particularly if they were without social support and hope. Conversely, if there were networks of support within the family, across extended family and with other families in the community, there was more optimism, and less family crises, despite job losses and financial strain. This research seems particularly pertinent at the time of writing this chapter, given the context of 'austerity' leading to massive cuts in both jobs and community services. As clinicians we know that hope is invaluable in effective therapeutic work (Snyder et al, 1999), but by building protective factors *in a community*, realistic hope (Weingarten, 2010) can be harnessed and sustained.

How can this way of working be centralised in CAMHS more?

With respect to my own experience of bringing these principles to the core of my work in community CAMHS I have been struck by the idea of 'leaning in' as a 'decolonizing' practice, rather than 'reaching out'. 'Leaning in' refers to a movement towards the other, which allows us to develop solidarity with them, from a position of humility (Reynolds, 2013). In my experiences, groups and multi-family groups can harness, sustain and develop resilience and emotional well-being very effectively. Of course, none of this is rocket science to any CAMHS clinician, but I think that we sometimes lose sight of the power of feeling connected within multiple relationships.

I have found it useful to draw on Freire's idea (1992) that providing groups of adults with a safe environment in which to express their opinions about the challenges of daily living is a more empowering basis for adult education, than an 'expert' approach of lecturing facts to people from a knowing position. Freire's belief that a more profound learning process occurs for adults if they feel that they can express themselves within a group of others who listen and exchange ideas, has the potential to radically challenge and change how we provide CAMHS interventions. We might then aim to develop more spaces for parents to support each other, within an enabling community of supportive others, in order for parents to discover much of what they know already. In addition to the community focus, the FAST programme draws on some of the tenets of structural family therapy (Minuchin, 1974) with respect to using coaching to reinforce the parental role. Thus it seems possible to *both* support parents to connect to their personal, relational and community resources, *and* offer more direct coaching to support them with the skills they need to fulfil their role.

Current fit and some potential pitfalls

Schools and CAMH services alike pay lip service to the concept of parent empowerment, but even within the setting up of a programme like FAST, parents can still be side-lined. The aforementioned values can pose a challenge for service providers and school staff. The reality of service user participation and feedback can mean extra work and being challenged in many other ways, such as feeling that our own position may be compromised when we see parents showing competence and agency. This is also potentially true of CAMH services, despite the fact that many of the ideals of the FAST programme fit well with our principles of centralising service user participation and feedback. One way of trying to ensure that parents are integral to our interventions, is utilising the concept of constant micro 'permission-seeking' (Aggett et al, 2015). This principle of shared governance, a non-hierarchical approach to intervention with families which gives them shared ownership, might be a challenge, if we struggle with 'shedding power' (Hoffman, 1993). However, shared ownership invites parents to invest more in the process, as it is viewed by them as being 'their' process rather than someone else's. For example, my experience is that parents always provide more food for the celebratory graduation, than the team expects. This observation alone can at times encourage more power 'shedding' from team members than would be usual.

The virtue and curse of manualisation

The manualised approach seemed to me not only clearly helpful in generating the 'hard' outcome data that government and commissioners find credible and persuasive, but for me it also meant that in subsequent FAST teams I was part of, we were all clear (including parents) how to deliver the programme with similar success. In addition, forty per cent of the programme can be adapted to fit a particular community (for example, changing the order of the two and half hour programme, singing different songs and other ways of adjusting components to fit with a particular cultural resonance), and in week five a special guest is always invited in, to run an activity that has been requested by the parents, such as managing debt, preventing gang membership, getting to know the free local sports and library facilities and Zumba for de-stressing. Despite the flexibility in the programme, this forty per cent adaptation does not always happen. Some tweaks are made but generally the programme runs in the way the manual suggests. It may be that the manualised approach stifles team members' creativity and responsivity. At the same time, school staff often like the clear instructions. After three weeks of delivering the programme in one school the SENCO wrote to me saying:

> *Really I could feel that FAST was having an effect. I think I began to see the wonder of the FAST programme yesterday. To see Mrs. Mohammed providing all of that food, reluctant to take money, take such pride ... It was truly magic. (To see) ... the Smith family, so many of them all coming, wanting to be part of it, really being so community spirited, it was truly magic to see. I began to see hope when I saw the families last night, community, sharing, joy, pleasure, laughter, relaxing. ... People working together ... what a wonderful evening. ... It is brilliant. ... I also enjoyed the fact that there were very clear instructions, and all we had to do was to deliver the script.*

Despite the benefits I have outlined I have some reservations about the FAST programme and how it is being rolled out in the UK, with the help of Save the Children. This financial support might at times compromise some of the underpinning values of FAST, given that being subsidised by a charity that has to promote vulnerability and weakness in order to attract funds, seems opposed to the idea that communities can create and sustain wellness for themselves. In addition, I wonder about the conflicted messages communities are receiving from our government about the value of community support when so many local services, such as swimming pools and libraries are closing.

Conclusions about what CAMHS can learn

The FAST programme exists in a wider culture of 'evangelical manual programmes' that present themselves as the ultimate answer to social problems. There may be elements of these manualised programmes (often developed in the US) that are alien to the British setting (such as the singing, the applause, the affirmations), but there are also elements that may fit more easily with families from diverse cultural backgrounds (such as the food making and sharing). The reader is invited to reflect on how they might draw from the programme's essential elements in ways that re-direct CAMHS work towards the gains of 'prevention' rather than the limits of 'treatment'. I myself cannot help wondering whether this approach to community empowerment might also let the state off the hook by empowering families *within* the current state of affairs rather than challenging the state of affairs. I have over the years racked my brains about how we might take this to another level and be even more responsive. I have flirted with ideas such as community therapeutic gardening projects, community cafés, groups for women, and multi-family mindfulness groups to name but a few, in order to introduce clients to each other, as sources of support.

I consider that the training of local people to deliver the programme and the fact that the team delivering it has to physically look and sound like the community they engage with as wonderful ideas. If a community CAMHS team could harness some of these processes that empower parents to be the *primary strengthening factor* in their children's lives, we could begin to really work with the idea that it is ultimately a happy family and community that will prevent mental health problems. The motivation for providing this type of intervention should come out of an ethical and moral respect for all parents/carers and our social responsibility towards our community. I am intrigued to continue reflecting on how we might use the elements of a FAST approach to think about prevention more imaginatively in CAMHS, in order to contribute to the promotion, enhancement and sustainability of familial emotional health and well-being.

References

Aggett, P., Swainson, M. & Tapsell, D. (2015). 'Seeking permission': an interviewing stance for finding connection with hard to reach families. *Journal of Family Therapy,* 37(2), 190–207.

Boss, P. (2002). *Family Stress Management: A Contextual Approach* (2nd ed.). Thousand Oaks, CA: Sage.

Department for Communities and Local Government (DCLG) (2012). *The Troubled Families Programme: Financial Framework for the Payment-By-Results Scheme for Local Authorities.* London, England: DCLG.

Freire, P. (1992). *Pedagogy of Hope: Reliving Pedagogy of the Oppressed.* New York, NY: Continuum.

Hardy, K. & Laszloffy, T. (1995). The cultural genogram: Key to training culturally competent family therapists. *Journal of Marital and Family Therapy,* 21(3), 227–37.

Hill, R. (1949). *Families Under Stress: Adjustment to the Crises of War, Separation and Return.* New York, NY: Harper & Brothers.

Hoffman, L. (1993). *Exchanging Voices: A Collaborative Approach to Family Therapy.* London, England: Karnac.

Lang, P. & McAdam, E. (1996). *Appreciative Work in Schools: Generating Future Communities.* West Sussex, England: Kingsham Press.

McDonald, L. & Fitzroy, S. (2010). *Families and Schools Together (FAST): Aggregate FASTUK Evaluation Report of 15 Schools in 15 Local Education Authorities (LEAs) across the UK.* London, England: Middlesex University.

McDonald, L., Fitzroy, S., Fuchs, I., Fooken, I., & Klasen, H., (2012). Strategies for high retention rates of low-income families in FAST (Families and Schools Together): An evidence-based parenting programme in the USA, UK, Holland and Germany. *European Journal of Developmental Psychology,* 9(1), 75–88.

Minuchin, S. (1974). *Families and Family Therapy.* Cambridge, MA: Harvard University Press.

Ncube, N. (2006). The Tree of Life Project: Using narrative ideas in work with vulnerable children in Southern Africa. *The International Journal of Narrative Therapy and Community Work,* 2006(1), 3–16.

Reynolds, V. (2013). 'Leaning in' as imperfect allies in community work. *Conflict and Narrative Explorations in Theory and Practice,* 1(1), 53–75. Can be accessed: http://journals.gmu.edu/NandC/issue/1.

Shotter, J. (2004). *On the Edge of Social Constructionism: 'Withness'-Thinking Verses 'Aboutness'-Thinking.* London, England: KCC Foundation Publications.

Snyder, C. R., Michael, S. & Cheavens, J. (1999). Hope as a psychotherapeutic foundation of common factors, placebos and expectations. In: M. A. Hubble, B. L. Duncan & S. D. Miller (eds.), *The Heart and Soul of Change: What Works in Therapy.* (pp. 179–200). Washington, DC: American Psychological Society.

Weingarten, K. (2010). Reasonable hope: Construct, clinical applications and supports. *Family Process,* 49(1), 5–25.

Wilson, J. (2007). *The Performance of Practice: Enhancing the Repertoire of Therapy with Children and Families.* London, England: Karnac.

Part IV

Challenging our assumptions

Learning from communities

Chapter 10

A systemic approach to community in family

Working with family mental health

Doreen Robinson

In this chapter I will explore how I have used a systemic framework to work with families and individuals from diverse cultural communities, who need support from a Child and Adolescent Mental Health Service (CAMHS). Through the presentation of case examples I will demonstrate how I have needed to hold multiple contexts in mind with respect to the communities within which the families existed. In particular, I present systemic work I have undertaken with three families: a White English family, a dual-heritage family and a family of Asian origin. To ensure confidentiality, I have given the families pseudonyms and changed some identifying information. I begin by introducing the context of the CAMHS work I engage in, introducing myself and the most pressing issues which impact on families from different ethnic and minority cultural backgrounds in the local community. I will also present a very brief introduction to systemic theory and to ways of working systemically. I will conclude with some reflections on the fit between a systemic approach and the need to address the mental health needs of families holistically within CAMHS.

Introduction

What is it like to be living in a densely populated inner London area, living cheek by jowl with ultra-modern transport and commercial developments and academic and health research centres on your doorstep? The British film director Shane Meadows made a film in 2008 called *Somers Town*, about a Polish boy living in a small community with his father who worked as a labourer on the then new St Pancras rail link, the Eurostar (Meadows, 2008). The film addressed themes of dislocation, 'outsider-dom' and the tensions between 'belonging' and 'being on the edge'. Silently, and solidly present, in between national and international railway junctions, this film is a reflection of the migrant experience of arriving, settling but always ever ready to move on again; sometimes physically but maybe often psychologically. This migrant experience is one of transience; of living with feet poised to step away from, and back to, where you live. In the borough served by the Community CAMHS team in which I work, lives Asian, Arabic, Eastern European, African and South American peoples speaking a myriad of languages in the midst of traditional English, working-class established communities and the multiple contexts of an urban inner-city. When the idea of writing this chapter about my work in the Community CAMHS was first suggested, I was excited about describing what our service does and why it is considered particularly unusual, compared to traditional CAMH services.

Moving into the community

I will start by providing a historical context to our team. In 2007, I was one of a group of clinicians from the Child and Family Department of the Tavistock and Portman NHS Foundation Trust who along with the Primary Care Team in Camden and a CAMHS in Schools Service, worked to establish a Community CAMHS team. I had been a member of the Asian Service in the Tavistock centre, so being part of a community team was a welcome opportunity to be based in the heart of the locality where the families with whom I worked, lived and went about their daily lives. While the number forty-six bus was a good conduit from Tavistock into the community, it also took a long circuitous route, interesting but time-consuming. Satellite projects from Tavistock were not new but the development of a Community CAMHS was exciting to me because, with a background in community work, social work and family therapy, I felt sure that we could engage more successfully with 'harder to reach' community groups such as those from communities for whom English is not a first language as well as those White British communities who for multiple reasons did not trust public and mental health services. It also offered the possibility of working more closely with voluntary groups who had already been working successfully with diverse communities. Through previous outreach work while working in the Asian Service I had already developed links in the community with the Hopscotch Asian Women's Centre, Asian Women Lone Parents Association (AWLPA) and the Bangladeshi Mental Health and Well Being Forum. As a family therapist I had worked using these links, meeting with clients in their own homes as well as at community centres with the aim of encouraging attendance at CAMHS. However, it was often the case that families felt that the Tavistock centre environment and its location were too foreign and far removed from their experience to attend appointments with me there. Interestingly, some colleagues from community projects had also voiced a reluctance to connect with Tavistock and did not necessarily associate the spirit of our Asian Service with the Tavistock centre.

Me, myself and mine

One of the reasons that I felt so excited about offering a Community CAMH service was that it meant making services accessible and non-stigmatising. This aim resonates with my personal values and experience. I grew up in West London in a community of Indian-Caribbean people who had come to England as economic migrants, invited by the British government. As in the film mentioned above, members of my Caribbean community also felt a belonging to England as well as an outsider-dom. Our parents found recognition in each other and resilience to manage the difficulties of working, living and raising their families in the context of prejudice and hostility. My parents, their friends and neighbours offered mutual support in physical, economic and emotional ways, and we, the children, grew up with a spirit of generosity, respect and kindness towards others and a sense of forgiveness instilled in us by the spiritual beliefs of our parents and elders. We saw how, in the face of adversity, our community drew upon deeply held strengths and fortitude in order to overcome hardships and to create a rich world of opportunities for us. There was a very strong sense of problem solving, and I remember my father expressing surprise, when I decided to take up social work as a career, that not everyone had the support networks that we had. His view, influenced by his cultural background and experience, was that people had the internal resources to find their ways through difficulties. In his modesty, he did not see how helpful he was to the many who sought his advice, good counsel and practical help. I also grew up to be mindful that there were often powerful explanations of ephemeral worlds beyond the human world to be curious about. Caribbean beliefs in Obeah, Shango, witchcraft and black magic and Roman Catholic beliefs in the influence of the devil and generally destructive forces in the world gave me a variety of perspectives on suffering, healing and well-being. Above all, my parents' Indian-Caribbean heritage and identity held a respect, care and concern for fellow Caribbean people of ethnicities including African and mixed heritage. This, I believe, filtered down to me and lead me to find a career in community and social work and later in family therapy.

A significant event in my life which may have lead me toward family therapy was when a student friend of mine at university began to feel unwell and behaved in ways which were outside my experience and understanding. She was an English woman who had been quite shy and became unable to manage socially or academically. At the time, we were lodgers with a landlady to whom I expressed my increasing concern about my friend's distress. The landlady's response was to contact my friend's parents who came and took her back home while I was out at lectures. I later found out that my friend had been diagnosed with schizophrenia before starting university. She had treatment at home and later returned to pursue her studies. Looking back, I imagine that there was a strong need to protect her and myself from the seriousness of her developing psychological distress. However, I do feel that the overriding factor explaining the ways in which her difficulties were hidden was the stigma associated with being diagnosed with schizophrenia and the fear of what that meant, for her, her studies and her social life. I was left with many questions and with sorrow that such psychological distress had affected my friend and how her parents and family seemed to withdraw and close down communication. I became curious about what mental health was and how people, their families and friends experienced mental ill health.

Systemic family therapy and community

As a student, I worked at night shelters and hostels for the homeless and people with mental health problems and this led me to social work. I qualified as a social worker working in generic social work and community teams as well as with specialist and complex child protection social work teams. The complexity of this work increased my curiosity about systemic ways of thinking, and this took me to training, qualification and practice in systemic and family therapy. In this journey I have been fascinated by the relationship between belief and behaviour and how these are a constant influence on each other. One can say that this is the most basic assumption of systemic thinking and practice. This means that the way people see the world, their beliefs and ideas, in other words their culture, has an important influence on the way they interact with others and do things, as well as on how they understand what they do and think.

My understanding and experience of 'community' has found an echo in Nancy Boyd-Franklin's work (2006), and I drew upon her ideas when meeting families and conducting family therapy with them. Nancy Boyd-Franklin (Boyd-Franklin & Hafer Bry, 2001) describes the multiple levels of context within which Black families in the United States of America live: these families tend to have strong relationships with extended family; they all live within communities, which are part of a wider district or region, which comes under local governmental administration; these regions in turn form part of the whole state, which in turn makes up the country. Each family member has a relationship to each other and with each level of context they are in. That is to say, each person in a family cannot operate in isolation from their immediate and extended family or from their community, region and ultimately their country of residence (and possibly their country of birth if different from their residence).

Families and persons have ways of describing their difficulties in unique ways that may or may not match a family therapist's view. It is the clinician's task to try to understand and put together different ideas and experiences and consider these in relation to the contexts in which they have been produced; whether as a response to national policies for example, and/or as a result of individual and intimate circumstances.

Mental health problems or psychological distress

It is important to think about the terms used to describe psychological distress. The term 'mental health', which refers to a state of functioning and perhaps an absence of suffering, is most often used by mental health professionals, in government policy documents and in guidelines. However, when some of the clients with whom I work hear the term 'mental health' they often think not of 'health', but of deficit. Any phrase with the term 'mental health' in it conjures up ideas about being very unwell, crazy or mad and triggers, above all, a fear that the person the term refers to may never recover. It may also refer to a much wider range of complaints, such as for Asian families for whom psychological suffering may include somatic/physical complaints and debilitation caused by bad fortunes or witchcraft and possession (Littlewood & Lipsedge, 1987). Of course there are differences also in how professionals working in the field of mental health categorise and name psychological distress. My own clinical and therapeutic approach to working with psychological distress and mental health problems is influenced by a combination of several systemic concepts. One such systemic concept is the idea of 'reframing' (Watzlawick et al, 1974) the problems which clients bring, so that they may be a more positive and forward-looking link towards finding a more surmountable story around a problem. I also draw on the narrative ideas of Michael White and David Epston (White & Epston, 1990; Epston et al, 1992; Epston, 1993), which allow for a greater degree of flexibility of approach to fit the families' own concept of psychological distress. A narrative is like a thread that weaves events together, as well as the meanings we attribute to them. As there are many stories occurring simultaneously, multiple contexts inform the stories we live and tell about lives. Narrative therapy seeks out alternative stories that the persons seeking help would like to live in their lives in order to challenge the influence of the problems they are facing.

Family therapy in the community and community in family therapy

One of the reasons for moving out of the Tavistock centre into the community was to be able to engage so called 'hard to reach' clients, by making our services 'easier to reach'. A systemic approach to this is to connect with those experiencing difficulties and also to connect with those who are able to offer support, such as the immediate family, nuclear or extended, as well as close friends, neighbours and community resources.

The Q family

Our Community CAMHS receives referrals from general practitioners (GPs) and other health services as well as from community projects and schools. For example, I have connections with the Asian Women's Project (AWP), where I offer consultation to the project's director as well as a clinical service seeing women who are isolated from their local as well as the wider community. It was there that I met Mrs Q, who had for some years been affected by serious family problems.

She was a rather distressed woman; the death of her husband and the stigma of being a single parent in the context of her Asian community left her with a profound sense of loss. She had concerns about her own family who lived abroad and had health problems associated with ageing. Mrs Q also worried about raising her children in a respectful way according to her Muslim faith so that she would receive the approval and admiration of other members of her local community. She felt that her reputation had been tarnished because of the way in which her husband died; he had suddenly died at home, and she, along with her children, believed that the causes of this sudden misfortune were malevolent spirits, who inhabited their home and caused them a huge amount of distress. When I explained that as well as seeing people at AWP, I also worked in CAMHS, Mrs Q told me that her daughter had in the past met with a psychologist from my team. Over time I found out that the other children had also attended CAMHS. In agreement with the mother, I spoke with a CAMHS colleague and we offered family therapy sessions to the Q family in the community, to support them with the impact of bereavement on the whole system. It seemed important to have a holistic approach to the family's expressions of distress. During the course of the sessions it emerged that the father had developed a mental health problem before his death. The family narrative about this, in keeping with their cultural outlook, was to see his mental health problems as caused by bad spirits that were present in their home. Therapy helped the family to voice their grief and shock at his death and try to understand their complex beliefs about it. Mrs Q was able to explain that they wanted to find a way to forgive their deceased husband and father for the way in which he had died, as well as develop a narrative in order to account for the mental health issues in the family. Mrs Q's culturally acceptable narrative about malevolent spirits in their home helped her to account for her husband's mental health problems, his death and the reason that she struggled to cope with his death. At the same time, the belief in the malevolent spirits in their home caused the family further distress.

Mrs Q looked to the Asian Women's Project for support and guidance for herself. She would not have been able to access support for herself from adult mental health services as she herself did not have a mental health diagnosis, however her psychological distress was very real. Once she became confident in my role as a Community CAMHS clinician, with her permission, I was able to connect with the AWP's practitioner in their individual work together, to provide a space for the children to share their feelings. By joining up the work between CAMHS and AWP, we perhaps acted as a professional surrogate extended family. Over time, in our family sessions with Mrs Q and her children, we were able to 'co–construct' (White & Epston, 1990; Epston, 1993; Epston et al, 1992) narratives, which gave new meanings about the father's psychological distress and the family's responses to it, that both respected their beliefs and enabled them to live in the way they wanted with less distress. I think that the family was able to connect with me because of my ethnicity, my cultural resonance with them, my understanding about spirits and my professionalism, which protected their privacy from their immediate community. I think that I was able to connect with them because of my ethnicity and my experience at university with my friend when I was faced with the impact of confusion and grief.

The U family

In another family I worked with, whom I shall call the U family, the members were of mixed English and Caribbean origin and consisted of children ranging in ages from six to twelve. They came to our CAMHS via a CAMHS clinician in a general practice, with concerns about one of the children who in a similar way to his mother was tearful and in low mood much of the time. The boy found it difficult to make sense of the emotional turmoil, unpredictable moods, stress and tensions at home and it was unclear where these feelings belonged. The children were often blamed and described as "squabbling" and not wanting to take instructions from their parents or do simple tasks around the house. This left both parents and children feeling exasperated. The parents seemed to join together in a parental subsystem and the children in another subsystem (Minuchin, 1974). This was highly upsetting for the children who felt criticised and in a session said "we can never get it right". At the same time, the parents conveyed that they felt disrespected and "never listened to". This description seemed to highlight the circular nature of unwanted repetitive patterns that can occur within family systems, which can so easily disguise the care which children and parents have for each other. Describing what an unwanted repetitive pattern might look like, Keith, et al (2001) notes: 'Naughty children arouse demoralized parents. Arousal is a form of being alive; a short acting anti-depressant. Anger temporarily interferes with depression. Children may frustrate parents as a way to keep them angry, because they cannot be rageful and depressed at the same time. Thus a child's depression often arises out of his inability to solve a problem of parental depression' (Keith, et al, 2001, p. 51). At the same time, parents may feel they are demoralised as a result of 'naughty' behaviour, hence the circularity.

The U family had never tried or heard of family therapy, but they were able to take the risk of trying something new because they were all at a point of despair with respect to how to manage the increasing arguments. Mr U seemed to be aligned with his partner, in order to comfort her when she was distressed but seemed upset himself about the behaviour of the 'naughty child'. Mrs U had not been able to work due to her tearfulness and low mood, and as a consequence the family had limited money. The situation felt stuck, and it seemed almost impossible to talk about what the distress was about. As described above, I had a hypothesis myself that the behaviour of the identified child was partly a response to his mother's distress, which was not being spoken about, as much as her distress was linked to her children's behaviour. It might have been that for the child, his mother's depression became intolerable, and he showed this by becoming 'naughty'.

I invited colleagues male and female, from different ethnic and racial backgrounds to create a diverse reflecting team to work with me and this family (Andersen, 1987; 1991; 1992). This involved the therapy reflecting team sitting behind a one-way mirror listening to the conversation between the family and therapist before coming into the session to reflect on what was being said; something which many families say they find helpful. We had noticed how the children described themselves and embraced how different their appearances were in line with their dual cultural heritage. We had also noticed how the 'naughty child' was quite different in appearance to his other siblings. He said that he felt as though he was a White child, and my colleagues and his parents were interested to know more about this. Together we drew a cultural genogram (Hardy & Laszloffy, 1995).

This is a family tree which includes at least three generations, which is used in order to map the different ethnicities in the system and to discover where parents and grandparents had come from and how they see themselves both in relation to their own familial heritage and in relation to each other. Different coloured pens can be used to represent each cultural group so that children of mixed parentage can represent each parent's culture. Cultural genograms may also include other information significant to the family such as gender, class and religion.

As clinicians we joined the family in becoming excited about locating the family roots in English, African and Scottish heritage. I suggested a game that would cast light on the complexity of 'race' and which illustrated how the same gene pool can have very different manifestations, that is, family members who are related can look quite different or perhaps persons who are unrelated might have traits in common. I put different coloured plastic cubes (and suggested that these could be considered to be a person's gene pool) in a bag and invited each member of the family to pick out four or five cubes each without looking. The children quickly caught on to the game and noticed that each time they picked some cubes different combinations of colours emerged. We talked about how the genes collected down through the generations had resulted in the children appearing physically different, while all originating from the same parents and grandparents. This exercise helped the child who felt White to appreciate how he was connected to his parents, all his grandparents and his siblings. This game led on to further explorations to include the likes and dislikes of the different persons in the family as well as the talents, skills and interests of the parents when they were younger, in order to highlight more connections between them. For example, Mrs U recalled how Mr U had always loved art and this was something reflected in what one of his children also enjoyed.

I had put together a book of photographs and articles about families of dual heritage, which I invited the family to look at. This exercise opened up a discussion about skin colour, ethnicity and racism. We heard about the parents' experiences as a young couple growing up, meeting and raising their family in a hostile environment where skin colour, rather than heritage, mattered; and the children had an opportunity to reflect on and ask questions about their parents' experience, gaining insight and knowledge about resilience in the face of adversity. As a result of feeling more connected with each other, Mr U started spending more individual time with each of his children, doing activities relevant to their ages. Mrs U felt stronger, less tearful and over time returned to work, which improved the family's finances. The emphasis had moved away from the problematic relationships between parents and children towards a recognition of what the family members shared with each other and what each individual member of the family contributed to the whole system, particularly in relation to their abilities and qualities.

The V family

The V family was a White middle-class English family consisting of two parents and three children. They came to the attention of our CAHMS, because Mrs V was particularly concerned about her middle child who had been seen initially through the CAMHS in Schools Service. The mother worried that her son was harming himself in some way. Mrs V was especially vigilant to any hints that her son was developing mental health problems as there was a history of mental health problems in her family. Thus the child's every action was seen through a lens of fearful anticipation. The CAMHS clinician at the school met the young person and felt that a child and adolescent psychiatrist should meet with him to find out more about possible self-harm and also felt that Mrs V herself might need some support. Mrs V agreed to have some family therapy sessions to think about what each family member may have concerns about and what they might want. Mrs V also requested some support for herself individually.

Mrs V attended family sessions, parenting sessions and some individual therapy sessions. It transpired that when she had been at university, one of her room-mates had, completely out of the blue with none of her friends having any indications of her distress, taken her own life. Mrs V had become highly focused on the middle son's emotional well-being at the same time as his older sibling preparing to leave home to go to university. Leaving home is often a big milestone and a significant change in the life cycle of the young person as well as his or her family, as was the case for this family (Carter & McGoldrick, 1980). At the same time, in this family academic achievement was highly valued, and there was a strong wish for all the children to achieve success, as members of the older generation had been unable to do so because of mental health problems. Mrs V was hyper-vigilant to any signs of emotional distress, as she assumed it inevitably led to serious mental health problems and consequently to being unable to pursue an education. There was a real fear of what Byng-Hall (1995) has referred to as 'replicative family scripts' in this family.

In our family therapy sessions we mapped out differences along a continuum of emotional health, from minor distress to acute ill health (Watzlawick et al, 1974). Life cycle events such as older children preparing to leave home and the accompanying feelings of loss and anticipation of unknown challenges related to social and academic accomplishments, seemed to create fear in family members of impending disaster. Thinking about this together helped the family share their feelings with each other, and separate out the less fearful from the very fearful. This enabled the older child to go to university less afraid, and in time it became apparent that the middle child, who presented as on the verge of developing mental health problems, in fact had a mild learning disability. This was discovered in his work with the child psychiatrist, and this discovery enabled strategies to be put in place by an educational psychologist to help the boy cope with the difficulties he had in school. However, while this was helpful to the child, the parents still held on to the fear of future mental health problems for that child, which they wanted to address. We were able to address this worry and opened it up by drawing on stories of resilience. For example, I drew upon my own experience of leaving home to go to university and my parents' and grandfather's views and opinions about my leaving home, as an Asian girl going to live independently. I acknowledged that these thoughts may or may not have connected to Mr and Mrs V's own views. I explained how although my family were concerned about my leaving, they were also fairly confident that I had some degree of resilience to manage without them. Introducing the idea of resilience, facilitated the possibility for this family to notice and acknowledge exceptions to their dominant stories about inevitable mental health problems (White, 2004).

Reflections

The beauty of Community CAHMS is that we are oriented towards trying to provide a bespoke service that is a good fit with the client and family. In the Q, U, and V families the parents were worried about an aspect of their children's welfare. All of the children's relationships to their parents were experienced as fraught and difficult. The U children felt that they were under scrutiny by their parents as did the V children. The Q children felt their mother was burdened and therefore they could not express worries directly to her. However, the nature of worry differed between the families. Offering a 'bespoke service' to these families meant joining with the particular experiences and circumstances of each family and exploring where they lived, worked, socialised, went to school and where they felt that they fitted in to their community. In addition, the therapeutic sessions took place outside the CAMHS base, in family homes, schools and community centres; wherever it was convenient and most comfortable for families; although some of the families felt able to come into the CAMHS base where we could use a family therapy reflecting team and the one-way mirror. Each family had a strong sense of their neighbourhood, class, culture, age, ethnicity, health, wealth and faith. One of my assumptions is that feelings of belonging contribute to resilience and an ability to manage adversity. Of course my path crosses with clients when they feel they are unable to manage, but family therapy is based on drawing on their resources and resilience, which they have temporarily lost connection to.

For each family, their immediate and wider cultural community was an important context to their experience of emotional distress, as well as well-being. For instance, the U family feared their child becoming unwell would make the family stand out amongst friends, wider extended family, the school and the local community. This family was well established in the local area, both parents having grown up there and the family reputation in the community was highly important to them. The parents had experienced racism both in their childhood and as a dual-heritage couple. In addition, there were concerns about the fall in income when Mrs U became depressed and unable to work and because her husband worked long hours in low-paid employment.

For the Q family, the crisis was related to an anticipated rejection by their close-knit community and a fear of being treated differently as a result of how the father's sudden death would look to their community. There was a worry that other people in the community might think that they had not cared enough about him and not looked after him well. For the V family the worry was that academic failure would mark them out within their circle where excellent educational achievement was accorded the highest social status.

The therapeutic work with the families that I have described in this chapter show how I have used systemic interventions to help meet families in their moments of psychological distress. Together with family members, we arrive at a kind of 'fit' allowing new meanings about how they conceptualise their moments of distress and help them find a different way to manage those moments, to emerge. A systemic approach to therapy works more successfully in a community setting as it takes into account the wider contexts within which the families exist. Our CAMHS base is geographically placed in the heart of where people live, shop, worship and work and this helps us to connect with them. We know exactly where the flats, streets, sports and community centres, playgrounds, and schools are. We may meet clients we know on the bus travelling around the area as we do home visits, and see our clients in places other than the Community CAMHS base. In short, we are part of the community. Apart from physical location, we are also mindful of how the differing levels of context affect our families. At the time of writing, the UK is in the grip of economic austerity. This has a very real impact upon families and how they are living. There is increasing poverty and cuts to benefits have far reaching consequences on living standards. As a systemic practitioner I must take these circumstances into account and be mindful of increased stressors upon families.

Conclusions

Before the Community CAHMS was established, my traditional CAHMS work was fairly restricted. We were constrained by how different disciplines structured interventions with families and confined to seeing families within the institutional base at Tavistock. This often led to a low take up of service. The positive aspect of community CAMHS is that we are able to offer interventions early because clinicians are physically situated in schools (the V family), in community centres (the Q family) and within GP (general practice) clinics (the U family) and therefore are able to talk to teachers, other health professionals and families themselves more easily. In the context of austerity and government cuts, clients have become even more vulnerable and statutory and voluntary agencies are facing significant challenges with respect to funding. Despite these complexities I am pleased that many years of outreach, including home visits, have meant that many clients and families now feel able to see our service as part of the local community; to use it and to develop an understanding and appreciation of what we can offer to them and their families.

References

Andersen, T. (1987). The reflecting team: Dialogue and meta-dialogue in clinical work. *Family Process*, 26(4), 415–28.

Andersen, T. (1991). *The Reflecting Team: Dialogues and Dialogues about the Dialogues.* New York, NY: Norton.

Andersen, T. (1992). Reflections on reflecting with families. In: S. McNamee & K. J. Gergen (eds.), *Therapy as Social Construction.* (pp. 54–68). Thousand Oaks, CA: Sage Publications.

Boyd-Franklin, N. (2006). *Black Families in Therapy. A Multi-System Approach.* New York, NY: Guilford Press.

Boyd-Franklin, N. & Hafer Bry, B. (2001). *Reaching Out in Family Therapy: Home-Based, School and Community Interventions.* New York, NY: Guilford Press.

Byng-Hall, J. (1995). *Rewriting Family Scripts, Improvisation and Systems Change.* New York, NY: Guilford Press.

Carter, E. & McGoldrick, M. (1980). *The Family Life Cycle. A Framework for Family Therapy.* New York, NY: Gardner Press.

Epston, D. (1993). Internalising Discourses Versus Externalizing Discourses. In: S. Gilligan & R. Price (eds.), *Therapeutic Conversations.* (pp. 183–96). New York, NY: W.W. Norton.

Epston, D., White, M. & Murray, K. (1992). A proposal for a re-authoring therapy: Rose's revisioning of her life and a commentary. In: S. McNamee & K. Gergen (eds.), *Therapy as Social Construction.* (pp. 96–115). New York, NY: Sage Publications.

Hardy, K. V. & Laszloffy, T. A. (1995). The cultural genogram; key to training culturally competent family therapists. *Journal of Marital and Family Therapy,* 21(3), 227–37.

Keith, D. V., Connell, G. M. & Connell, L. C. (2001). *Defiance in the Family. Finding Hope in Therapy.* Brunner, England: Routledge.

Littlewood, R. & Lipsedge, M. (1987). The butterfly and the serpent. *Culture, Medicine & Psychiatry,* 11(3), 289–335.

Meadows, S. (2008). *Somers Town.* Film: The Works, UK.

Minuchin, S. (1974). *Families and Family Therapy.* Cambridge, MA: Harvard University.

Watzlawick, P., Weakland, J. H. & Fisch, R. (1974). *Change: Principles of Problem Formation and Problem Resolution.* New York, NY: W.W. Norton.

White, C. & Epston, D. (1990). *Narrative Means to Therapeutic Ends.* New York, NY: W.W. Norton.

White, M. (2004). *Narrative Practice and Exotic Lives: Resurrecting Diversity in Everyday Life.* Adelaide, Australia: Dulwich Centre Publications.

Chapter 11

Developmental hope

Rethinking professional roles and values

Ana Rivadulla Crespo

Developmental hope: the shadow of a crisis

> *Maybe this is why we have to suffer—so that hope will be revealed in all its depth.*
>
> (Zambrano, 1999, p. 173)

In this chapter I wish to draw attention to and reflect on those areas of Child and Adolescent Mental Health Services (CAMHS) work that may influence the emergence of a sense of hope, both that of young people and of our own, described by Zambrano. Young people, at least in the UK, are experiencing increasing rates of self-harm (Wood, 2009) and inpatient admissions (McDougall, 2013). A recent report estimated that, just in the UK, 2 million more adults and 100,000 more children and young people will have mental health problems by 2030 than at present (Mental Health Foundation, 2013). Young people who are referred to CAMHS also often experience long periods of hopelessness until an adult (family member or a professional) may be able to offer help. Although I refer to hopelessness and hope separately, my approach is based on the idea that there is always a relationship between the two (Flaskas, 2007).

Hopelessness is often associated with mental health problems, despair and pathology, while hope is associated with good mental health. However, here I wish to describe a process, which I call 'developmental hope', which is a reciprocal experience that comes from the integration of the systolic and diastolic movement between hope and hopelessness, where hopelessness is influenced by past experiences and hope develops from current reparative relationships. In this approach, crises are opportunities to access what we might call 'unconscious hope' or 'unrealized resilience' that, when contained and explored in a relationship, will enable development. There are two main steps or questions in my argument. First, how the experience of a 'good enough' community (which includes CAMHS as part of a sustainable and preventative public health collaborative system) can contribute to the reparation of deficits arising from early attachment trauma. Second, how reflective practice can promote an environment in which we are able to wait for the process of transformation of hopelessness into hope. In order to help young people find hope, we as mental health professionals need to be able to help them understand what hopelessness means to them, as well as understand what it means to us.

Impaired emotional development may result in disturbed interpersonal relationships and behaviours as well as mental health symptoms that often do not fit well into specific diagnoses. Many young people with what is often referred to as 'complex' emotional, behavioural and relational difficulties are only able to access CAMHS during severe crises. A crucial area of prevention should be working with parents with mental health problems, such as 'personality disorders' (Adshead, 2015). Insufficient preventative interventions result in high levels of emergencies and intensive CAMHS interventions including treatment under Tier 4 CAMHS (inpatient adolescent units) far away from the home environment. These gaps in the allocation of resources raise important clinical and ethical questions that I wish to explore with the help of the case of Juan[1]. I want to make an argument for a 'values-based' CAMHS in which developing hope for young people is at the heart of everything that we do.

The 'maternal and paternal functions' of developmental hope

Juan was a seventeen-year-old White and Afro-Caribbean dual-heritage adolescent boy living in a children's home when he was referred for a psychiatric assessment by his social worker because of concerns about his mental state. Juan became a Looked After Child when he was thirteen years old following his mother's suicide. Juan never met his father, and the only thing he knew about him was that he was of a different race and cultural background to his mother. As there was no available extended family, Juan underwent a trajectory of foster care placements. He had already been assessed repeatedly by different CAMHS professionals while he was in his mother's care and he was diagnosed with ADHD (aged seven) and conduct disorder (aged twelve). At the age of fifteen, following a series of failed foster placements, Juan was arrested for shoplifting, aggressive behaviour and possession of cannabis. While he was in the police cell, Juan attempted to commit suicide by hanging himself. Juan then had a Mental Health Act (MHA) assessment, and he was found to be emotionally aroused, paranoid and at risk to himself. He disclosed that he had been using various psychoactive substances and was admitted to an Adolescent Unit (Tier 4) under Section 2 of the Mental Health Act (MHA, 1983) for several weeks. Here he was treated with antipsychotic medication before being discharged to a new foster placement and to CAMHS (Tier 3) for follow-up. Juan remained mentally stable and seemed to engage with CAMHS, where he met with a psychiatrist for medication reviews. However, after a few months Juan stopped the medication and disengaged from CAMHS. The social worker remained involved as the main professional providing some consistency, but when she left and a new social worker took over his case, Juan absconded from his foster placement. He disappeared for several weeks living with a 'gang' until he was severely stabbed and required hospitalisation. After his discharge from hospital, Juan was persuaded by his new social worker to move to a children's home where he became increasingly withdrawn and guarded. This concerned his new carers and precipitated a new referral to CAMHS, but Juan refused to engage.

A diagnosis of inclusion

There is evidence that specialist CAMHS are functioning 'in an environment where demand frequently exceeds capacity', that thresholds to access CAMHS are 'being set too high' (Royal College of Psychiatrists, 2013a, p. 12) and CAMHS receives only six per cent of the current spending on mental health. These worrying facts result in few resources and few therapeutic relationships being available; more vulnerable young people being excluded from CAMHS; the medicalisation of social, psychological, emotional difficulties because of this being relatively less resource intensive; and high-risk behaviours being the key to accessing therapeutic support. This is very concerning, particularly when we know that in addition to the adolescent need to feel included in a peer group, young people under CAMHS are likely to feel stigmatised and may have a more challenging adjustment process to their identity perception after being given a diagnosis. Group therapeutic interventions in CAMHS have reduced despite the awareness that these have the potential to bring additional 'curative factors' (Yalom, 1972), which are aimed at increasing interpersonal skills and hope and therefore very relevant to adolescents. Similarly, individual longer-term psychodynamic psychotherapies have also been replaced by short-term interventions that can effectively treat specific symptoms and behaviours. However, short-term symptoms-based interventions are not sufficiently effective when treating more serious psychopathology and in understanding the underlying complexity of factors that perpetuate the symptoms of mental disorders.

Juan's case raises an initial dilemma for professionals in relation to whether we should or should not intervene when someone does not wish to engage (with health/life/development enhancing behaviours) because holding out hope for change and improvement has slipped away. Our ability to engage with young people who have lost hope depends on our having space to think about them. With the current high demands on CAMHS and less opportunity for reflection and analysis of systemic and unconscious processes, we are at risk of colluding with a social outlook that mostly values increased productivity at the expense of quality and psychological development. The 'maternal function' (which I explain in more detail below) within the role of the psychiatrist is suffering from the increasing overemphasis on quick and financially measurable outcomes. However, if health is a human right (Article 25 (1): The Universal Declaration of

Human Rights, 1948) this raises important questions in relation to what we value as health, what should we research, which services and interventions should be funded to promote health and for whom (Maitra & Krause, 2014). For example, despite the high risk of suicide and many other serious and costly public health concerns, many young people at risk of developing 'personality disorders' in adulthood are not receiving treatment and they do not access any mental health services. The reduction of psychotherapeutic interventions (both direct and indirect, individual, groups and institutional reflective practice) in the NHS is very concerning especially considering that, despite suicide being preventable, it is 'the second most common cause of death for young people', 'globally the most common cause of death for female adolescents aged fifteen to nineteen' and 'the UK has one of the highest rates of self-harm in Europe (at 400 episodes per 100,000 population)' (Royal College of Psychiatrists, 2014, p. 4).

It is important that we reflect on how policies and guidelines are interpreted and influenced by our values and how these translate into the decisions that we make in clinical practice and those we support in political agendas. Despite having major advances in scientific research, medical treatments, greater life expectancy and improved technology, the 2007 UNICEF study showed that the UK ranked at the bottom on children's well-being compared with North America and eighteen European countries, and in another 2009 survey ranked twenty-fourth out of twenty-nine European countries (Bradshaw & Richardson, 2009; Royal College of Psychiatrists, 2010). Young people appear to feel increasingly more hopeless 'driven to consume and with little or no community life' (Wilkinson & Pickett, 2009, p. 3). Recent research by the government reveals that thirty-three per cent of children in England live in poverty, that it has 'more than doubled compared to what it was 25 years ago' and that 'several cross-country studies indicate that the rate of child poverty in the UK is one of the highest among developed countries' (Pedace, 2008, p. 5). Pedace (2008) also suggests that when we compare the emotional well-being outcomes across countries and look closely at research there is evidence that the most important determinant of child outcome seems to be parenting quality, and income is only a crude measure of this (Heckman, 2008). Yet we live in times in which diagnosing, too often and too generally, appears to be replacing good enough parenting and relationship values.

Given Juan's past history and the presenting concerns raised by his carers, in his case we would have had sufficient justification to attempt to assess his degree of risk. The dilemma remained in relation to how much and in which way I as a psychiatrist should intervene and where was I to draw the line of my responsibility in my intervention. What should I/we do if Juan was not able to accept relationships with adults which may help him to be able to develop in a healthy way? How could I/we respond to Juan's resistance when we know that his refusal to engage was also a manifestation of feeling hopeless and excluded from the system that was attempting to pursue him? And from Juan, more general questions arose in relation to the community: who is responsible for promoting mental health prevention for young people? What is 'mental health prevention'? How do we respond to these complex questions during times of scarcity? How do our values influence how we think about these dilemmas?

The maternal function of developmental hope

The application of psychoanalytic theory in child and adolescent psychiatry can help us understand the developmental, emotional and unconscious dynamics between patients, families, professionals, groups and institutions. The term 'patient' may be controversial as for some people it may have connotations of submission and implied passivity. As a psychiatrist (Good Medical Practice: GMC, 2013) and psychodynamic psychotherapist (Code of Ethics: British Psychoanalytic Council, 2011), I use this term to describe a person who is under the care of a health professional. The term implies that the professional has clinical responsibility over the patient's clinical care and therefore has to adhere to specific ethical and professional guidelines and code of conduct. In this chapter, I reflect on the doctor/therapist and patient relationship that involves both conscious and unconscious exchanges.

I suggest that in Juan's case we may start by creating the conditions for a 'thinking space' (Lowe, 2014) in which a reflective process can be safeguarded as a vital part of CAMHS work. Such a process involves creating a holding environment in which a young person may be able to discover, experience or re-experience themselves in relationships. This is the 'maternal function,' and it may belong to or be incumbent upon any person, group and institution promoting development and the internalisation of being able to provide this life giving function to oneself as well as to others (hope).

Freud defined the 'ego' as the part of the mental apparatus that mediates between the 'id' (instinctual drives) and the external world. He also described how the 'ego' creates defence mechanisms such as 'repression' to protect the 'id' from the external world (Freud, 1923). According to Klein, during the early stages of development, 'internal objects' or internal representations of external objects are felt to be undifferentiated, physical, emotional and psychological concrete experiences. Klein described that, the immature 'ego' protects itself from 'annihilation anxiety' by splitting the perceived 'internal objects' into good or bad (persecutory) parts. She used the term 'paranoid-schizoid position' to describe this complex process that also involves projecting outwards anything that the 'ego' perceives as a threat (Klein, 1988, p. 34). The 'maternal function' provides a developmental space to both hold and attempt to emotionally understand the projections that the primitive ego is not yet able to own. My view is that this fundamental function is crucial to all the various interventions offered by CAMHS. With the increasing pressures to provide interventions that result in short-term measurable outcomes, my concern is that we are at risk of prematurely discharging young people who have not yet developed sufficient internal ego boundaries that will provide them with a secure enough maternal function. If young people are fortunate, they may have sufficient parenting/community resources to compensate for that deficiency but many young people do not.

The mistrust in mental health services and refusal to engage is not uncommon in people who have suffered from trauma and/or neglect. There is evidence that adolescents from Black and Minority Ethnic (BME) groups who suffer from psychosis have more compulsory admissions (Corrigall & Bhugra, 2013). It is therefore helpful to think about the person in terms of their emotional state, development and sociocultural history rather than simply about their symptoms or symptom clusters. When someone does not engage with mental health services in a sufficiently safe way, mental health professionals have a duty to intervene when there is a suspicion that the individual suffers from a mental disorder of a nature or degree that could put any life at risk. Unless the person warrants an assessment under the Mental Health Act (MHA, 1983), the higher the risk involved, the greater the inter-agency conflict in relation to areas of responsibility. In my view, instead of falling into the hopelessness of defensive practice, we could move towards a culture of prevention and collaboration with the community to provide the necessary engagement, which would lead to hope.

The skills of multidisciplinary teams working in CAMHS offer opportunities to provide an in-depth and integrated understanding of complex aspects involved in child and adolescent mental health (emotional, psychological, social, systemic, cultural, medical, legal). This may be experienced by a young person as a kind of 'holding' and provides a 'maternal function' both for the patient and for the professionals, enabling both sides to survive the feelings of hopelessness and despair that young people may need to communicate to us both overtly through their actions and through less discernible unconscious projections. After sufficient exposure to the 'maternal function', the young person may begin to get in touch with some hope for himself. Until a young person like Juan decides for himself to become our 'patient', he and the people working with him may need to experience a period of ambivalence characterised by anxiety and subsequent resistance to the potentially destructive internalised persecutory or/and abandoning 'bad breast'. If the process of engagement is experienced as secure enough, the young person will gradually move towards being more able to experience his feelings of dependency and vulnerability in a more realistic way. During this process of engagement, the young person may begin to choose to engage in a therapeutic relationship with professionals that will facilitate other relationships that are necessary for his development. The young person may then begin to accept his role of being a 'patient', which will influence the development of his identity[2] depending on how the experience of being a patient is perceived. The new relationships developed by being in a 'patient' role may bring both anxiety of a 'claustro-agora-phobic' nature (Rey, 1994) and hope for reparation. For an environment to provide an enabling 'maternal function' it has to provide both good enough nourishment and sufficient space to promote a secure enough separation and identity differentiation. In contrast to what is often not possible within the current fragmented CAMH services, a transitional approach would promote more secure attachments. During a crisis, the development of hope will depend on the ability of the young person to modify his 'internal objects' while making use of the available past and current 'maternal functions'. This transformative process may aid the unlocking of hope, which was previously split off and encapsulated. Freud considered that resistance to receiving the 'maternal function' was a manifestation of a 'death instinct' (Freud, 2010)[3]. I wonder if when young people engage with self-destructive behaviours and manifest psychosomatic symptoms, they are offering us opportunities to access the unconscious tension between life and death and of encountering hope. The process of 'developmental hope' represents this tension in which hope breaks through the boundary of the unconscious to begin a new stage of consciousness to transform hope into trust.

Although Juan was not yet ready to engage, we in CAMHS accepted the referral to assess whether he had a mental health problem, to offer him an opportunity to engage with his personal crisis in a different way and to support his carers. Our initial work became part of that maternal function.

The paternal function of developmental hope

While the 'maternal function' signifies dependency, the 'paternal function' facilitates a process of differentiation, which is necessary to enable the development of the 'superego'. This term was coined by Freud (1923) to describe the aspect of the mental apparatus that regulates our internal moral rules and our capacity to bear guilt, psychic pain and assume responsibility. As the infant develops, and is more able to differentiate from the (external) objects that interact with him, he or she gradually gets in touch with 'depressive anxiety' (Hinshelwood, 1991) and becomes fearful over losing the loved object. This leads to the development of guilt feelings, concern for loved objects and feelings of responsibility. This developmental experience was described by Klein as the 'depressive position' (Klein, 1988, pp. 71–80) and perceived to start around four to six months of age and to continue to develop in an oscillating way throughout life. The 'paternal function' regulates the anxiety and guilt generated by the 'depressive position' during the process of separation. In their work CAMH professionals can promote the development of this function by working together with young people, as well as their families and the community. An example of such an intervention is the psychoanalytically oriented group work carried out in a deprived area of London by the Brent Centre for Young People with adolescents who have been sentenced to a community order (Armstrong & Rustin, 2015).

We know that young people of Afro-Caribbean origin, Looked After Children and young people with low-socioeconomic backgrounds are more often diagnosed with conduct disorder which tends to be a diagnosis of exclusion from CAMHS despite being associated with higher co-morbidities and negative social outcomes (NICE, 2013). We know that there is a relationship between conduct disorder in childhood and subsequent adult depression (Stringaris, Lewis & Maughan, 2014). It has also been reported that about seventy-three per cent of young people reoffend within a year (Ministry of Justice, 2013) and that psychiatric morbidity in prisons is an epidemic as 'seventy-two per cent male and seventy per cent of female sentenced prisoners have at least one mental disorder, and one in five prisoners has four major mental health disorders' and 'boys aged fifteen to seventeen are eighteen times more likely to kill themselves in prison than in the community' (Mental Health Foundation, 2007, p. 34). But despite these tragic figures, many vulnerable, socially excluded young people in search of containment end up using prisons as concrete boundaries or 'brick fathers', if we paraphrase the concept of 'brick mother' (Rey, 1994) rather than relationships. These findings and statistics confirm the pressing need for CAMH services to work with other agencies in order to promote healthier relationships and to develop a psychological (and psychoanalytic) understanding of the antisocial behaviour of adolescents as a potential for the development of hope (Winnicott, 1986).

With Juan's story, I wish to illustrate how the working through of the maternal and paternal functions at different levels (from individuals to environment) gradually brought more hope into his internal objects and helped him to safely bring together the different parts of himself and reach a 'depressive position' in a more secure way.

Despite Juan's reluctance to engage with CAMHS, we worked on the maternal and paternal functions by regularly supporting him, his carers and the social worker. The idea of a 'third position' 'from which object relationships can be observed' (Britton, 2005, p. 42) and of a cohesive family was modelled to Juan through this process of different adults working together to think about his needs. The role of CAMHS was also important to contain the anxiety experienced by the adults who lived with him. Gradually, Juan began to engage with his carers and, eventually, he accepted an appointment with a psychotherapist and myself.

Meaningful responsibility and caring beyond the self

Juan began to attend appointments at CAMHS in a cautious way. He found it easier to engage with the psychotherapist by combining talking with art work as he could share both silence and conversation while they squiggled (Winnicott, 1971). Juan eventually agreed to meet with me for monthly psychiatric reviews. His engagement with his carers improved and he began to attend some lessons at a local college. Despite the improvement, concerns about his mental state remained. As we anticipated, Juan's past trauma began to erupt with unpredictable aggressive feelings that manifested in occasional suspicious behaviour and anger outbursts. The more hopeful curiosity towards his new relationships seemed to put him in touch with intense difficult feelings related to his past experiences. This created a strange infectious paralysis in the group of adults working with him which required more conversations with his carers to help them understand Juan's behaviour and to contain him. At some point Juan had an argument with one of his carers, which resulted in having an alcohol binge. He became angry and paranoid and disappeared for one night. The police were called, but eventually, Juan returned home and asked to see his psychotherapist. He was also able to admit to having self-harmed and to feeling suicidal. This coincided with Juan's key worker leaving her job without warning. I was able to join the psychotherapist in order to complete a psychiatric assessment, and our impression then was that this brief but mentally disturbed episode was a fearful reaction to the reminiscence of previous traumatic losses evoked by an unexpected and sudden loss of someone he had become intensely attached to in the present time; 'when hope is disappointed, hope turns into delirium' (Zambrano, 1999, p. 176). As Juan had already engaged in treatment, this crisis also became an opportunity to further assess Juan's needs and to make a plan about subsequent treatment. On this occasion, Juan was more able to engage and to get in touch with his feelings of sadness and vulnerability. He showed insight in relation to his interpersonal difficulties and his need for ongoing treatment to learn to understand and to manage his emotions. Juan then agreed to more intensive psychotherapy and regular psychiatric reviews. The focus of the psychiatric care was to monitor his mental state while providing psycho-education and contributing to the creation of a resilient team that could safely engage with him. Working together we managed to prevent an inpatient admission.

Where there has been failure of containment in childhood, there are likely to be greater difficulties during adolescence to separate from one's 'internal objects' (as well as from actual carers) in a healthy and safe way. Even when young people run away from home, they carry their internalised parents with them who become manifest during states of emotional arousal generated by the emergence of new relationships. This is the point at which a mental health crisis might ensue. Freud proposed that the ego's defence mechanisms also appeared 'as resistances against recovery' and that 'the ego treats recovery itself as a new danger' (Freud, 1937, p. 237). Although Juan's internal sense of hope was still in the early stages of development, he began to share it with others and with his community by engaging with a horticultural group (Haigh, 2012). I suggest that when he began to develop a 'good-enough' internal sense of hope, a need to transcend this hope emerged. I associate this aspect of hope with Maslow's 'self-actualisation' process (Maslow, 1943) because it enhances the curiosity one might have about oneself that longs to connect and to contribute to something beyond the self. To hope is to dream of something bigger than oneself, to enjoy the process of wishing and to feel part of a relationship that hopes for others. The risk is that, once hope has been experienced after a state of extreme hopelessness, the need to develop omnipotent solutions to prevent another fall into the abyss of hopelessness, may reinforce splitting defences to keep the dynamic of hope and hopelessness apart, as though they cannot exist together. In my clinical experience it seems that the more traumatic and fragmented childhood development has been, the more unpredictable and abrupt the transition between hope and hopelessness.

Despite ongoing concerns about the possibility of Juan suffering from a psychotic illness I did not find enough evidence to support this concern. Giving Juan a diagnosis would have had repercussions for the type of treatment indicated (such as specific guidelines and medication), services available (adult mental health services) and legal responsibility (the perception of Juan's capacity to make decisions). I found it much more helpful to understand Juan as a developing adolescent whose emotional and psychological development had suffered because he needed to rely too much on primitive internal defences to protect himself after suffering from very negative experiences throughout his life. Past trauma emerged from his unconscious mind in the form of persecutory feelings that often divided him and deprived him from his sense of hope and self. My judgement was that Juan would need to continue to have ongoing therapeutic support beyond his eighteenth birthday to help him integrate his sense of self. The problem was that, without a diagnosis of some kind of mental illness, Juan did not meet the criteria for many services. He could have accessed short-term cognitive behavioural therapy, but no longer-term relationship-based therapies (individual and group) or even psychiatric care would be available. The multidisciplinary team therefore decided to set up a transitions consultation group with Juan and other adolescents that were attending CAMHS to think with them about our dilemmas and concerns about their ongoing care. We had several workshops that led to the creation of a Transitions Pilot in partnership with a charity from the local community. The aim was to provide continuity of care for young people attending CAMHS until they were developmentally ready to end their therapeutic work, while at the same time, to facilitate them building interpersonal, social and life skills by joining flexible therapeutic group activities.

Hope, the light of a crisis

Juan's story is not atypical. It shows how, in an apparently complex and difficult case, the consistent and collaborative work of a multi-agency team managed to help a young person rescue his buried hope from his personal and collective past traumas. Through his crisis, Juan accessed new possibilities of maternal and paternal care that enabled him to discover the consciousness of his emotional pain. With Juan's story I have shown how accessing hope which is unconscious and buried in a young person's past experiences, gradually can become possible when experienced through the eyes of other people who are able to receive and understand hopelessness while providing caring and emotional nourishment. The unlocking of unconscious hope and resilience requires the availability of someone who provides a 'maternal function' to 'contain' the frightening (persecutory, murderous) internal objects that emerge in every crisis. The realisation of 'the maternal function' involves a relationship in which there is emotional contact with someone who is able to recognise and legitimise the crisis, and enable the development of hope. Hope has to travel from the unconscious of the young person to the therapist who will have a capacity to receive it and recognise it and return it in the form of an expression of care. This care may then become what I have referred to as 'developmental hope' derived from the values of respect, dignity, inclusiveness and care that we aim to embody in every aspect of what we do to enable young people to understand and to forgive themselves. Forgiveness comes from having experienced being listened to in a particular way, where the shadow aspects of human experience are not denied and where young people can allow themselves to have an authentic relationship with themselves and with the community. Henri Rey described the relationship between forgiveness and hope: 'Only when the super-ego becomes less cruel, less demanding as well of perfection, is the ego capable of accepting an internal object which is not perfectly repaired, can accept compromise, forgive and be forgiven, and experience hope and gratitude' (Rey, 1986, p. 30).

In our CAMHS it is therefore important to allow sufficient time and continuity so that the young person is able to experience an integrative process, which through the making of relationships can promote the transformation of more rigid experiences of hopelessness into more flexible areas of *developmental hope*. Financial pressures are not just excluding vulnerable young people who do not meet diagnostic and arbitrary political criteria, but are also leading to a competitive culture that mostly values visible 'objective' outcomes while excluding subjective human experience from psychiatry and CAMH services. DeJong (2010) poses an important question in relation to young people who present with mental health symptoms after experiencing severe trauma. While acknowledging the limitations of our current diagnostic system, she asks: 'How do we marry a developmental psychopathology perspective with our current diagnostic system?' (DeJong, 2010, p. 596). In her paper she proposes prevention, improved inter-agency communication and the creation of more 'developmentally sensitive' assessment standardised tools to allow for research comparisons' (DeJong, 2010, p. 596). I agree that we need to improve our research tools and systems to better understand young people and to provide safe, quality and fair services. However, I think that we need to work within local and global health care systems to instil hope in young people while minimising the bureaucracy involved. Hope starts from unlocking the silence (Segal, 1987), by acknowledging the shadow of both individual and collective crises. Young people learn to understand and manage their conflicts according to how their caregivers and their communities, including statutory services, respond to them. However, the current defensive system appears to be conducting us towards an aimless 'morally blind' (Bauman & Donskis, 2013) hyperactivity in which 'the capital of fear can be turned to any kind of profit, commercial or political' (Bauman, 2007, p. 12).

I suggest that in CAMHS we need to promote an environment of responsibility and trust (Royal College of Psychiatrists, 2013b) instead of just looking for short-term solutions. By valuing relationships that promote the maternal and paternal functions, we will contribute to 'developmental hope', which can enable young people to transform their initial resignation into a more hopeful acceptance (Sábato, 2000, p. 118). I see it as a crucial aspect of our professional roles in CAMHS to both hold in mind, and speak up on behalf of, the needs and creative potential of all the young people in our communities.

Notes

1 In order to provide an illustration I have constructed Juan's case as a composite of many typical patients I have come across in many years of psychiatric practice. Any similarity with real cases only demonstrates that these themes are common. For the purpose of consistency, I will use masculine pronouns when I refer to an individual young person (in the community) or a patient (under the care of CAMHS).
2 Here I do not make a distinction between the terms 'identity' and 'personality'.
3 The death instinct is the drive towards death, self-destruction and the return to the inorganic. In Freudian thinking this drive stands in opposition to the tendency toward survival, propagation, sex and other creative, life-producing drives.

References

Adshead, G. (2015). Parenting and personality disorder: Clinical and child protection implications. *British Journal of Psych Advances*, 21(1), 15–22.

Armstrong, D. & Rustin, M. (2015). *Unconscious Defences Against Anxiety in a Youth Offending Service*. London, England: Karnac.

Bauman, Z. (2007). *Liquid Times. Living in an Age of Uncertainty*. Cambridge, England: Polity Press.

Bauman, Z. & Donskis, L. (2013). *Moral Blindness. The Loss of Sensitivity in Liquid Modernity*. Cambridge, England: Polity Press.

Bradshaw J. & Richardson, D. (2009). An index of child well-being in Europe. *Child Indicators Research*, 2(3), 319–51.

British Psychoanalytic Council (BPC) (2011). Code of Ethics. London, England: British Psychoanalytic Council (BPC).

Britton, R. (2005). *Belief and Imagination*. London, England: Routledge.

Corrigall, R. & Bhugra, D. (2013). The role of ethnicity and diagnosis in rates of adolescent psychiatric admission and compulsory detention: A longitudinal case-note study. *Journal of the Royal Society of Medicine*, 106(5), 190–5.

DeJong, M. (2010). Some reflections on the use of psychiatric diagnosis in the looked after or "in care" child population. *Clinical Child Psychology and Psychiatry*, 15(4), 589–599.

Flaskas, C. (2007). The balance of hope and hopelessness. In: C. Flaskas, I. McCarthy & J. Sheehan (eds.), *Hope and Despair in Family Therapy: Reflections on Adversity, Forgiveness and Reconciliation*. (pp. 24–35). Hove, England: Brunner-Routledge.

Freud, S. (1923). *The Ego and the Id*. The Standard Edition of the Complete Works of Sigmund Freud, vol. XIX, London, England: Hogarth Press.

Freud, S. (1937). Analysis terminable and interminable. *Standard Edition*, 23, 209–54.

Freud, S. (2010). *Beyond the Pleasure Principle* (J. Strachey trans.). Seattle, WA:: Pacific Publishing Studio and CreateSpace (originally published in 1922).

General Medical Council (GMC)(2013). *Good Medical Practice: Working With Doctors Working With Patients*. London, England: GMC. Available online at http://www.gmc-uk.org/guidance.

Haigh, R. (2012). The philosophy of greencare: Why it matters for our mental health. *Mental Health and Social Inclusion,* 16(3), 127–35.

Heckman, J. J. (2008). Schools, skills and synapses. *Economic Enquiry,* 46(3), 289–324.

Hinshelwood, R. D. (1991). *A Dictionary of Kleinian Thought*. London, England: Free Association Books.

Klein, M. (1988). *Envy and Gratitude and Other Works 1946–1963*. London, England: Virago. (first published 1975).

Lowe, F. (2014). *Thinking Space. Promoting Thinking about Race, Culture and Diversity in Psychotherapy and Beyond*. London, England: Karnac.

Maitra, B. & Krause, I-B. (2014). *Culture and Madness. A Training Resource, Film and Commentary for Mental Health Professionals*. London, England: Jessica Kingsley.

Maslow, A. (1943). A theory of human motivation. *Psychological Review,* 50(4), 370–96.

McDougall, T. (2013). *Quality Network for Inpatient CAMHS (QNIC) and Quality Network for Community CAMHS (QNCC) Position Statement: Hospital Access, Admission and Discharge*. London, England: Royal College of Psychiatrists' Centre for Quality Improvement.

Mental Health Foundation (2007). *The Fundamental Facts. The Latest Facts and Figures on Mental Health*. London, England: Institute of Psychiatry.

Mental Health Foundation (2013). *Starting Today. The Future of Mental Health Services. Final Enquiry Report*. London, England: Institute of Psychiatry.

Ministry of Justice (2013). *Proven Re-offending Statistics Quarterly Bulletin, October 2010 to September 2011, England and Wales*. London, England: Ministry of Justice.

National Institute for Health and Care Excellence (NICE) (2013). *Antisocial Behaviour and Conduct Disorders in Children and Young People: Recognition, Intervention and Management*. London, England: NICE.

Pedace, L. (2008). *Child Wellbeing in England, Scotland and Wales. Comparisons and Variations*. London, England: Family and Parenting Institute.

Rey, J. H. (1986). Reparation. *Journal of the Melanie Klein Society,* 4, 5–35.

Rey, J. H. (1994). *Universals of Psychoanalysis in the Treatment of Psychotic and Borderline States*. London, England: Free Association Books.

Royal College of Psychiatrists (2010). *No Health Without Public Mental Health. The Case for Action*. Royal College of Psychiatrists Position Statement (PS4/2010). London, England: Royal College of Psychiatrists.

Royal College of Psychiatrists (2013a). *Building a Sustaining Specialist CAMHS to Improve Outcomes for Children and Young People*. Update of Guidance on Workforce, Capacity and Functions of CAMHS in the UK. College Report (CR182). London, England: Royal College of Psychiatrists.

Royal College of Psychiatrists (2013b). *Enabling Environments Standards*. College Centre for Quality Improvement (CCQI). London, England: Royal College of Psychiatrists.

Royal College of Psychiatrists (2014). *Managing Self-Harm in Young People*. College Report (CR192). London, England: Royal College of Psychiatrists.

Sábato, E. (2000). *La Resistencia*. Una Reflexión Contra la Globalización, la Clonación, la Masificación. Editorial Seix Barral, 2011. Colección Booket, primera edición 2007 y tercera impresión en 2011.

Segal, H. (1987). Silence is the real crime. *International Review of Psychoanalysis,* 14(1), 3–12.

Stringaris, A., Lewis, G. & Maughan, B. (2014). Developmental pathways from childhood conduct problems to early adult depression: Findings from ALSPAC cohort. *British Journal of Psychiatry,* 205(1), 17–23.

The Department of Health (2015). *Mental Health Act 1983: Code of Practice.* London, England: The Stationery Office.

The Universal Declaration of Human Rights, (1948). Article 25. United Nations. Available online http://www.un.org/en/documents/udhr/index.shtml.

Wilkinson, R. & Pickett, K. (2009). *The Spirit Level. Why Equality is Better for Everyone.* London, England: Penguin Books.

Winnicott, D. W. (1971). *Playing and Reality.* London, England: Penguin Books.

Winnicott, D. W. (1986). *Home Is Where We Start From: Essays by a Psychoanalyst.* London, England: Penguin Books.

Wood, A. (2009). Self-harm in adolescents. *Advances in Psychiatric Treatment,* 15(6), 434–41.

Yalom, I. D. (1972). *The Theory and Practice of Group Psychotherapy.* New York, NY: Basic Books.

Zambrano, M. (1999). *Delirium and Destiny. A Spaniard in Her Twenties.* New York, NY: University of New York Press.

Chapter 12

Making meaning around Female Genital Mutilation (FGM)

From contentious debate to ethical dialogue

Taiwo Afuape and Inga-Britt Krause

Introduction

Being situated in the multicultural context of a London inner-city borough the practitioners of our CAMH service are working daily with diverse cultures and therefore often with persons who have experienced racism, racialisation[1] and discrimination based on where they are from, the colour of their skin and their beliefs, practices, emotions and relationships. This poses a challenge for CAMHS practitioners, because no matter how hard they may try to be respectful, not contextualising and critically reflecting on the ideas we hold about right and wrong, the human rights of adults as well as children and what it means to be free, to choose and to exercise agency over our lives, may interfere with our ability to engage in ethical dialogue. Ideas about freedom are always relative and contingent upon other ideas about relationships, responsibilities and possibilities. As described in Chapter 2 relational orientations (sociality) varies according to the way persons and groups engage with different styles of community. Thus persons who emphasise loyalty to kin and locality, as well as hierarchical ideas about gender, sexuality and procreation may have a different outlook with regards to personal agency and freedom than persons with relational outlooks based on choice, individual autonomy and fluid, perhaps less permanent, social networks. It is not surprising then that these two orientations may give rise to polarising, even hostile debates.

The challenges posed by the debate around female genital mutilation (FGM) is an example of such polarisation fuelled not just by different cultural points of view but also by feminist critiques and safeguarding legislation articulated in high-profile worldwide anti-FGM campaigns (World Health Association, 2008). Given the numbers of women and girls in the UK from countries in which FGM is practiced, CAMHS clinicians have the challenging task of both meeting statutory responsibilities with respect to safeguarding the well-being of children and of respectfully engaging in enabling and therapeutic relationships with families, who are from FGM-practicing communities. It may even evade our attention that there is indeed a diversity of perspectives on this issue, given that there is ample media and political attention to the violative nature of FGM and less attention given to the critique by some African women of the negative impact of the way the anti-FGM agenda positions itself and 'others'. As a result, there is a relative dearth of reflective, dialogical and clinical-based material for CAMHS clinicians working with families affected by FGM and affected by the FGM debate. There is a danger in the present climate of blanket condemnation, of unwittingly conveying horror and revulsion toward women and girls who have experienced FGM, shutting down dialogue with them and therefore failing to meet them with the dignity and respect they deserve. In fact, we may fail to engage such girls, women and families in our services all together.

Our aim in this chapter is to reflect on the significance of *meaning* when trying to understand both our own feelings, responses and responsibilities and the feelings, responses and responsibilities of our clients. We refer to this as an 'ethical dialogue', and we emphasise that this involves practitioners being aware of the social, cultural and political context in which particular statements are made and views are held in relation to FGM. In the first part of the chapter we consider, our statutory responsibilities as CAMHS practitioners; some patterns of cultural and social processes which FGM articulates; different types of practices and what they may involve; the complexity of defining such practices in the context of current legislation; and then we share our personal contexts and how these shape *our* meanings. The second half of the chapter is comprised of a dialogue between us (Taiwo and Britt), which shapes our understanding of the importance of 'ethical dialogue'. We aim to encourage the reader to reflect on meanings, in order to (re) consider ways of moving out of polarised positions and develop more engaging services.

Our statutory responsibility

As a result of *Every Child Matters*, which includes the *Children's National Service Framework*[2], the Department of Health, Home Office and Department for Education's *Working Together to Safeguard Children* 1999 and the *Children's Act* 2004[3], practitioners from all statutory and voluntary agencies have a statutory responsibility to safeguard children from FGM[4]. With respect to international legislation, the UN Convention on the Rights of the Child[5], and the UN Convention on the Elimination of All Forms of Discrimination against Women[6] contain articles, which oblige signatory states, like the UK, to take legal action, by identifying when a child may be at risk of being subjected to FGM and responding appropriately to protect them; identifying when a child has been subjected to FGM and responding appropriately to support them. While these government policies reflect UK/European law and policy, they are also influenced by, and in turn influence, the worldwide increase in campaigning for the criminalising of FGM. The tone of these campaigns are often emotive, such as for example, the 'End FGM European Campaign' by Amnesty International in partnership with NGOs, with a logo depicting a beautiful pink rose stitched up in the centre.

Regardless of their own position on FGM, this kind of highly emotive message inevitably shapes the views of CAMHS professionals, encouraging them to just act, rather than to reflect and act.

Many governments in Africa and elsewhere have taken steps to eliminate FGM in their countries, through criminalisation, education and outreach programs, and preventative use of civil and administrative regulations. In the UK all types of FGM are illegal (carrying a maximum penalty of fourteen years in prison) under the Female Genital Mutilation Act 2003, which states:

> *(1) A person is guilty of an offence if he excises, infibulates or otherwise mutilates the whole or any part of a girl's labia majora, labia minora or clitoris. (2) But no offence is committed by an approved person who performs—(a) a surgical operation on a girl which is necessary for her physical or mental health, or (b) a surgical operation on a girl who is in any stage of labour, or has just given birth, for purposes connected with the labour or birth.*

FGM is an offence, which extends to acts performed outside of the UK and to any person who advises, helps or forces a girl to inflict FGM on herself. However, when referring to 'the offence to excise, infibulate or otherwise mutilate the whole or any part of a girl's labia majora, labia minora or clitoris', the UK law explicitly states that the term 'girl' includes 'woman'. Whereas the US Federal Prohibition of Female Genital Mutilation Act, and the provision of the Canadian Criminal Code condemn the practice only when 'performed on minors' or those under eighteen years old; therefore it is not an offense if 'the person is at least 18 years of age and there is no resulting bodily harm' (section 268 of the Canadian Criminal Code).

What does FGM involve?

The World Health Organisation splits the practices into four different types:

1 *Circumcision* : Removal of prepuce (foreskin) and some or all of the clitoris
2 *Excision* (clitoridectomy): Removal of the clitoris and some or all labia minora (small lips which cover and protect the opening of the vagina and the urinary opening)
3 *Infibulation*: Removal of part or all of the external genitals and stitching/narrowing of the vagina
4 *Unclassified*: Various procedures to narrow the vagina (although this does not include Western cosmetic and intersex surgeries as they are not illegal)

This classification organises the practices in order of increasing degree of severity, and specific practices from diverse locations 'are forced into one or another of these categories' (Njambi, 2004, p. 283).

Definitions and meaning

Definitions are highly contentious, and it is impossible for any label to be value-neutral. The definitions we use are assumed to elucidate the position of the definer on this polarised issue (complicit or challenging; judgemental or neutral), and there are supporters and critics of every possible position. Being neutral means being too uncritical of such practices, whereas naming the practices in such a way as to highlight the violence of it, may not match with the experience of all women who experience it.

The language used has the power to mobilise allies with similar views, and impact on wider social discourses, attitudes, law and policies. Davis (2004) prefers the term 'genital cutting', 'above "female genital mutilation", which obscures the agency of women who participate in the practice. "Genital surgery" medicalises the practice, while "circumcision" underplays risks, pain, and impairment' (p. 309). La Barbera (2009) adds the word 'ritual' ('ritual female genital cuttings') to highlight the inherent cultural dimensions to the practice. Mabilia (2013) prefers the term 'female genital modification' in order to facilitate our listening to those women who do not regard themselves as mutilated and as a reminder that the variety of acts that are referred to as FGM should not be reduced to a set of mere acts of violence (Mabilia, 2013).

The context in which FGM is performed varies from place to place. Some communities perform FGM at home in the presence of female family members, whereas other communities perform them away from home, or outdoors. Some are performed by elders of the family or community while in other cases the incisions/cutting calls for an expert practitioner. Although the age varies among different communities, with some groups practicing it a few days after birth (Bradley, 2011), usually the practice marks the entrance into adulthood. As these rituals constitute a celebratory occasion, they are traditionally accompanied by special foods, dance and songs.

Just as definitions are arrived at from a particular point of view, definitions never stand alone, but reflect the context around that which is being defined. Thus persons and groups who carry out the practice do not tend to use a term which denotes something as negative as 'mutilation'. Rather since the practice tends to be central for identity and relational orientations (sociality) the term used in specific localities tends to vary and have wider meanings. Thus Talle (1993) reports for Somalia where infibulations are practised that the girl who has had this procedure is referred to as *gabar tolan/qodban* 'a girl who is sewn/joined together' and she translates this as a 'virgin'. However, 'sewing' and 'closing' also have much wider meanings in Somali society. The excision of the clitoris (*xalaalays*, from the Arabic *xalaal* in praise) (Talle, 1993) was considered an act of purification, which removed 'hard' and 'dirty' parts, that is to say the 'male' parts from a woman's genitalia. The ritual not only marked a girl's transformation into womanhood it also at the same time transformed, 'joined' or enclosed her into a circle of her father's kin. At this point she was no longer an androgynous child but had been 'reborn' as a person with a female identity and could now be ready to marry. Defibulation or sexual intercourse was thought of as an inversion, namely in terms of 'separating' and 'opening' (Talle, 1993).

We have opted in this chapter to use the language of the current UK legislation of 'female genital mutilation' (FGM), in order to highlight, rather than obscure, the ways in which this language and the legislation that uses it, was specifically conceived as a tool to protect women and girls against mutilations. Although we use the term FGM, it is important to note that no labels can fully grasp or describe the range of experiences women have. For example, while some women who have undergone the practice feel that "circumcision" is too lenient and uncritical a term, others do not consider their bodies mutilated. We hope to reflect on the complex consequences of how we as service providers position ourselves whilst not shying away from taking some kind of position ourselves.

Some cultural meanings

Clinicians in the UK who work with culturally diverse communities may encounter people who adhere to practices they do not understand, or agree with. In the countries where FGM is not practiced, there is a widespread belief that it is an inherently barbaric, misogynistic and abusive practice, harmful to female bodies and sexuality; as well as evidence of the universal oppression of women by male dominated social structures. Whereas the wider UK social, cultural and political context tends to draw on ideas about barbarity, as well as rational and irrational belief systems, in order for practitioners to engage in ethical dialogue with service users, it is important to reflect on the complexity of the meanings we hold in the West, as well as what these practices might mean to the people who come to our services.

Although there is no single cultural explanation for FGM, and the origins of it are unknown, several studies analyse the symbolic meanings related to gendered and social relations, social roles, familiar relations, constructions of female identity, conceptions of the human being, aesthetics of the body, and spiritual beliefs. Such meanings are often misunderstood as they reflect different orientations to bodies, 'the self' and social relations than those taken for granted in the West/Minority World[7]. At the same time these understandings provide some insight into the persistence of these practices, and why women, rather than men, are often strong supporters of it, as well as some of the complex, multi-layered relationships people from FGM-practicing communities may have with the practice. They also suggest that although there are some meanings shaped by patriarchy not all meanings (at all times, in all places) relate to the idea that women are inferior to men. Despite the focus in the anti-FGM literature on harm, experiences are by no means universal and uniform. Isha Abulkadir's chapter 'Somali Memories of Female Genital Mutilation' (Abdulkadir, 2011) describes how some women she interviewed could remember 'excruciating pain', and violence, while other women remembered the procedure itself being painless and being cared for by senior female figures. In other literature, there are accounts of girls and young women fleeing in order to escape having the procedure done, while other accounts by women describe how they threatened to run away if their parents, who did not agree with the practice, did not allow them to have it done (Njambi, 2004).

With respect to historical context in Europe and America, forms of FGM were carried out in the past as interventions for issues such as nymphomania ('uncontrollable sexual desire') in women was thought to be linked to the cerebellum, ovaries, uterus, and/or clitoris, insanity, epilepsy, masturbation, lesbianism and hysteria (Toubia, 1993). In the United States until 1905 the labia were sewed together (i.e. infibulated) to prevent masturbation, and until 1935 clitoridectomy was used in mental hospitals to treat epilepsy, catalepsy, melancholy and even kleptomania (Sheehan, 1981). In addition, Sigmund Freud himself, stated that 'masturbation, at all events of the clitoris, is a masculine activity, and the elimination of clitoral sexuality is a necessary precondition for the development of femininity' (Freud, 1925, p. 255).

Taiwo Afuape: My multiple perspectives in relation to my personal context

How I am positioning myself in this paper is complex: I am a British-born Nigerian woman. In Britain I am 'other' (that is, I am non-Western), and yet I am 'other' in the context of my cultural heritage (that is, I am also to a large extent 'Western'). As a woman and a mother, I am deeply disturbed by the various forms of violence perpetuated against, and global exploitation of, women and children (sexual abuse, rape, trafficking and poverty), as well as the ways in which powerful systems and institutions have been shown to engage in, be complicit in, and/or cover up such abuses. I am uncircumcised and strongly believe that girls should not be circumcised because they cannot consent to this practice, although I do not hold such strong beliefs about male circumcision. The issue of FGM performed on girls is particularly poignant for me as, at the time of writing this, I have a baby daughter and would hate for her to undergo any form of 'cutting', and have even opted not to have her ears pierced until she is old enough to choose this for herself. At the same time I know adult women who have gone through FGM when they were young, who do not regard themselves as harmed or abused and would be confused and perhaps offended if I suggested they were. I know of women who have gone through FGM but would not have this procedure performed on their own children; not because they view FGM as abusive but because the meaning has changed for them over time, and in another context. I am uncomfortable with the idea inherent within the UK legislation that adult women from FGM-practicing communities should not be considered able to make their own decisions about their bodies. Under the UK legislation (Female Circumcision Act, 1985; Female Genital Mutilation Act, 2003), women from FGM practicing communities are considered equal to legal minors and therefore unfit for self-government. As a feminist my ideas about women's liberation and what is liberating for women and their bodies have become more and more complex and less certain over time, and as I engage in dialogue with a diverse array of women. It has become clearer to me that ideas I once had are not as straightforward as I originally thought. For example, is it oppressive or liberatory to expose our bodies as much as we want? (or neither, or both?) Is it oppressive or liberatory to cover our bodies up? (or neither, or both?) Are women who sell their bodies exploited and abused by patriarchy or exploited and abused by the lack of recognition (and protection) of their 'work'? (or neither, or both?) Are transgendered women oppressed by Western society's binary definitions of gender, or by the oppressive nature of the disconnect between their gender certainty and the biology they were born with? (or neither, or both?)

Although I am critical of sexist, restrictive and harmful views about the female body and sexuality that often shape the context for 'cosmetic surgeries', I also believe that adult women have a right to do what they want with their bodies, despite my awareness that 'choice' and 'rights' are not uncomplicated, timeless or universal concepts. My preference would be to critique FGM in light of cosmetic surgery or surgery on intersexed children performed in the West, rather than condemn it in such a way as to revive colonial ideas about civilised and uncivilised cultural practices. We have become so accustomed to, at times rather voyeuristically[8], Western cultural body practices that are violent, intrusive, and based on idealised notions of beauty, that we are in danger of focusing our horrified gaze elsewhere, at those we position as culturally inferior.

As a person of Nigerian heritage I am sensitive to the ways in which African and Islamic societies are widely regarded as backward, superstitious and primitive, where women are oppressed and unspeakable things are done to their bodies, whereas the Minority World is viewed as liberated, free and a progressive place and culture. In this neo-colonialist context, African brutality is often highlighted while Western brutality is obscured (such as in the case of the mainstream media coverage of the people of Congo—see Afuape, 2006). This 'backwardness' is often portrayed as the reason for Africa's political and economic position in the world; therefore the only way to liberate it is to civilise it. At the same time, the discourses surrounding FGM in non-practising countries, that largely regard these practices as an oppressive and regressive relic, should also be understood in light of the historical context of FGM practice in the West, as described above, as well as the present context of global exploitation and harm of women and children. Although, as an African person, I am more aware of how spiritually and socially evolved much of the culture is, than most non-Africans, I do not want to overly romanticise the continent and its people. I believe that progression (as defined by African people themselves) is just as important, and inevitable, in the vast and varied continent of Africa, as tradition. For me, understanding FGM practices is complicated further, with respect to, the complexity of our personal, cultural and historical context; living in a society that often uses language to obscure violence;

as well as the diversity and heterogeneity of these practices and the different responses women have to them.

My own views about FGM have changed over time, and in dialogue with others. In the past I assumed that African women who support the practice of FGM are in Njambi's words: 'not only victims of their own ignorance, but are themselves 'prisoners of ritual'' (Njambi, 2004, pp. 28–56). In hindsight, it makes little sense to view African women as upholding such practices because they lack 'education' and 'empowerment' when in the Minority World women, who view themselves to be empowered, increasingly undergo painful and health-hazardous cosmetic surgery, such as hymen repair, vaginal tightening, clitoral hood removal (clitorodomy), lifting and reduction of the labia and breast implants, in spite of their level of education (La Barbera, 2009).

How I feel about the terms and words used to describe such practices, are shaped by my concern about the ways in which violence can be obscured by the language we use, and my belief in the importance of descriptive, accurate language in order to ensure social justice and positive social responses to harm through violence. This is particularly important because perpetrators of violence often use language to obscure their responsibility for it, to blame those who are harmed and conceal their forms of resistance to harm (Coates & Wade, 2004). Professional language too may be used in ways that obscure the events in question; for example referring to violence in a domestic setting as 'a domestic' or referring to rape as 'sexual assault' or a 'sex attack'. At the same time, the anti-FGM movement, in an attempt to challenge violence, often uses sensationalist language which might in itself be regarded as harmful, by depicting 'others' as uncivilised and describing in graphic detail, practices that have not been substantiated as true. For example, the American Medical Association (AMA) claims that 'the instruments most commonly used to perform FGM are razor blades, kitchen knives, scissors, glass, and in some regions, *the teeth of the midwife*' (AMA, 1995, p. 1714, emphasis added), while, as Njambi (2004) argues, 'not a single group is identified which employs such crude instruments' and yet, 'such statements are presented as a matter of "fact"' (Njambi, 2004, p. 284). As a Nigerian feminist I agree with Sudanese surgeon and women's health rights/feminist activist Nahib Toubia when she states that, while it is important to challenge abusive practices against women and girls, inaccurate, sensationalist and offensive language understandably generates resistance and counter-challenge from those who feel objectified, not by FGM, but by anti-FGM discourse. This 'only makes real change more difficult to achieve' (Toubia, 1993, p. 35).

Perhaps 'change' is a more complex task than the anti-FGM discourse implies. In the context of our legislative responsibilities and personal ethics, we might also need to understand FGM in ways that respects that other contexts, worldviews and embodiments generate unique dilemmas and challenges for those affected by it.

I am reminded of this when I think about the ways in which FGM practices might for some people in Africa, come to symbolise cultural identity, freedom and resistance against colonialism (Presley, 1988), particularly given the historical link with local movements against colonial power which banned FGM. This is clearly represented by the Kenyan story of *Ngaitana* (meaning 'I will circumcise myself'), which made up part of the Mau Mau revolt. In 1956, the male-formed Meru town local council—under colonial administration—voted unanimously to ban clitoridectomy. In response to this, groups of teenage girls calling themselves *Ngaitana* circumcised themselves, without ceremonies (Morinis, 1985). For *Ngaitana* girls FGM was a way to rebel against the oppression of Kenyan men attempting to control female bodies, *and* colonial power attempting to control Kenyan culture (La Barbera, 2009). My inability to comprehend this form of rebellion does not automatically make it invalid; it does however, remind me of the need to be careful not to consider feminist politics as universal, without listening to the voices of women in other contexts to mine. The anti-FGM movement subsumes diverse and heterogeneous practices under one umbrella, and yet this umbrella does not include the genital mutilations performed on non-consenting 'intersex' children, for reasons related to ideas about gender, sexuality, sex and aesthetics.

It seems to me that both sides of the debate are in danger of assuming that all experiences and all women are the same or that all voices are equal or chime together. Within any culture there are different experiences mediated by our many different identities and positions based on gender, ethnicity, class/caste/status, age, religious/spiritual beliefs, sexuality and so on. It would be equally oppressive to ignore the African women and feminists in the continent working to outlaw the practices and/or suggest that they are brainwashed by Western ideology. Nor does it make sense to say that all those 'outside' a culture should not interfere in that culture or have an opinion about it, as this might encourage indifference to the plight of others and a reluctance to engage with issues outside our own cultural domain. It also seems to me that both sides of the debate assume homogeneity in the opposing camp. Not all those who oppose FGM hold the same views and oppose the practices in the same way and not all those who oppose the anti-FGM movement do so from the same stand point. It may even be possible to have some sympathies with both sides of the debate.

It is important to acknowledge that not all women regard their experience of FGM as harmful; however many women do and therefore want to challenge the aspects of their culture that uphold it. Most importantly, the responses and relationships women from FGM-practising communities have to FGM, may be much more complex and subtle than we realise. We may assume the most traumatic aspect of a given woman's experience is being what we regard as physically brutalised, whereas that woman may also have very painful and difficult feelings about the contradictions, relational dilemmas and negative social positions which come with being from an FGM-practising community within the context of Western condemnation. As an African feminist and CAMHS clinician I believe we cannot provide services that engage helpfully with diversity and complexity without moving beyond the limits of our worldviews and engaging in dialogues that enable us to meet people in their unique experience, based on *their* social, cultural and political world. Only then can we engage with the diverse views and positions of power/disempowerment that may exist within the communities we serve and the diverse views and positions of power/disempowerment that exists within a family system.

Britt Krause: My reflections about myself in relation to FGM

As I was growing up FGM never entered my thinking or experiences. Being born in Denmark, a country with a strong tradition of democracy and women's rights in laws of inheritance, the labour market and sexual politics, I grew up expecting to be able to decide for myself who I would marry or have sexual relations with and what I would do with my life. However, growing up was not free of problems and worry. I remember the agonising, anxiety-provoking processes around menstruation and early sexual experiences, about body shape and development in PE and about being popular with boys and girls. I remember feeling that I ought to wear a bra and have sexual intercourse. I was a shy, although quite tough girl and I remember struggling with these issues largely on my own. I did not feel that members of my family or kin group in any way were involved in helping me with these worries and thinking back perhaps I would have wished that they could have been, that they could have been more of a collective reference point for me. Perhaps this is why I became first a social anthropologist studying kinship and family relationships in different cultures and later a family therapist.

Looking back I might say that I would have liked a more collective body of relationships in my life. Perhaps this is why I cherished rituals. I was baptised after birth in Church (*Den Danske Folkekirke*) when I received my name and as far as it goes that aspect of my identity. I was also confirmed, reciting the Cate-chism[9] wearing a white dress and receiving presents, many of these gold and silver jewellery from my family and acquaintances. I was brought up a Protestant, and although I have since stepped out of the Church, the Church has had a profound influence on me as it has on most Danes both in the past and currently. The Church in Denmark is closely associated with the State, but this does not mean that Denmark is a religious state. Rather the Church (*Den Danske Folkekirke*— 'The Danish Folkchurch') constitutes a kind of symbol of being Danish; it refers to the notion of folk (*'folk'*) as a revered albeit profane collective. This aspect of being Danish, which is expressed in the language, in the rituals we carry out over the year, in the food and in style, I cherish. Later when I trained as a social anthropologist and carried out fieldwork I found that being sensitive to and taking seriously ritual processes also resonated with many peoples across the world.

My personal experiences described above may seem a world away from the situation in reference to understanding the practices of FGM. However, I think rituals of transition, the marking of life stages, which is one aspect of FGM, reso-nates with me as a process through which individual persons, in this case women, make sense of the bodily transformations and expectations of sex and sexuality, taking place during puberty and adolescence. These are embodied experiences, although I do not want to downplay the difference between the rituals I underwent and those which involve inflicting pain. Nevertheless, a collective recognition of pain, transformation and of belonging may ease and make sense of individual suffering (Morinis, 1985).

To me then my first association to FGM may be seen to be that of a typical social anthropologist, namely one of noticing and even valuing the collective belonging which FGM in many instances symbolises. This resonates with me personally both in terms of my own wishes and desires and in terms of my social identity. However, I am also aware that this contrasts with the emphasis on choice and autonomy celebrated as an absolute right of individuals in many Western societies. The FGM debate articulates this dichotomy, so that those who condone, promote and carry out a practice apparently so 'foreign' to dominant views on gender, bodies and sexual relationships must be mistaken and slaves to their 'culture', whereas for us in our knowing better and being more rational, we mostly do not consider the role culture plays in our own world-views. This tends to depict 'others' and in particular, women touched and involved with FGM, as 'traditional, culture-bound, uneducated and ... coerced into mutilation' (Ahmadu & Shweder, 2009, p. 17) regardless of what goes on, on the ground and how women themselves understand and experience FGM. As a Danish woman I know that not all Danish women are like me or share my experiences or points of view, so how can I assume that women from different backgrounds and different social contexts with different experiences are any less diverse?

One of the problems, which continues to emerge and re-emerge in the FGM debate I think, derives from a kind of essentialist thinking. I do not think that there is a universal category designated 'women' other than in a biological and somewhat simplistic sense. As a social anthropologist I am often taken aback by equally simplistic approaches to 'culture'. The term and the idea 'culture' is complex and even those who know that 'culture' may refer to many intersecting layers of social relationships forget this. In particular there is often in the literature about FGM a reference to the role of patriarchy in the oppression of women (Bradley, 2011). Patriarchy means that men hold power. In different societies this idea intersects with other political and economic structures to different degrees, but there are very few societies in the world where patriarchy does not play a role. For example, even in Denmark, women struggle to be considered equal with men in many spheres of life. I think that much writing and thinking about FGM conflate patriarchy with patriliny. Patriarchy is not the same as patriliny. Patriliny refers to the principle of tracing significant relationships through men. In societies in which relationships are based on a principle of patriliny this principle also intersects with many other ideas such as the formation of groups, references for identity and selfhood, marriage patterns, etc. Societies in which FGM is practiced also tend to be patrilineal and although it is true that this may mean that men dominate women in many spheres of life, this also intersects with fundamental ideas of relatedness in these societies. In other words, women who accept and promote FGM themselves are not necessarily just accepting the pain, they may also be safeguarding particular ideas and processes of how they and their children relate to others. Such ideas and processes may be oppressive to men as well as to women. I think that the way men may be oppressed themselves by certain traditional practices and expectations have escaped from view in most of the FGM debate.

I am worried that the seemingly reasonable and ethical message of the anti-FGM campaigns to free women from painful bodily mutilation, poor health and problematic sex, obscures other less overt messages, which are symbolically violent and also likely to perpetuate cruelty. For example, questions have been raised about why modify the body at all? Why not accept the body as it is in its natural state, sometimes exemplified by the bodies of Western women. This suggests that there is such a thing as a 'natural body' and turns a blind eye to all the different ways Western women modify and beautify their bodies. I myself and women who might be ethnically more or less like me, shave their body hair, straighten and whiten their teeth, have piercings, tattoos, breast implants, Botox treatment, nose jobs, facelifts, tummy tucks and various other modes of body modification for cosmetic reasons or reasons of sexual enjoyment. Can we condone these other violent practices while being critical of FGM? On what grounds?

One aspect stands out, namely the idea of choice. I agree with TA that I would not choose for my two daughters or my son to have these kinds of procedures done to them and I know in an absolute way I am not able to understand parents who do this. On the other hand, I also know that my understanding derives from my own experiences and outlooks situated in a certain cultural, historical and social context as I have sketched above. I know that pain and hurt can take many forms and that there are no societies or cultures in the world (including Western ones) in which individual persons do not suffer at collective hands. I value choice for myself and for everybody else, but I also know that choice itself is contingent on context, experience and social relationships (Henriques et al, 1984). Paradoxically, the FGM campaign may contribute to minority women from societies in which FGM is practiced and who themselves perhaps have undergone the procedure, feeling under pressure to restructure their identities to pacify competing ideologies. Choosing not to have their daughters undergo the procedure while complying with the law, may alienate men and women from their own communities, while choosing to follow tradition means that they will be looked upon with disdain by the majority and punished. Perhaps this is why so many immigrant women feel that in many ways life in the West is even more isolating for them than their lives back home and that despite the emphasis on choice and individuality around them, they cannot talk openly about the things they would like to change in their lives. This does not seem much like being able to exercise choice.

I think that as both a social anthropologist and as a family therapist I must be concerned about the individual women and clients I meet and how to help them think about solutions under these very difficult circumstances. In order to do so I think that I have a duty to acknowledge that FGM does not *only* involve violence and to understand the circumstances and worries which women themselves experience when faced with the dilemmas which FGM poses for them. I think that essentialist thinking is not helpful, because we are then likely to turn a blind eye to the specific circumstances of particular women and their families. Only through aiming to access the details of every situation can I begin to understand the scope and limits of individual agency and choice and how I might be able to contribute to women from different backgrounds deciding for themselves. I think that to frame the debate and the issues which I face as a woman working in mental health services in the UK with women and families who have been touched by FGM, in terms of feminism versus multi-culturalism is simplistic and misguided. Both sides are right; both sides are wrong. Through this maze it is my job to find connections which can articulate and address the needs and worries of particular women, men and families in particular contexts.

FGM and CAMHS—'opposites' in 'ethical dialogue'

The recently evolved campaign to eradicate FGM practices has formed into a powerful discourse with powerful figures. The law is clear, as are our responsibilities in safe guarding; what is less clear is *how* we go about enforcing it and the intersections between culture, power, ethics and child protection, inherent in the *how*. This is because, the focus of the dominant discourse on FGM is on eradicating the practices, which relegates all other concerns—such as those that relate to making meaning—as secondary. What is missing from the official discourse are the voices of women who argue that in our attempt to protect them, we might do harm, by taking an expert 'educator' position in relation to families from cultural contexts different from our own. So the question arises: how can we be *reflexive*, *responsive* and *respectful* while being *protective*?

Taiwo and Britt in dialogue

We started our dialogue by asking each other to share aspects of our personal and professional contexts that make sense of where we were both coming from, as described above. This enabled us to be honest about our complex positioning, challenge the assumption that feminists are White and Western and multi-culturalists are Black and male, and enabled us to reflect on the complexity of power and oppression.

BRITT: I'm also aware that the FGM agenda and the incredible attention it's had is also a way of avoiding something; putting on to it the 'gender agenda' and hiding the 'race agenda'. So when they say 'well, how barbaric! How bad!' are they really talking about gender here? Are they really thinking about what is done in *our* society to women?

TAIWO: [also] when you're a very political person, from that point of view you're supposed to have a very clear idea about the stand you're taking and that says something about the commitment you have; but in doing that maybe we are creating another orthodoxy in shutting out other ideas and maybe we might be hiding another kind of oppression.

Our dialogue highlighted the importance of reflecting on the contexts of our ideas no matter how inherently ethical they seem to be, in order to create a clinical space that allows for service users to reflect on their own complex positions. For example, women may experience tensions between being valued for having undergone FGM in one community but devalued by the same experience in another.

BRITT: ... ideas have contexts; but contexts do not stand by themselves, they always stand in relation to persons and relationships. But the other bit is that all that complexity is *inside* persons.

In another part of our dialogue we reflected on the role CAMHS practitioners might have in supporting families affected by FGM with respect to the impact of multiple contexts and relationships, and the importance of practitioners reflecting on their taken for granted assumptions about the link between the individual and community.

TAIWO: But in the context of CAMHS, even though we try to work with the idea that parents are trying to do the best for their children, we are also responsible for protecting children, because we often know and often see that sometimes, even within trying to do their best, and within the choices that people have, parents *are* harming their children.

BRITT: So in CAMHS, the challenge for us, is how to work with a carer in such a way that areas of possibility open up?

TAIWO: ..... if you're from a culture that sees the individual as part of the collective, it's very hard to see your needs and your bodily integrity as separate from the needs of your family and culture; so if you are having an experience that is different from the collective view, it is very hard to challenge that.

BRITT: ... but I think individual and collective is not a dichotomy ... there's nowhere in the world where there isn't also personal choice; that's what the collective is, it's a mass of heterogeneous stuff that kind of starts to have some pattern to it.

TAIWO: But because there is personal choice that means that there isn't one voice within the African context ... and there isn't one culture within those cultures, there are differences in terms of gender, age, sexuality, status.

Our dialogue allowed for possibilities to emerge in our understanding that might not have done so otherwise, or might not have seemed immediately obvious or relevant from the start. For example, we started our dialogue reflecting on the obvious themes of violence and choice and finished by reflecting on the less obvious theme of loss.

BRITT: … another level to that is to acknowledge that because of the law that makes it illegal it is a loss for some people … the fact that this is something that maybe they're expected to do, that this is something that has meaning in terms of including their girls in the extended family… it is a loss. We may need to acknowledge that it is a loss, not that it is a triumph for progress as it were…

TAIWO: … and loss might result from having it done too.… One of the problems with the discourses around FGM … is that they shut down dialogue … about the complexity of how people are left feeling and thinking. Even though we have to say 'this can't happen', what is left? How can we engage with what is left for women, girls and families? What do we do next? What do women, girls and families want help with?

Final reflections

Issues related to FGM are often identified during a woman's pregnancy or during the summer break if school girls of a certain age are travelling back 'home' to FGM-practising countries on holiday. Increasingly CAMHS practitioners are working in schools, GP surgeries, children's centres and with medical profes-sionals working with family health such as midwives, health visitors, paediatri-cians and obstetricians. Given that communication between medical professionals and women who have experienced FGM is often poor (Bradley, 2011) with the women feeling looked down on and stereotyped, there is a role for CAMHS prac-titioners offering consultation to medical staff to encourage them to reflect on their attitudes and assumptions in order for them to better understand the needs of families. In addition, CAMHS professionals need to reflect not just on the impact of the practices, but of the impact of prejudice, discrimination and invalidation on women and girls relationships and well-being. Much of the text created in the UK about FGM relate to the need to educate professionals and communities by pro-viding access to 'facts' and clarifying statutory responsibilities. Less of it reflects on meaning and context with respect to the services we currently provide and the services we are yet to provide to support families affected by FGM. Rather than reinforcing the notion that we just need more information (for example, reading, attending information days, training, conferences and reading case examples) we wanted this chapter to reflect on the uniqueness of each individual's, and/or each family's experience as well as on the work we, as professionals, need to do, in order to enter into dialogue with families who can explore with us *themselves* what positions, services and ways of talking are most helpful.

In this chapter we have explored the complexity of how our various identities linked to a variety of community connections create the context for our responses to FGM. It is important as CAMHS clinicians to explore meanings, but not just stay with the meanings for persons in 'other' societies, but spend a considerable amount of time reflecting on our own meanings and the contexts in which they emerge. These contexts inevitably involve aspects of our experience we would like to challenge and weaken (such as sexist, racist, imperialist and other types of oppressive discourses) as well as values we would like to uphold (such as a commitment to securing the safety and well-being of all people and in particular, children). In doing so we might create the context for engaging in dialogues with families about the fluid, contextual and complex nature of the aspects of their culture *they* want to challenge and to uphold, as well as the different positions, experiences and connections to power, each family member holds. This is what we mean by ethical dialogue, keeping in mind not just the physical body, but the whole person, including all aspects of the complex contexts in which we all exist. It is necessary therefore to move beyond contentious debates, where each side defensively reinforces the rightness of their position, towards ethical dialogue.

Notes

1 Racialisation refers to the practice of using 'race' as a justification for any purpose.
2 National Service Framework for Children, Young People and Maternity Services: http://www.dh.gov.uk/PolicyAndGuidance/HealthAndSocialCareTopics/Children-Services/ChildrenServicesInformation/fs/en.
3 http://www.opsi.gov.uk/acts/acts2004/20040031.htm.
4 For example, under the Children Act 1989 Local Authorities can apply to the Courts for various Orders to prevent a child being taken abroad for FGM.
5 http://www.unhchr.ch/html/menu3/b/k2crc.htm.
6 http://www.un.org/womenwatch/daw/cedaw/text/econvention.htm.
7 Minority World culture is European culture since Europeans and the cultures they have created represent a minority in global terms, and those of Latin America, the Far East, the Middle East, Africa and Asia as Majority World cultures, since they make up the majority of the world.
8 Such as '20 years younger', 'botched.'
9 Cathechism refers to a written summary—a question and answer designed instruction in Christian core beliefs.

References

Abulkadir, I. (2011). Somali memories of female genital mutilation. In: T. Bradley (ed.), *Women, Violence and Tradition: Taking FGM and Other Practices to a Secular State*. (pp. 51–72). London, England: Zed Books.
Afuape, T. (2006). Subjugating nature and 'The Other': Deconstructing dominant themes in Minority world culture and their implications for Western psychology. *Journal of Critical Psychology. Counselling and Psychotherapy*, 6(4), 238–55.
Ahmadu, F. S. & Shweder, R. A. (2009). Disputing the myth of the sexual dysfunction of circumcised women, *Anthropology Today*, 25(6), 14–7.
American Medical Association (1995). Female genital mutilation. *Journal of the American Medical Association*, 274(21), 1714–16.

Bradley, T. (2011) (ed.). *Women. Violence and Tradition: Taking FGM and Other Practices to a Secular State*, London, England: Zed Books.

Coates, L. & Wade, A. (2004). Telling it like it isn't: Obscuring perpetrator responsibility for violent crime. *Discourse and Society,* 15(5), 499–526.

Davis, K. (2004). Responses to W. Njambi's 'Dualisms and female bodies in representations of African female circumcision: A feminist critique'. Between moral outrage and cultural relativism. *Feminist Theory,* 5(3), 305–23.

Freud, S. (1925). Some psychical consequences of the anatomical distinction between the sexes. In: S Freud, *The Standard Edition of the Collected Work of Sigmund Freud,* vol. XIX (pp. 2415–8). London, England: Hogarth Press.

Henriques, J., Hollway, W., Urwin, C., Venn, C. & Walkerdine, V. (1984). *Changing the Subject. Psychology, Social Regulation and Subjectivity.* London, England: Methuen/ Routledge.

La Barbera, M.C. (2009). Revisiting the anti-female genital mutilation discourse. Palermo, Italy: *Diritto & Questioni Pubbliche,* 9, 485–507.

Mabilia, M. (2013). FGM or FGMo? Cross-cultural dialogue in an Italian minefield. *Anthropology Today,* 29(3), 17–21.

Morinis, A. (1985). The ritual experience: Pain and the transformation of consciousness in ordeals of initiation. *Ethos,* 13(2), 150–74.

Njambi, W. N. (2004). Dualisms and female bodies in representations of African female circumcision: A feminist critique. *Feminist Theory,* 5(3), 281–303.

Parliament of the United Kingdom (2003). *Female Genital Mutilation Act.* Charter 31. Legislation.gov.uk.

Parliament of the United Kingdom (1985). *Female Circumcision Act.* Legislation.gov.uk

Presley, C. A. (1988). The Mau Mau rebellion, Kikuyu women, and social change. *Canadian Journal of African Studies/Revue Canadienne des Études Africaines,* 22(3), 502–27.

Sheehan, E. (1981). Victorian clitoridectomy: Isaac Baker Brown and his harmless operative procedure. *Medical Anthropology Newsletter,* 12(4), 9–15.

Talle, A. (1993). Transforming women into 'pure' agnates: Aspects of female infibulation in Somalia. In: V. Broch-Due, I. Rudie & T. Bleie (eds.), *Carved Flesh, Cast Selves. Gendered Symbols and Social Practices.* (pp. 83–106). Oxford, England: Berg.

Toubia, N. (1993). *Female Genital Mutilation: A Call for Global Action.* New York, NY: Women, Ink.

World Health Association (2008). *Eliminating Female Genital Mutilation: An Interagency Statement by UNAIDS, UNDP, UNECA, UNESCO, UNGPA, UNHCHR, UNHCR, UNICEF, UNIFEM, WHO.* Available online at http://www.un.org/womenwatch/daw/ csw/csw52/ statementss_missions/ Interagency_Statement on_Eliminating FGM.pdf (accessed 23 January 2013).

Chapter 13

Working together

Unearthing community connections in parental mental health

Jasmine T. Chin with contributions from 'D'

Introduction

This chapter focuses on therapeutic work with parents, informed by narrative and systemic theory, in the context of a Child and Adolescent Mental Health Service (CAMHS). I am a Black British woman, trained as a clinical psychologist and working as a parental mental health professional in a CAMHS. I aim to help parents reflect on the reciprocal relationships between their well-being, the well-being of their children and the well-being of their family as a whole, so as to enable them to make preferred choices about how to live. In this chapter 'D'[1], who is of an Irish British working-class background and who I worked with, has generously shared her thoughts about the impact of this work on her and her family. Traditionally, psychological therapy with adults comes under the domain of 'adult mental health' and so I will outline the political context of adult mental health work in the British National Health Service (NHS) as I see it, and describe some effects of this on the therapeutic space. I will describe my attempts at working with parents in CAMHS in ways that take account of these wider issues as well as the parents' own specific community connections. In addition, I illustrate the ways I, together with parents, attempt to draw resources from, *and* make separate spaces from, these community connections as appropriate. I hope to invite the reader to consider different ways that they might attend to community in their own work. The chapter begins with some considerations about our local community and how it can be a potentially influential context. I then move on to describe the wider social contexts to addressing parents' emotional well-being as well as my specific contexts. I end with examples of ways I have tried to keep community in mind, using some principles from systemic therapy to support me.

Our local context

The population in our services' locality is dense and diverse and typical of an inner-city. Within the space of a day I might see parents who come from widely different economic backgrounds, whose families originate from the UK or from other countries around the world, for whom life in the city may be settled or transient, and who for one reason or another have chosen or found themselves raising their children within a relatively small radius. In this context, developing a sense of connection to other people allays the feelings of loneliness and isolation that can plague us all and which often can become a foundation to psychological distress. As such, the notion of 'community' can be thought of as a constructed phenomenon which parents have to develop for themselves; finding others who they can share their values and principles with, who can support them and who can validate the history of their lives beyond their immediate and current experiences. In an urban environment, the varying community contexts in which parents participate provide multiple and rich possibilities for developing new relationships and, consequently, accessing new and different resources. This is no less true for me than for my clients. When thinking with another colleague who, like me, is also a parent, about the various networks and communities from which we drew strength, we generated a long list including our children and their schools and nurseries, our work contexts, our education experiences, our shopping places, ethnic heritage, cultural heritage, social media and family. We thought together about how some community contexts felt more influential than others and how we intentionally seek out opportunities to connect with the values represented by some, while distancing ourselves from those that seem less helpful. Parents seeking support from CAMHS also bring with them membership of many contexts and communities. One way of understanding their lives is to think with them about their problems and hopes in relation to their different positions in these collectives; exploring with them which communities speak to them best about their preferred ways of living and which speak the least. With support, parents can be helped to shift their relationships to others in the community so as to live in ways, which are more attuned to their particular values and aims. Well-being and sound mental health are undoubtedly influenced by the general quality of one's life and, more specifically, the quality of the relationships one has with friends, family and wider members of the differing communities one belongs to. I therefore believe that exploring these with parents is central to working with them to create optimal well-being for themselves and their families.

Providing a service to parents in CAMHS

There is compelling evidence about the prevalence of distress in the parents of children who attend CAMHS (Mordoch & Hall, 2002; Aldridge & Becker, 2003; Göpfert, Webster & Seeman, 2004; Tunnard, 2004; Mordoch, 2010). Many parents fall between the borderlands of different specialities, presenting as beyond the parenting remit of CAMHS, but finding themselves either "not complex enough" for specialist adult mental health teams or not presenting with a "specific treatable condition" for generic, adult psychology services. In the meantime the need of the child to have a mother, father or carer who can provide good-enough parenting never stops but may go unmet, if parental needs go unmet. Our Parental Mental Health Service was developed to address this; initially in a generic and paediatric

CAMHS, extending to children's centres and adult psychology services, and more recently encompassing a neurodevelopmental team as well as a local non-statutory provider. In each service context we have aimed to provide an in-house adult psychology (or referred to as adult mental health) service to parents who report distress and dissatisfaction that interrupts their ability to move forward in their life and parent their child (or children) in their preferred way. D provided some thoughts about this. D lived alone with her teenage children and over the time that I met with her obtained a first-class degree while working part-time. Her children were referred to CAMHS for support, before D sought individual support for herself. D describes the value of what she calls "family-based therapy" and why this was so beneficial to her:

> "I had sought out help before at my doctor's surgery on a particularly bad morning when I was so badly suicidal that I knew if I went back home I would end my life and I felt that the resulting prescription of an antidepressant wouldn't really sort me out, just cover the issue up as it seemed to do with my mother's anxiety and depression; and the way the doctor seemed to be 'listening' without sympathy or empathy really didn't do it for me. I wanted responsibility of the management of my mental health issue. To gain back some control wherever I could. I felt ashamed that as a parent I couldn't cope with my life. Also the fact that the therapy (in this service) was family centric, dealing with the family rather than the individual made me consider how my progress slotted in with my children and how it affected them. ... It seemed that becoming a parent meant I had to face my own demons about how my parents brought me up. No running away from it. Did I want to repeat history or change it? I found myself repeating things which I couldn't tolerate in my parents which made me feel bad about myself. Family-based therapy helped me to realise that I didn't have to be anything like them and helped feed back to me what my own children thought of me. How I fitted in to the equation. I don't think I would have got this feedback had I undergone individual therapy."

Although our sessions occurred alongside traditional 'family work' where D and her children met with a therapist, the work D describes above as "family-based therapy" was indeed individual work; a strong endorsement perhaps that the family did not have to be in the room at all times to be kept in mind by both of us.

Welcoming 'difference'

As I suspect is the case with other practitioners, I have been drawn to work in ways which fit most with my personal outlook, professional orientation and values. Whenever I encounter a family, a number of theories and stories about their experiences come to mind. This process is unlikely to be random but deeply connected to my own membership to a wealth of contexts: British-born, descended from an African-Caribbean migrant community, fluid social class membership, mother of sons, educated, able-bodied, leftist political leanings and so on. As such the meanings I give to every utterance and movement in the therapy room will be influenced by the beliefs and values generated from my life experience. An important aspect of my work with this service has been to acknowledge that the same is true for the people I see: the different communities to which parents belong are likely to have imbued their experiences with a wealth of different meanings.

Practising within this array of 'difference' and diversity has the potential to be overwhelming, and one way of managing this might be to try to metaphorically 'leave it outside of the therapy room' and adopt a position of presumed neutrality (Selvini Palazzoli et al, 1980). Neutrality[2], as I use the term here, refers to an assumption that all perspectives are equal and that as a therapist I am seeking to make sense of each member of the system's view, as if on a level playing field – for example not differentiating in any way the views held by a man and a woman. If I were to take a stance of neutrality in my work I might be seeking to minimise the artefact of 'difference' as less relevant and amplify other aspects of experience, perhaps drawing more on the universality of human suffering. However, this would not account for the different effects of my clients' social contexts on their world-view, and on their lives, which I see as one of my responsibilities in the therapy room. Instead my preference has been to choose methods, which explicitly acknowledge context using it as a resource from which parents and I can draw. Remembering that 'difference' is socially constructed can help to manage the challenges that this can also bring. For example, I recall speaking to a woman who described her identity as British Asian, about her friendship group which was predominantly White British and asking questions about belonging, fit and connection amongst her peers. For this woman her British identity rather than her cultural heritage was the most relevant point of connection. My curiosity arose from my own personal experiences of heritage differences at times being an important organising principle for friendship. However, it might at times feel risky to bring up such issues and in my experience, my stance of curiosity and attempt to be tentative and responsive helps with such risk-taking.

Ethics as a foundation to practice

A fundamental influence on my work has been to keep an ethical approach at the fore. Following the Oxford Dictionary definition, 'ethics' refers to the moral principles that govern behaviour or conduct and from a philosophical position leads to the greater benefit of all beings. Part of ethical practice is therefore seeking to hold a just disposition to benefit the other and wider society, which by implication includes myself. This involves me aspiring to be with people in a way that does not perpetuate the social inequalities and oppressive ways of thinking, which I view as inherent in our society. I hold the view that people in a help-seeking position are likely to be much more susceptible to the negative effects of these ways of thinking and can go some way to shaping aspects of their identity (I will say more later about the construction of identity and how it can be influenced by wider cultural and specifically oppressive stories). Unpleasant or difficult emotional experiences which people find overwhelming are not a desired cultural experience in our society and are frequently constructed as something that only happens to an unlucky minority, rather than to the masses. So I aspire to work respectfully with parents and honour the expertise and knowledge they have about their own lives; that is to say that I aim to work alongside them *collaboratively*. But of course there are significant challenges to this and aspirations are not always obtainable in every moment of contact and some of which will be palpably obvious while some remain hidden despite my best efforts. For example, while I may intend to work alongside a parent, taking their perspective as the meaningful focus of therapy, I am also required to work in the best interests of the wider service such as simultaneously requesting the completion of 'mood ratings' which may construct their difficulties differently. Maintaining ethical practice therefore requires a firm commitment to self-reflection: becoming aware of what I think I know and naming it explicitly; recognising that there are many things that I do not know; learning to be comfortable with this uncertainty and ignorance, and having the confidence to ask questions to find out more. In particular, self-reflexivity refers to practitioners intentionally acknowledging the many influences on their practice; be it the theories they hold, their political leanings, their prejudices or their other biases. In my practice, this has taken different forms. For example, when considering sharing ideas from a theory which I know could have a blaming effect on a parent, I might name the theory, ask if they would be interested in hearing what this approach has to say about their difficulties and evaluate with them the effect and usefulness of this particular idea. Another form this has taken has been to ask parents for feedback about how I am working with them and being genuinely prepared to accept the feedback and make adjustments to my own practice as necessary, what Burnham (2005) has referred to as 'relational reflexivity'.

Other influential theoretical models

Centralising ethics in this way could be thought of as my professional rules (Fredman, Johnson & Petronic, 2010); my beliefs and values about how to be a 'good therapist' which contribute to shaping my professional and personal identity. In this way, professional or theoretical discourses, the stories we tell ourselves about why problems occur for people and how they are maintained, have the potential to shape both clients' and professionals' identities, by either reinforcing or conflicting with our values. My work has been predominantly grounded in a systemic therapeutic model which, as D endorses, follows the 'Think Family' approach (SCIE, 2009), which aims to support, rather than pathologise, families by preferring overall to see problems as existing within contexts and relationships rather than within people themselves. In some ways, theoretical models can be viewed as maps, which guide practice. Choosing to rest my work on this theoretical foundation has not been an accidental process and as described earlier is probably influenced by my own multiple identities. More specifically in my clinical practice I have been influenced by theories derived from the social constructionist[3] tradition in systemic therapy such as Narrative Therapy (White & Epston, 1990; White, 2004). In the Narrative model, an assumption is made that the stories people tell themselves and others about who they are and how they live hugely influence how they come to know themselves, and it is difficult (if not impossible) to tell stories about our lives that are not influenced by wider cultural stories dominant in the societies in which we live. These stories that speak of value and worth tend to be told and shaped by the most powerful groups in society. In this approach people are invited to notice the effect of these dominant discourses on their lives; take a reflective stance to the existence of problems; and develop the hidden or shy discourses, which may speak to their own mostly hidden abilities and strengths. Michael White spoke of people not being the problem but instead identified 'problems as the problem' (White & Epston, 1990), allowing for an exploration of the space between people and their difficulties. I have found that people are acutely aware of the wider cultures and sub-cultures, which influence their lives, and only a few questions seem to stimulate interest in the many taken-for-granted stories we all live with. Narrative Therapy facilitates this exploration bringing it to the centre of therapy.

Another model helpful in elucidating the influence of wider community contexts on people's lives is Cronen and Pearce's (1980) model of communication: the Coordinated Management of Meaning or CMM. CMM suggests a reciprocal rather than a linear relationship, between action, meaning and context. In brief, it highlights how there can be contextual forces which influence individual meaning, action and language and that in turn the individual's perceptions can have a significant effect on their social context. In this way the individual is not viewed as a passive object with regards to the influences of context but has an agentive role in their own world; nor can any perceptual experiences be immune from the effects of the wider social world (Cronen & Pearce, 1980; 1985). An aspect of CMM which I find most helpful is its detailing of the levels of contexts which can give meaning to our actions and the stories we have about ourselves and the world, whilst being in interaction with each other. Following Afuape's (2011) expanded list of levels of contexts, meanings can be derived from: the content of a statement made by someone, bodily sensations, speech acts, the particular episode, life scripts, interpersonal relationships, family, culture, spiritual beliefs, and the political or global arena. Drawing from models such as these allows me to prioritise context and communities with parents in a helpful way. I will return to the influence of these particular theoretical contexts throughout this chapter where I will use fictional, composite and anonymised examples of practice to detail these approaches further.

With an underlying foundation of ethical practice, my practice has allowed for interventions from a range of models in addition to those from the broad systemic field including cognitive-behavioural therapy, mindfulness and attachment theory, to name but a few. Burnham's (1992) model of Approach Method

Technique is helpful here and describes the *why* (Approach), *how* (Method) and *what* (Technique) of therapeutic work. Burnham describes how therapeutic and supervisory encounters can be understood at three different levels. The Approach details the worldview and assumptions, which underpin the work (synonymous perhaps with my 'professional rules' as described earlier). The Method is concerned with how the encounter is structured and put together (what you might see the practitioner doing in the room). The level of Technique covers what the therapist actually does, what is said, how it is said and what is asked of the person seeking help. In this regard, an ethical systemic Approach allows for the integration of Methods and Techniques from other theoretical models including those most promoted in the National Institute for Health & Care Excellence (NICE[4]) guidelines, if done in a collaborative, non-expert and responsive way that underpins the spirit of social constructionist approaches like Narrative Therapy. Whilst my attempts have been to provide a hopeful, non-stigmatising approach to tackling the problems adults can face, the wider context of adult mental health service provision has nonetheless been a powerful backdrop to how problems can be understood and what it is possible to do in response to them. I will now describe aspects of this context and the effect it can have.

I have found it important to stay open to a range of models and hold onto the both/and position (Burnham, 1992) to acknowledge that all models have opportunities and constraints; this means that any model can be helpful if approached ethically and with consideration of the effect on the parent at multiple levels. For example, I agree with Simblett (2013), who as a psychiatrist clearly demonstrates this in the title of his paper 'Dancing with the DSM' (Simblett, 2013) integrating diagnostic and social constructionist models in his work with adults, and reminding us that DSM-V[5] is but one way of organising information. I have had personal experience of mindfulness, cognitive and attachment models and found these helpful in making sense of my own experience and in alleviating my own distress. I do not intend to disregard the usefulness of different ways of working, but rather to point out that all models and theoretical approaches have constraining effects; some constraining effects are likely to be more disregarding of the influence of community on the individual, and risk further promoting disadvantage. For some of the parents with whom I have worked, the adult mental health service context is a powerful but nonetheless helpful presence in their lives. Thinking with them about new ways to stay connected to it that feel more satisfying has helped to reveal aspects of this relationship that they prefer and those that they would like to change.

The political and financial contexts of adult mental health services

Like many strands of the British NHS, the adult mental health field has been rapidly changing over the last few years. Services have been streamlined into diagnostic service lines, funding has flowed (or more often the case is, not flowed) along the same streams, and those individuals not fitting into these rigid pathways are required to find their own way back to recovery. Such restructuring is not new. Wherever boundary lines have been drawn in services there have always been those that meet the criteria and those that do not. This is in stark contrast to my own professional ethics: I believe that the uniqueness and complexity of people far extends the somewhat arbitrary divisions that are made for administrative, financial and political reasons. Most obviously in this recent shift has been the effect on fundamental understandings of mental health. I know I have not been alone in waiting for a paradigm-shift to move thinking about people using mental health services to less stigmatising and more hopeful approaches. However the recent political context has arguably resulted in a 'paradigm-strengthening', where more than ever before people have come to be defined at an organisational level by their particular presentation of distress (for example, as 'having a personality disorder', or 'being psychotic'), moved to the corresponding service line, and within tight time constraints become understood and treated primarily within an expert model which privileges internal experience. Again this is a significant challenge to my preferred way of thinking and professional ethos and presents real dilemmas when needing to secure further support for parents. I have wrestled with decision making when considering if parents might benefit from the advantages of a team approach to their care, knowing that this will involve referring them on to a team where, at least initially, they will be defined by a diagnosis. Being honest with parents about my own dissatisfaction has helped to alleviate the discomfort felt about being part of this process.

Embracing and resisting the mental health context

Yet within service restructuring and the reformed multidisciplinary teams that deliver the services, professionals working on the ground acknowledge other contributory factors to distress. Often there is much talk of and attempts to provide more holistic ways of working with people so as to attend to wider aspects of their lives: their physical health, the impact on carers, and financial and housing needs. However, compounded by limited social resources (for example, the impossibility of affordable, satisfactory and permanent housing and impoverished employment opportunities), and an emphasis on time-limited outcomes to stay competitive with other providers, the internalising model of distress becomes an easy, achievable default position. For example, following a referral of a person 'feeling low', it would be quite easy to choose to begin to story someone's life in accordance with a depression diagnosis, listening out for 'features of depression', asking questions informed by this construction, perhaps completing appropriate standardised measures and further reinforcing the idea of depression as the problem, held within the adult mental health arena. This need not be a thoughtless or heartless act: I have known adults to describe relief at being given a formalised name for their problems and feeling as if they now have a way of making sense of their difficulties. And there would, of course, be ample guidance in the NICE guidelines on how I could then help, which again many people would attest to. Alternatively, I might begin by exploring all of the influences on their difficulties including, but not exclusively focusing on, internal processes. And then we might decide together which to prioritise; learning new ways to cope with problems. For example, where 'feeling low' is influenced by housing constraints, rather than focusing on the effect of poor housing on their mood we might instead spend the session addressing the housing difficulties directly, developing skills in articulating their concerns to their housing officer, formulating a letter together which I might send on their behalf or weighing up the pros and cons of writing a letter of complaint to their housing organisation. Therapeutic moves such as these represent small but important ways of challenging the effects of an unhelpful context on an individual's identity.

When internal processes are placed at the centre of the help given, and particularly when this is primarily led by the therapist, there is a risk of meaning becoming divorced from its context. As a result, the rich knowledge which people hold about themselves and their communities becomes minimised in favour of a particular way of knowing about people. For the majority of the psychotherapeutic professions, this knowledge base is traditionally derived from specific ways of thinking which match the identities of its originators, typically male, middle class, heterosexual and broadly European in heritage. This may not match the worldview, intentions, hopes and priorities of the people seeking help, and as a result many contextual influences become forgotten when working in this way, both by the therapist and the individuals seeking help.

Another potential constraint of the current dominant ways of promoting wellbeing, is that the hard-to-ignore relationship between presentations of emotional distress and various forms of inequality, disadvantage and abuse in the wider social context becomes minimised. For example, there is much written about the increasing prevalence of emotional distress for people with experiences of trauma, abuse, and social inequalities based on gender, for example, Belle (1990); 'race', for example, Patel & Fatimilehin (1999); sexuality, for example, Bridget & Lucille (1996), and class, for example, Gomm (1996)—to name but a few (Afuape, 2011). Most of the parents attending CAHMS that I have worked alongside have lived at least one of these experiences of social inequality, as well as other contextual struggles. In my own experience, it is much more difficult to attend to an individual as belonging to a wider community, or to take their idiosyncratic community connections seriously when they are primarily thought about internally or diagnostically.

In busy and demanding working environments, it is an easy therapeutic move to rest in the dominant stories of the adult mental health context. Self-reflexivity has been an aide in helping me to notice the insidious effects of this context on my practice. Doing so provides me with the necessary space to make a choice about how I work with someone. So instead, many practitioners, myself included, actively seek small ways to resist these quite linear and narrow ways of thinking about people, their relationships and their lives.

Keeping 'relationships to context' in the room

Many of the ways in which I have stayed attuned to and aware of the influence of the adult mental health context, have also helped me to stay aware and mindful about other contexts and significant relationships. However, doing so requires an active intention by the clinician, as this case example demonstrates:

> *A colleague came to consult with me on the work he had been doing with Miriam and Esther, both White British medical consultants and parents of nearly six-year-old Peter. They had been finding the transition from couple to parents difficult and were considering separating. They had been meeting with my colleague, a therapist, since Peter did poorly in an exam at a local independent school and the couple's relationship more rapidly declined after this, at which point they sought help. However, one year on they and their therapist, described feeling incredibly stuck. As my colleague spoke I noticed my own assumptions regarding 'high-achieving couples' gathering strength within me. I began to ask myself questions informed by unhelpful assumptions: 'why didn't they separate when life was clearly so miserable for them together?', 'if they do separate they'll probably be battling endlessly in court', 'is it fair that they are placing their own high standards on their son and entering him into an overly-academic school?', 'are they just good at thinking (hence their academic achievement) but not good at feeling ...?' As these assumption-informed questions and statements continued, I too noticed a sense of hopelessness overcoming me as the "stuckness" became infectious. Reflecting on how this had come to be, and allowing myself to question the assumptions I was making, helped me to return to a more curious stance as opposed to a knowing one. I then started to become interested in the meanings they might give to their actions, their strengths and what they did well as a couple, as well as what they hoped for themselves.*

As illustrated here, therapists, too, are vulnerable to pervasive, unhelpful discourses in the wider context, and arguably, given our positions of power, susceptible to reifying and perpetuating these. Taking my responsibility as a therapist seriously involves acknowledging the power I have in producing and reproducing existing power relations in the therapy room (Winslade, 2005); as a therapist from communities which are routinely disempowered, this is very important to me. As described earlier, what I choose to give focus to in the process of conversing with someone is likely to be highly influential of the narratives the person will develop about him- or herself. They are then likely to take these new narratives back to their relationships and the meaning becomes further endorsed. Within the local geographical area of our service clinic, a narrative of high achieving, conflictual couples has from time to time dominated and in the case example above, I was being influenced by it. Staying aware of my own inner speak (Rober, 1999; 2002; 2005) and taking a 'curious stance' (Cecchin, 1987), where I acknowledged that my own views and ideas about the family might not be shared by them, made it possible for me to listen for the unique story that the family might wish to tell; or the story about themselves as resourceful and hopeful which even they may have lost sight of. As a result, I was better able to remain questioning and doubtful of my own theories and stories, and have this doubt inform the questions I went on to ask.

Staying curious extends to giving importance to the client's words and language and not making assumptions about the meaning or significance of the words they use. This allows me to support parents in describing their experience in their own words and treating these as valid and meaningful in their own right: I see my role here not as interpreting what they mean by the words they say but aiming to develop a shared understanding or construction of their problems and lives. So rather than producing a therapeutic encounter which replicates existing narratives, curiosity-derived questions enable me to help parents create openings for exploration and possibilities for change, and consequently develop new stories about themselves.

Tuning in to resources and listening with an appreciative ear have been two additional systemic concepts, which have been particularly helpful to me in attending to context and honouring the relationships and 'communities' important to parents. As highlighted earlier, difference can easily be thought of as a complicating factor and by listening with an appreciative ear—listening out for aspects of their living and life which I might appreciate or admire—helps to give a different focus to the work, away from problem-filled stories to those where hope is strengthened. As a therapist and more broadly as a person in the world, I try to hold the belief that all individuals and systems already have resources which can help them to move towards their hoped for lives. By intentionally tuning into these, either during a consultation with colleagues or direct work with a family, their resources have the potential to become the beginnings of change. With the couple above, using these principles may have led to questions rather than assumptions which were more hopeful: I may have wondered what was important for them in staying together; what they were holding on to and appreciating about each other as co-parents; what their hopes and dreams were for their son that had perhaps been taken away from them when he did not pass the exam and whether there were other ways they as a couple could work together towards these. I have found this to be a more enlivening and enriching process for me and as feedback has suggested, for those parents and colleagues I work alongside too. D describes the meaningful effect of this approach on her:

"I remember when we were talking about my description of depression ('the black hole') and you would use the same terms as I used, the same visual descriptions—colours, shape, size. As I am a visual person these things appealed to me. Speaking my language as it were. Climbing in to the situation with me as an observer. It helped me to feel that whatever emotion I described (and the way I described it) that I wasn't alone. I guess the person's (I come from an educational background) learning style (for example, visual, auditory, kinaesthetic), whichever one that may apply to the person receiving the therapy, could make them more receptive to it. I think your use of the same language that I used didn't only create rapport but also meant that strategies suited to my visual sense meant that I could get something more out of it."

For D it seems that having me stay close to her words extended her ability to make sense of her experience. Unexpectedly for me, staying close to D's words helped her feel as though I was staying close to her, by diminishing feelings of loneliness.

Naming the community context

Connections to other people are important and I will now go on to explore how community contexts can influence even the most casual of relationships with wide-ranging effects.

Patrick was a thirty-eight-year-old new father. Having been born in Nigeria he had been living in the UK for the past twenty years, and working for a competitive consulting firm. I met with him after he had lost his mother eight months previously and grief had become a pervading influence in his life; something he was particularly struggling with at work. He described feeling the weight of others' expectations when in conversation with colleagues that he would have had a "brilliant, amazing, weekend". In contrast to life before his bereavement when this would have fit for him, his experience now was vastly different. I asked if it felt possible to talk more honestly with anyone at work about his experience and he spoke with sadness and frustration as he said that conversations about "down days", stress or even mundaneness were implicitly forbidden amongst his peers. He told me, "After all this time, staying positive is what people expect of you, isn't it? No-one's got any sympathy for losing Mum anymore. I should be over it by now, shouldn't I?"

In this example, Patrick is identifying the influential voice of his peers on his experience, implicitly naming the powerful discourses prevalent there and in wider society which speak first to the length of time one is permitted to grieve and second where 'negative' feelings tend to be marginalised and minimised, and 'positive' feelings and experiences are amplified. Patrick felt unable to share his emotional experience with others for fear of being ostracised and not fitting in with the community norms of his work place. However, staying silent intensified his feelings, such that it was no longer only grief that was affecting him but also sadness and annoyance with himself that he was not measuring up to the standards expected within this local community. In such instances, it can be useful to amplify the wider context and spend time exploring the development of these pervasive stories, so as to create space between the person and these constraining ideas. So in this case I might become curious with Patrick about who else might hold this view that "he should be over it by now" and how that idea might have gathered dominance, both for him and others. I could ask him who it might work for to have this idea of "staying positive in the face of grief". I could then ask if he knew of others who might hold a different view. Helping Patrick to uncover and name wider societal discourses would hopefully enable him to make a choice about the position he takes in relation to them; continuing to "do what society expected of him" or something else, perhaps more in line with a value from another community context he felt he belonged to. I might also invite him to think of one or two colleagues who he might be able to connect with in a more authentic way and who might be more accepting of the whole of his experience. Finally, I might think with him about small acts of social action that he might engage in that would contribute to undermining at a broader level the social injustice, which was connected to his life difficulty.

White (2004) describes a similar process using the idea of 'modern power' borrowed from Foucault (1980; 1982). White (2004) described Foucault's notion of modern power as a system of social control, which encourages individuals to regulate themselves in accordance with the norms of wider societal values. People then develop their worth in accordance to their adherence to these, tending to feel good about themselves when they comply. Rather than being seen as socially con-structed, these pervasive values take on the position of 'normal', with those that hold different ideas and inclinations implicitly encouraged to view their actions and subsequently their identities as failures. Of course, the pull of 'modern power' is equally applicable to therapists and so continuing to stay reflexive to its effects is important for us too.

Conclusions

This chapter has described my attempts to stay close to parents' experiences as they navigate their way towards hoped-for-lives, for themselves and their children. In seeking guidance from CAMHS professionals they put themselves at the mercy of our professional models and personal views at a vulnerable time in their lives. In this chapter, I have hopefully emphasised ways that I have taken this respon-sibility seriously by, acknowledging the impact that my own worldview has on others; remaining sensitive to this impact; honouring the communities in clients' lives, in all of the layers this involves, including the parts of their lives that I do not see, and reflecting on the connections to others that are most meaningful to them as well as the values that they hold dear. I have also hopefully spoken of the challenges our services and institutions face in holding community values at the forefront of practice.

The process of writing this chapter has in itself been a method for keeping me closer to the values that are important to me, reminding me that it helps to remain creative with how I strengthen my connection to community in my work. And as I reflect on the content of this chapter, I am aware of a heartfelt wish that I practiced in this way all of the time, with the very many moments where this approach does not feature in a significant way easily coming to mind. Constantly attending to community is not an easy task: meeting parents and making visible their contexts whilst staying mindful of the influence of mine takes effort and perseverance. It has required me to take stands against the norm and resist the status quo, which can sometimes feel uncomfortable, unsettling and consequently easy to turn away from. If this sounds familiar then I would invite others to face this discomfort rather than avoid it, and notice how it can enhance the therapeutic relationship and the work overall. D agrees, and her advice to therapists is to:

> "Relate, using your own background experience and not what you think the person's experience would be like and ... be honest if you cannot relate to it".

Notes

1 'D' is the name chosen by this parent.
2 Selvini Palazzoli and colleagues used the term 'neutrality' to encourage practitioners to actively avoid taking sides with one person or another in a family or system, or viewing one perspective as more correct or truthful than another.
3 Hedges (2005) has been a particularly influential text for me on social constructionist ways of approaching individual adult therapy.
4 In the UK, NICE aims to provide national guidance on best practices in order to improve health and social care. The guides for providing interventions for mental health disorders are typically based on meta-analysis of published studies. More often the published studies use a cognitive-behavioural intervention.
5 DSM-V is a classification system of "mental disorders" developed by North American psychiatrists.

References

Afuape, T. (2011). *Power, Resistance and Liberation in Therapy with Survivors of Trauma: To Have our Hearts Broken*. London, England: Routledge.

Aldridge, J. & Becker, S. (2003). *Children Caring for Parents with Mental Illness: Perspectives of Young Carers, Parents and Professionals*. Bristol, England: The Policy Press.

Belle, D. (1990). Poverty and women's mental health. *American Psychologist, 45*(3), 385–9.

Bridget, J. & Lucille, S. (1996). Lesbian Youth Support Information Service (LYSIS): Developing a distance support agency for young lesbians. *Journal of Community & Applied Social Psychology, 6*(5), 355–64.

Burnham, J. (1992). Approach—method—technique. *Human Systems, 3*(1), 3–26.

Burnham, J. (2005). Relational reflexivity: A tool for socially constructing therapeutic relationships. In: C. Flaskas, B. Mason & A. Perlesz (eds.), *The Space Between: Experience, Context and Process in the Therapeutic Relationship.* (pp. 1–17). London, England: Karnac Books.

Cecchin, G. (1987). Hypothesising, circularity and neutrality revisited: An invitation to curiosity. *Family Process, 26*(4), 405–14.

Cronen, V. E. & Pearce, W. B. (1980). *Communication, Action and Meaning: The Creation of Social Realities*. New York, NY: Praeger.

Cronen, V. E. & Pearce, W. B. (1985). Towards an explanation of how the Milan Method works: An invitation to a systemic epistemology and the evolution of family systems. In: D. Campbell & R. Draper (eds.), *Applications of Systemic Family Therapy: The Milan Approach.* (pp. 69–84). London, England: Grune and Stratton.

Fredman, G., Johnson, S. & Petronic, G. (2010). Sustaining the ethics of systemic practice in contexts of risk and diagnosis. In: G. Fredman, E. Anderson & J. Stott (eds.), *Being With Older People.* (pp. 181–210). London, England: Karnac Books.

Foucault, M. (1980). *Power/Knowledge: Selected Interviews and Other Writings 1971–1977.* New York, NY: Harvester Wheatsheaf.

Foucault, M. (1982). The subject and power. In: H. Dreyfus & P. Rabinow (eds.), *Michael Foucault: Beyond Structuralism and Hermeneutics.* (pp. 208–26). New York, NY: Harvester Wheatsheaf.

Gomm, R. (1996). Mental health and inequality. In: T. Heller, J. Reynolds, R. Gomm, R. Muston & S. Pattison (eds.). *Mental Health Matters: A Reader.* (pp. 110–20). London, England: Macmillan in association with the Open University.

Göpfert M., Webster, J. & Seeman, M.V. (eds.) (2004). *Parental Psychiatric Disorder: Distressed Parents and their Families.* Cambridge, England: Cambridge University Press.

Hedges, F. (2005). *An Introduction to Systemic Therapy with Individuals: A Social Constructionist Approach.* London, England: Palgrave.

Mordoch, E. (2010). How children understand parental mental illness: "You don't get life insurance. What's life insurance?" *Journal of the Canadian Academy of Child and Adolescent Psychiatry,* 19(1), 19–25.

Mordoch, E. & Hall, W. A. (2002). Children living with a parent who has a mental illness: A critical analysis of the literature and research implications. *Archives of Psychiatric Nursing,* 16(5), 208–16.

Patel, N. & Fatimilehin, I. (1999). Racism and mental health. In: C. Newnes, G. Holmes & C. Dunn (eds.), *This Is Madness: A Critical Look at Psychiatry and the Future of Mental Health Services.* (pp. 51–73). Ross-on-Wye, England: PCCS.

Rober, P. (1999). The therapist's inner conversation: Some ideas about the self of the therapist, therapeutic impasse and the process of reflection. *Family Process,* 38(2), 209–28.

Rober, P. (2002). Constructive hypothesizing, dialogic understanding and the therapist's inner conversation: Some ideas about knowing and not knowing in the family therapy session. *Journal of Marital and Family Therapy,* 28(4), 467–78.

Rober, P. (2005). The therapist's self in dialogical family therapy: Some ideas about not-knowing and the therapist's inner conversation. *Family Process,* 44(4), 477–95.

Selvini Palazzoli, M., Boscolo, L., Cecchin, G. & Prata, G. (1980). Hypothesizing, circularity, neutrality: Three guidelines for the conductor of the session. *Family Process,* 19(1), 3–12.

Simblett, G. (2013). Dancing with the DSM—The reflexive positioning of narrative informed psychiatric practice. *Australian and New Zealand Journal of Family Therapy,* 34(2), 114–28.

Social Care Institute for Excellence (SCIE) (2009). *Think Child, Think Parent, Think Family: A Guide to Parental Mental Health and Child Welfare.* London, England: SCIE (updated December 2011; Review: December 2014).

Tunnard, J. (2004). *Parental Mental Health Problems: Messages from Research, Policy and Practice.* Totnes, Devon, England: Research into Practice (RiP).

White, M. (2004). *Narrative Practice and Exotic Lives: Resurrecting Diversity in Everyday Life*. Adelaide, Australia: Dulwich Centre Publications.

White, M. & Epston, D. (1990). *Narrative Means to Therapeutic Ends*. New York, NY: W.W. Norton.

Winslade, J. (2005). Utilising discursive positioning in counselling. *British Journal of Guidance and Counselling,* 33(3), 351–64.

Chapter 14

A responsive approach to urban communities? concluding reflections

Taiwo Afuape and Inga-Britt Krause

In the introduction we described the ways in which this book represents an approach to child and family mental health work in which diversity and responsiveness are integral to our working models. As we respond to the diversity in our communities we inevitably change what we do; and changing what we do changes what and how we understand, which in turn, potentially transforms the services we offer. In this process we value equity in service delivery, but equity does not always mean approaching clients in the same way or offering identical solutions to everybody. Reflecting on *a responsive approach to urban communities* from the diversity of viewpoints within a community CAMHS, inevitably involves describing a variety of approaches, focussed on general notions such as 'process', 'values' and 'complexity' rather than on specific ideas related to 'outcome', 'techniques' and 'certainty'.

Although originally a modest undertaking, the chapters of this book have gone further than simply describing the methods of clinicians in an urban CAMHS; they have opened up and renewed our notions of 'community'. In doing so they have demonstrated that being a 'community service' does not just mean being located outside clinics, but also being fully present to and engaged with, the multiplicity of connections and meanings of those living in communities; that is, CAMHS work *with,* and not just *in,* communities. This necessitates noticing, acknowledging and working with the unique resources and challenges of the urban context.

So what is 'community'?

All the chapters of this book explore, what is 'community'? from the point of view of mental health work, and how our understanding of it contributes to our ability to be responsive to the children, young people and families we meet. What might seem obvious and axiomatic in our everyday use of terms, like 'community', is exposed as far more complex. In keeping with the dictionary definition of 'complex', 'community' itself 'consists of many different and connected parts', is 'a group or system of different things that are linked in a close or complicated way', is 'a network' made up of fluid channels—which joins two areas together and directs elements towards a particular end—and is often 'a complex structure', 'denoting or involving quantities containing both tangible and intangible parts' (Oxford University Press, 2008). Tangible aspects of community relate to geography, environment and place; whereas intangible elements might reflect a cluster of feelings associated with relatedness, communion, belonging or a desire to belong. Community might refer to a real experience—such as where we come from—or an imagined one—what we want to retreat to and/or create. Britt Krause reflected on this complexity in the first chapter, being sure to include the often forgotten importance of physical environment (travel and traffic systems, communication systems, surveillance, housing and architecture, the availability of parks and public spaces, as well as access to services and education), to our sense of self and community. Whatever definitions or personal leanings we have in relation to what community means to us, it is clear that wellness happens not just in our psyches, but also in our relationships with each other and the environment.

Despite the circumstances they find themselves in, Britt demonstrated the ways in which communities are not fixed but fluid and multi-various; therefore 'community' is open to continual construction in favour of which experiences most fit and are most conducive to the well-being of members. An urban context in particular comes with many potential challenges or risks (for example, poor and overcrowded housing or more opportunities for gang affiliation), as well as many possibilities and freedoms (for example, opportunities for people to construct, and combine different aspects of, identity and belonging). Perhaps this is why the multidisciplinary aspects of CAMHS is favourable, allowing for the availability of a variety of approaches that tackle the concrete and the intangible elements of community, as well as the links between them. Thus, 'community' calls for cross fertilisation between CAMHS and non-CAMHS workers as well as between different CAMHS professionals. What 'communities' find less helpful seems to be the breaking up of services into separate and distinct parts.

CAMHS as community

Britt's chapter reminded us that CAMHS teams cannot work together as though they are in the community but not themselves a community. CAMHS as a community holds tensions between different approaches, in order to better respond to the complexity of the internal and external, personal and interpersonal, social and political elements of 'community'. Most people, perhaps everybody, participate in multiple communities that can vary across time, place and circumstance. Similarly, CAMHS workers make up a community of people who are also part of other professional and personal communities. As in any community, CAMHS workers may feel supported or constrained or both at different times, within their personal communities and/or within the CAMHS community. Team members in multidisciplinary teams can get to know each other well through close working, despite the potential for members to be unduly competitive with each other and perceived privileges. The complexities inherent in the visible and invisible differences between people create challenges for CAMHS clinicians but also come with a kaleidoscope of possibilities which make responsiveness both possible and feasible.

What does it mean to be 'responsive'?

The Oxford English Dictionary defines 'responsive' as: 'reacting quickly and positively' and more specifically, 'a flexible service that is responsive to changing social patterns' (Oxford University Press, 2008). In the case of CAMHS, being responsive means clinicians and clients/the community working in close relationship with each other and within each other's context, with the former adjusting flexibly to create services that are engaging, accessible and meaningful to the latter. Whereas, being unresponsive means that practitioners and clients/the community are unconnected, functioning separately without integration or cooperation, with incompatible agendas that are not shared or negotiated. In an unresponsive service, practitioners continue to offer what they believe to be helpful and regard those who do not engage with what is being offered to them, as 'hard to reach'. What is implied by such turns of phrase, about the relationship between services and communities, is a gulf that needs to be bridged in some way, to allow easy access between distinct places, with communities, not services, being problematised. Alternatively, the contributors used a variety of other concepts and analogies that helped to illustrate what responsivity means. In different ways they all suggest that being responsive requires a particular awareness of 'difference' and 'context'. In what follows we discuss the various ways in which 'difference' and 'context' intersect in our work as CAMHS professionals.

Working together across different professions, systems and contexts

The contributors used different concepts to highlight the role of cross-fertilisation in a responsive approach to communities. Zoe Dale referred to a *tripartite intervention structure* when describing the assessment and intervention process that, although primarily group-based, also involved the family, the school and CAMHS. Combining group work and school and family approaches in their intervention enabled the group facilitators to explore the links between the challenges in school, experiences at home and social disadvantages within the community. Doreen Robinson described Nancy Boyd-Franklin's '*multi-systems*' approach to 'community' (Boyd-Franklin, 2006); similarly Taiwo Afuape described Co-ordinated Management of Meaning's (CMM) levels of context, utilising notions of co-ordination (how we live alongside and interact with each other), coherence (how we make sense of life) and mystery (that which is beyond rationality) (Pearce, 2007) that help us notice, honour and nurture clients' creative responses to adversity. For Esther Usiskin-Cohen, systemic and narrative concepts, 'a gracious invitation' (Lang & McAdam, 1996) and 'leaning in' (Reynolds, 2013), are useful for grounding this process in humility, respect and compassion.

Each person, each system and each moment simultaneously, is influenced by and shapes multiple contexts (Pearce, 2007). For example, the family and school system exists within a wider context of oppressive discourses related to gender, ethnicity/'race', sexuality, class and so on, and other social issues that impact on the lives of young people and their families. A head teacher of a secondary school might be trying to manage a hundred employees without receiving proper budget forecasts, while costs are going up and there are pressures from Ofsted[1]. Such pressures on head teachers can trickle down to teachers who may then experience an imperative to 'teach for testing' by improving and achieving better results year after year. A teacher who has an Ofsted inspection the next day may have less headspace to attend to a pupil's non-academic needs when approached, if they feel nervous and/or have things to plan. A pupil may be experiencing peer difficulties, struggling with academic work and strained relationships at home alongside a growing and changing body. Parents may have a number of stressors impacting on their lives ranging from personal difficulties in their home life, worries about housing, employment and finances, mental health difficulties, as well as the historical context of their own experience of being young and at school.

The different contributors of this book have all highlighted the impact of these multiple levels of context, at times focusing on some more than others, while being mindful of them all. For example, Ana Rivadulla Crespo described Heckman's conclusion that the emotional well-being of children and young people is mostly determined by parenting quality rather than income (Heckman, 2008), while Taiwo Afuape also highlights the ways in which the government's change in approach to poverty has deliberately focused on the behaviours of parents (unstable adult relationships, addiction and joblessness) at the expense of measuring and monitoring the impact of discriminatory economic and social structures, such as lack of income, that form the context these parental behaviours may exist within. Chris Glenn in his chapter referred to a *joint systems approach* to joining up the school and home systems around the child, in order to overcome differences and bring together knowledge and resources, rather than these being polarised and oppositional. Similarly, Rachel James and Kanan Pandya-Smith referred to *partnership working* that responds to the cultural, political and social contexts of clients' lives. As demonstrated in the chapters of this book, this type of work involves developing working relationships with: hospital and community midwifery services, social care services, multi-agency children's centre teams, community CAMHS and adult mental health services, health visitors, voluntary sector community organisations, general practitioners, community nurses, teachers, head teachers, teaching assistants and educational mentors. There is often some sort of joint appointment with the referrer and a comprehensive assessment, which draws information from multiple perspectives, systems and teams.

Engaging other professionals in the mental health/well-being agenda of CAMHS can create opportunities for non-CAMHS workers to better understand the needs of young people and parents with respect to context. This was epitomised by Esther Usiskin-Cohen's use of Russian dolls within dolls to exemplify the multiple contexts within which a child and family are located. This shared understanding of the importance of context made it easier to develop interventions that drew on a variety of people within the community to support families. In the FAST programme school staff, parents, CAMHS professionals and local people from youth work, library, sports, or religious settings, all worked together, creating the potential for such links to continue; making the community a more engaging and enabling place.

But what might need to happen in order to work with 'difference' in a non-colonising and creative way? What might this process entail? Louise Emmanuel argued that working in the community and bringing community into psychoanalytic work requires 'crossing a border' into settings, contexts and communities less familiar to us. 'Crossing' in this metaphor is less about clients being 'hard to reach' and more about the need for clinicians to challenge their own assumptions about what is right, true, helpful and just; bringing us closer to the ways in which these are always socially, culturally and politically constructed. The 'border crossing' analogy conveys certain images of adventure, anxiety, possibility and uncertainty. It requires us to reflect on the taken-for-granted values, assumptions, responsibilities and 'rules' that we live by, as well as those which other people live by. 'Border crossings' have resemblances to Madsen's (2007) idea of taking an *anthropological approach* to all encounters with families, and not just those deemed to come from 'different' cultural contexts from our own (Madsen, 2007). Madsen argues that 'we can think of ourselves as cultural anthropologists who have been given the opportunity to enter into the life space of clients and learn from them about their unique multi-layered experiences' (Madsen, 2007, p. 160).

Holding on to different positions at the same time

Being responsive is a complex task, not just because communities and persons are embedded in multiple levels of contexts, but also because clinicians are required to hold on to different viewpoints, ideas, perspectives and positions at the same time. As an example, Leila Bargawi, Lousie O'Dwyer and Louise Emmanuel argued that doing child psychotherapy in General Practice means going beyond the internal world of the child and holding in mind the opportunities and constraints of the contexts they are working within, the personal and professional experiences, values and beliefs of their colleagues, as well as their own personal and professional experiences and training, while trying to adapt to and connect with the cultures and experiences of families. As well as working jointly with other professionals, the psychotherapists aim to be part of, *and* outside of, the systems they work within, in order to use psychoanalytic thinking to reflect on what is happening within the system. In addition, they use personal reflections on the moment-to-moment experience with clients to better understand the clients' internal and external context, as well as the links between them. All this necessitates an awareness that with the challenges of 'difference', are always opportunities to be creative with, and responsive to them.

Growing from the challenges of 'difference'

There is a danger in books like this about urban communities, that people from 'other communities' deemed to come from 'difference' and 'deprivation' are exotisised. Indeed the idea of 'difference' is contentious given its association with power—that is, who has the power to define 'others' and in so doing engage in the process of 'othering', which in itself can be oppressive to groups of people whose access to social and political power is limited? It seems common sense to say that we are *all* 'different' from each other and yet at any given moment, some groups of people (for instance, women, Black and Minority Ethnic people, people with disabilities, Lesbian, Gay, Bisexual, Trans, or Questioning people, working classes and so on) are deemed 'different', when defined in relation to visible and invisible dominant discourses. As a result 'difference' is often associated with problems—leading to a quest to somehow 'overcome' it, which suggests that a movement towards homogeneity is desirable.

A number of contributors challenged this usual approach to 'difference'. Jasmine Chin reflected on 'difference', not as a thing to avoid or ignore, but a useful process to engage in. Britt Krause quoted Gilroy (2008), who highlights the potential in the urban context for valuing the opportunities to experiment with identity and belonging that come with 'difference'. Being responsive involves an understanding that with 'difference' comes the opportunity to learn, grow and develop richer and more responsive services, as we are shaped and influenced by young people, families, communities and colleagues.

The inclusion of a chapter on female genital mutilation (FGM) by Taiwo Afuape and Britt Krause was an attempt to face the complexity of 'difference' head on; by reflecting on, rather than shying away from, a controversial and emotive issue. Knowing how to respond to individuals, families and communities with different life experiences, values and beliefs from us is challenging enough, but this challenge is further exacerbated when the issue at the centre of the clinician-client interaction brings up difficult, and at perhaps dissimilar, feelings in both parties. Being responsive is not easy, straightforward and uncomplicated, and FGM is a topic that highlights this complexity in a profound and powerful way. Britt and Taiwo offered some reflections on 'ethical dialogue', which focuses on the ethics of the dialogue itself not just on the ethics of the subject matter being discussed. Most importantly, ethical dialogue allows for possibilities to emerge that might not seem obvious or relevant at the start.

The contributors of this book did not shy away from the complexity of responsivity and the challenges they encounter. However, even within the sometimes relentlessness of despair, adversity and oppression, the authors reflected on the possibilities that can emerge. For example, Taiwo Afuape wrote about using the possibilities inherent within creativity, while Ana Rivadulla Crespo emphasised the importance of igniting hope in our work with our clients in crisis. In this vein, rather than the hackneyed focus on the challenges of working with interpreters, Louise Emanuel described ways in which her 'professional couple' relationship with an interpreter contributed to her ability to 'cross a cultural border' between herself and her 'patient', into a worldview with which she would otherwise not be familiar.

Making adaptations to traditional approaches

Responding to the needs and experiences of communities requires first a continuous process of reflection, in order to unearth our taken for granted assumptions, preferences and ways of being, and second feedback from clients about how they experience our services/interventions. Taiwo Afuape and Jasmine Chin described self and relational reflexivity (Burnham, 2005) as the central ingredients of respecting the world of the other as 'different' from our own and adapting our ways of being. Rachel James and Kanan Pandya-Smith described ways in which they approach communication with families that encourages engagement, such as using SMS reminders and mobile phones that show the caller's number for clients who are reluctant to answer their phone to unknown numbers. Zoe Dale's group drew heavily on traditional group psychotherapy models but combined this with a socio-centric tripartite structure; this addition to the traditional group therapy approach, allowed for the exploration within the group, of wider social issues.

Adapting our approach requires reflecting on clients in context, but it also requires reflecting on ourselves as clinicians in the context of our own personal, professional and historically situated lives. As such, the authors of this volume reflect on their personal experiences and how these shape their approach to and relationships with children, young people and families. Trying to stay curious about, challenge and expand what we come to know are crucial clinical skills. As our reflective spaces (in the form of supervision, consultation, peer support, case discussion and so on) are being eroded by the pressures of bureaucracy, austerity, increasing demand and dwindling resources, we need to be able to safe-guard spaces to reflect *about* and *with* clients.

Helping people better understand and communicate with each other

Despite major rifts between the boys in Zoe Dale's group, their school and their parents, for many of the group's participants, the group enabled them to strengthen parent-child and pupil-teacher relationships, as understanding and meaning making was shared from young person to adult and vice versa. From the outset it was clear that how the boys related to both their parents and teachers had a profound impact on their capacity to relate interpersonally and socially and their interpersonal and social experiences likewise influenced how they related to their parents and school staff; thus communication was viewed in circular rather than linear ways (Dale, this volume Chapter 14).

Doreen Robinson described using systemic theory to help families understand the impact of their membership of communities on their family relationships, and Jasmine Chin drew from the ways in which community membership can help people move towards their preferences for living. In addition, bringing community into clinical work involves elucidating the influence of levels of context on each other, such that social circumstances might impact on a family's functioning which in turn might impact on the identity of a young person and vice versa. Rachel James, Kanan Pandya-Smith, Louise Emanuel, Leila Bargawi and Louise O'Dwyer all described how they helped parents reflect on the impact they have on their children, given that parents are the primary point of reference through which cultural, social and political contexts are expressed in a child's world. Esther Usiskin-Cohen chapter suggested that how parents interact with their children can be viewed as a collective issue that requires a collective intervention, while Doreen Robinson's chapter reflected on the cultural issues impacting on all the relationships constituting the family system.

Attempting to be inside another's experience

Crucially responsiveness involves aiming to enter into an experience that is not our own and allowing ourselves to exist there, even if temporarily, in order to ensure that meaning making is connected to the experiences of others. Jasmine Chin's client 'D' described this as "Climbing in to the situation" with her so that she "wasn't alone". A number of contributors described engaging in parallel processes, mirroring that of their clients—for instance, Zoe Dale described how she went through 'transitions and rites of passage' as one of the group facilitators, at the same time as the group itself went through this process. Similarly, Louise E, Leila and Louise O described how the mirroring in their emotional experience of the emotional responses of their clients, supported their connection to their clients' lived experience. Those working with the under-fives described the ways in which they notice and comment on how babies and infants respond emotionally and psychologically and not just physically to their experiences. Entering into the world of the other was also described in relation to close working, joint working and partnership with colleagues outside of CAMHS that enable clinicians to better understand the pressures their colleagues face, and how their world-view is shaped by their context. In addition, home visits meant understanding the family's context more immediately.

Services based on resilience and resourcefulness rather than pathology

A responsive approach challenges mainstream and dominant discourses in the mental health field that focuses on pathology and deficit. As Jasmine Chin pointed out it is much more difficult to attend to an individual as belonging to a wider community, and the unique resilience, creativity and resourcefulness of those community connections, if we continue to base our assessments, formulations and interventions on diagnoses. In Ana Rivadulla Crespo's words 'a diagnosis of inclusion', would mean providing young people with the relational experiences they need rather than diagnosing them with mental deficits. Chris Glenn highlighted research that suggests that children and teachers alike, champion the idea of CAMH services being available in schools in order to prevent mental health problems deteriorating, normalise mental health services and make access easier. In her chapter Esther Usiskin-Cohen reflected on the benefits of a universally given school-based intervention which, rather than receiving referrals from professionals, was based on word of mouth and offered to a target year group, rather than a target child. As Zoe Dale explained, responsive services bring systems, professions and contexts together in ways that are not precipitated, and thus shaped, by the emergence of a crisis. Having CAMHS available in everyday community settings potentially places our attention on wellness, rather than illness, a goal everyone aspires to. It also fosters collective responsibility for well-being that challenges the notion of individuals and families being solely responsible for themselves.

The positive qualities that enable people to survive adversity do not exist within the minds of individuals but are processes that emerge in relationships and communities. The collective and relational nature of resilience and hope means that the task of working with, as well as in, communities is pressing. Hope is far from the musings of an optimist, or a desperate victim needing comfort, as though hope is achieved purely by conjuring up a feeling from the dark recesses of personality or mind. Hope is a doing, a process, a relationship that exists in the in-betweenness of inter-action. When hope is viewed in this way we take pressure off the individual who may or may not be able to bring it forth by themselves given the adverse contexts of their lives. In this way we place responsibility on a community to notice it, support it and as Weingarten describes, hold it for others while they are unable to hold it for themselves (Weingarten, 2007).

Communities, by virtue of their complexity, do not only create, but also hold tensions, allowing for the co-existence of apparent opposites. As Ana Rivadulla Crespo points out 'a good enough community' and a responsive community, allows for the co-existence of hope and hopelessness, not as opposites, but as bedfellows. 'A good enough community' is creative in that it helps to create the context for new expressions of identity and possibility to emerge where none previously seemed to exist. Despite often being regarded as 'anti-social', disrespectful and challenging in their behaviour, the boys in Zoe Dale group expressed their shared interest in fairness and justice. Despite being viewed as 'non-cooperative' and 'non-engaging', many families not only engaged in the FAST programme but became its strongest advocates.

Final reflections

We hope these chapters written by CAMHS clinicians from one service, who work together in the two CAMHS teams (North and South), highlight how different ways of working can co-exist and function together, resulting at times in tensions, conflicts and misunderstandings but most often leading to creative and responsive interventions. By inviting members of the same team to write chapters we have tried to highlight, rather than water down, their differences.

To answer the question of whether our CAMH services are responsive to the urban communities they serve and what this responsiveness looks like, we have reflected on these terms with genuine curiosity; as though wanting to start their usage afresh. Despite the negative associations with the word 'urban', this is not a book about lack; here, 'urban', chimes with possibility and creativity. Each chapter in this volume demonstrates that 'community' is much more than location, and therefore a responsive community CAMHS does more than locate itself in the community. A responsive service strikes a balance between offering relationships and experiences that are close enough to what is familiar and everyday, and therefore safe and containing, and offering something that moves clients and clinicians towards new possibilities; a combination of 'a secure base' in Bowlby's (Bowlby, 1978) terms and 'the difference that makes the difference' in Bateson's (Bateson, 2000). It is clear therefore, that the notion of 'community outreach' commonly proposed in mental health literature and in government policies does not go far enough. A genuine movement towards bearing 'community' in mind is both actual and symbolic. It means being more present in community contexts *and* responding to the needs people have within them. A responsive approach requires a readiness to re-examine, change and adapt our practices to have a good enough 'fit' with our local contexts.

In summary, responsiveness involves, working across different professions, systems and contexts, holding different positions at the same time and growing from the challenges of difference; delivering community services aimed at the general population, making adaptations to traditional models, supporting people in the community to better understand each other's context, creating space for reflection and responding to client feedback, and using our skills to attempt to go 'inside' the client's experience as well as witness, honour and encourage their resilience and resourcefulness. Being responsive takes time, effort and perseverance; it also requires that we utilise the multiplicity of identities and belonging (to multiple communities) that exist within CAMHS. To us, responsivity means being changed by our relationships with clients and a willingness to embody that change in our thinking, commitments and actions. A responsive approach is necessarily a political one. If we take our engagement with communities seriously, are we not compelled beyond amelioration and even social connection, towards transformative social action? Being responsive is more radical than we might initially think. It requires us to ask searching questions about what roles and functions we are willing to redefine, which aspects of our powers we are willing to forego and which we are willing to make use of in order to facilitate progressive and socially impacting changes.

Note

1 Ofsted is the Office for Standards in Education, Children's Services and Skills. They inspect and regulate services that care for children and young people, as well as services providing education and skills for learners of all ages.

References

Bateson, G. (2000). *Steps to an Ecology of Mind: Collected Essays in Anthropology, Psychiatry, Evolution, and Epistemology*. Chicago, IL: University of Chicago Press (first published in 1972, Chandler Publishing Company).

Bowlby, J. (1978). *Attachment and Loss. Vol. I: Attachment*. London, England: Penguin Books (originally published in 1969).

Boyd-Franklin, N. (2006). *Black Families in Therapy. A Multi-System Approach*. New York, NY: Guilford Press.

Boyd-Franklin, N. & Hafer Bry, B. (2001). *Reaching Out in Family Therapy: Home-Based, School and Community Interventions*. New York, NY: Guilford Press.

Burnham, J. (2005). Relational reflexivity: A tool for socially constructing therapeutic relationships. In: C. Flaskas, B. Mason & A. Perlesz (eds.), *The Space Between: Experience, Context and Process in the Therapeutic Relationship.* (pp. 1–17). London, England: Karnac Books.

Gilroy, P. (2008). Melancholia or conviviality. The politics of belonging in Britain. In: S. Davidson & J. Rutherford (eds.), *Race, Identity and Belonging.* (pp. 48–60). London, England: Lawrence & Wishart.

Lang, P. & McAdam, E. (1996). *Referrals, Referrers and the System of Concern.* unpublished manuscript. Available online at http://www.taosinstitute.net/Websites/taos/Images/ResourcesManuscripts/McAdam-lang-%20Referrals,%20Referrers%20and%20the%20System.pdf (accessed 30 March 2006).

Oxford University Press (2008). *Oxford Pocket Dictionary*. Oxford, England: Oxford University Press.

Pearce, W. B. (2007). *Making Social Worlds: A Communication Perspective*. Oxford, England: Blackwell.

Reynolds, V. (2013). "Leaning in" as imperfect allies in community work. *Conflict and Narrative Explorations in Theory and Practice,* 1(1), 53–75. Available online at http://journals.gmu.edu/NandC/issue/1 (accessed 8 July 2014).

Weingarten, K. (2007). Hope in a Time of Global Despair. In: C. Flaskas, I. McCarthy & J. Sheehan (eds.), *Hope and Despair in Family Therapy: Reflections on Adversity, Forgiveness and Reconciliation.* (pp. 13–23). Hove, England: Brunner-Routledge.

Index

.